The
Invisible
Powers

The
Invisible
Powers

The Language
of Business

John J. Clancy

Lexington Books

D.C. Heath and Company/Lexington, Massachusetts/Toronto

Library of Congress Cataloging-in-Publication Data

Clancy, John J. (John Joseph), 1937–
The invisible powers.

(The issues in organization and management series)
Bibliography: p.
Includes index.
1. Business—Terminology.   2. Businessmen—Language.
3. Metaphor.   4. Paradigms (Social sciences)   I. Title.
II. Series.
HF1002.5.C57   1989   650'.014   88–23109
ISBN 0–669–19542–1 (alk. paper)

Published simultaneously in Canada
Printed in the United States of America
International Standard Book Number: 0–669–19542–1
Library of Congress Catalog Card Number: 88–23109

The paper used in this publication meets the minimum requirements of
American National Standard for Information Sciences—Permanence
of Paper for Printed Library Materials, ANSI Z39.48–1984.

89 90 91 92 8 7 6 5 4 3 2

For Sue—
"Who can find a virtuous woman?
For her price is far above rubies."

Contents

Acknowledgments   xiii

1. Introduction   1

Part I.   Metaphor in Business   7

2. The Web of Language   9

   Metaphor   9
   Historical Perspective   14

3. The Bearer of Truth   23

   Theory of Metaphor   23
   The Metaphor in Business   28

4. The Journey: Leadership and *le Voyage sans But*   35

   The Journey in Literature   35
   The Journey in Business   37
   Entailments of the Journey   38
   Strengths and Weaknesses of the Metaphor   40
   Summary   42

5. The Game: The Playing Fields of Business   45

   Early Examples   45
   Taylor, Too   46
   Modern Usage   48

The Structure of Games   50
Goals and Difficulties   52
Unpredictability   53
Fun   54
The Team and the Risk   55
Strengths of the Metaphor   56
Weaknesses of the Metaphor   57
The Team Leader   58
The Infinite Players   60
Summary   62

6. War: Soldiers in Pinstripes   63

Historical Background   63
Business Usage   65
The Good Side of War   67
The Janus Face of War   69
The Dogs of War   71
The War Leader   72
Strengths and Weaknesses of the Metaphor   73
Summary   74

7. The Machine: Taylor and Positivism   77

Background   77
Entailments   79
The Machine's Impact   82
The Soulless Machine   85
The Machine Gone Awry   86
The Leader   87
Summary   88

8. The Organism: Evolution and the Good Shepherd   91

Background   91
Business Usage   93

Romanticism and Complexity 96
Darwin and Evolution 98
Other Entailments 99
Guides to Action 102
Strategy 104
Strengths and Weaknesses of the Metaphor 106
Ambiguity Overdone 110
The Leader 110
Summary 114

9. The Society: Shamans and Statesmen 117

Background 117
Types of Societies 120
Business Usage 122
The Entailment of Meaning 128
Culture 130
Myths, Rituals, Symbols 134
The Ills of Society 138
Politics and Power 141
Shared Entailments 143
The Leader as Shaman 145
The Statesman 149
The Hero and the Saint 152
Strengths of the Metaphor 154
Weaknesses of the Metaphor 157
Summary 162

Part II.   Purpose in Business   165

10. Purposes and Paradigms 167

The Shifting Tides 167
The Work of Thomas Kuhn 171

Purposes   177
Summary   182

11. The New Messiah: The Paradigm of Production   183

    Background   183
    Production and Economics   184
    The Actors   186
    Ford the Exemplar   190
    Some Puzzles   193
    The Problems Left Behind   197
    Incommensurate Thinking   201
    The Metaphors of Production   203
    Production: Pro and Con   207
    Summary   211

12. Treasures upon Earth: The Paradigm of Wealth   213

    Background   213
    The Actors   219
    Sloan the Exemplar   222
    Kuhn and Sloan   226
    The Metaphors of Wealth   229
    The Eye of the Needle   231
    Summary   237

13. Stonecutters Fighting Time: The Paradigm of the
    Institution   239

    Institutions   239
    Origins   241
    The Actors   245
    Jones the Exemplar   247
    The Puzzles   249
    The Metaphors of the Institution   251
    Institution: Pro and Con   254
    Summary   261

14. Fin de Siècle   263

    A Taste for the Apocalypse   263
    Economic Trends   264
    Cultural Trends   268
    Trends in Thought   272
    Failures of the Paradigms   275
    Legitimacy   281
    Summary   283

15. Voyaging, Voyaging, Voyaging   287

    Things Fall Apart   287
    Drucker's Paradigm: The Eclectic   288
    The Shape-Changers   293
    Metaphors   297

Notes   301
Bibliography   319
Index   327
About the Author   333

Acknowledgments

This book was written as an independent study project under the aegis of Washington University's Master of Liberal Arts Program. Professor Walter Nord of Washington University's Business School supervised the work, and I am deeply indebted to him; his encouragement, suggestions, and counsel were invaluable.

I also received encouragement and advice from others who reviewed the work at various stages, including Eugene Powers and my novelist brother, Ambrose Clancy.

Finally, there would be no book without the tireless efforts of my friend of many years, Eva Conley, who typed the manuscript and persevered through many drafts.

1
Introduction

In truth, the ideas and images in men's minds are the invisible powers
that constantly govern them.

—John Locke[1]

This is a book about business, but not from the perspective of
economics, marketing, or administration; it is about business
as a cultural artifact, a critical component of Western civilization.
The structure of business has of course been studied extensively in
terms of basic economic forces and other exogenous factors—for
example, political theory and sociology. Any good MBA program
provides these perspectives to the student. More important in the
long run, perhaps, have been the thought processes, the "mental
furniture," of those who build and operate business enterprises; it
is these "ideas and images in men's minds" that have produced
today's industrial civilization. The purpose of this work is to chart
these ideas and images, seek their sources in larger cultural movements, and determine the impact of these "invisible powers" on
the structure of business and on society at large.

How does a book like this come to be written? I cannot pretend
to an "epiphanal" moment—like Gibbon in the ruins of the Forum,
grasping in an instant the long decline and fall of Rome. Rather, a
series of readings and observations set me on the course of this
inquiry; I was particularly influenced by Lee Iacocca's autobiography, Thomas Kuhn's *The Structure of Scientific Revolutions*, and
the business press's coverage of the acquisition wars. In Iacocca's
book, I was struck by the flood of metaphors—his constant use of
analogies to describe his business: war, organisms, societies, games,
journeys. I wondered if Iacocca was unique in this regard and went
then to Alfred Sloan's and Henry Ford's autobiographies to see if

such metaphorical use was common in business writing. I found that it was, indeed, but I noted something else as well: a fundamentally different purpose for business, expressed by men in the same time and same industry. While speculating on the implications of these business metaphors and the disparate purposes of business leaders, Kuhn's book—one I had long planned to read—rather fortuitously came into my hands. Kuhn writes about scientific theories, the manner in which they change, and the behavior of scientists who are committed to a theory. He proposes the idea of a "paradigm"—a fundamental set of beliefs about the world—which is usually established by one person's unique and exemplary work. Further—and an illumination for me—Kuhn notes that metaphor springs from paradigm; the scientist's basic model of the world seems to generate the metaphors he uses in describing it. The implications for business thought seemed obvious. When business people use metaphors, the metaphors probably say something about their view of business and probably "govern" their actions. And the metaphors probably signal something about their purpose—their paradigm—what they believe their business is really all about.

Another set of observations took me further. Like many in business, I have followed with fascination—and some dismay—the recent spate of multibillion-dollar mergers and acquisitions. Business acquisitions have been a commonplace for generations, but the recent activity seems to signal not just a change in magnitude and intensity but a change in kind. Few of these transactions are spurred by the need for expanded markets or new product lines—the principal strategic reason for acquisitions in the past. Rather, the new wave is led by "raiders," men whose motives appear to be entirely financial. What is especially striking about the recent acquisition contests is the disparate language and intentions of the protagonists. The raiders have a very clear intention—indeed, a clear ideology: corporations are sets of wealth-producing assets; as such, they should be in the hands of those who can maximize the return on those assets, which, by the laws of the market, means those who can bid the highest for the assets. The managements of the target companies do not express nearly so clear a view; their response is more emotional, but also broader in terms of the potential impact on society. Their concerns (I discount their personal motives) are for employees and communities, but also for society's loss of essential products and services.

I sense a radically different philosophy of business between the raider and management, a fundamentally different purpose that each attributes to a corporation. The raider's purpose is clear: a corporation exists to produce wealth. The management's purposes are also valid, though often not so well expressed: a corporation exists to produce goods and services; or alternatively, it exists as an institution to benefit all its "stakeholders"—employees, shareholders, suppliers, customers, and communities. This disparity in expression and in world view struck a familiar chord; it sounded much like Thomas Kuhn's analysis of the change in scientific theories—and it sounded like the different views of Sloan and Ford.

Also, and—as Kuhn foresaw—closely related to these divergent purposes, I have noted different forms of expression between the contestants.

The raider talks in terms of "cash cows" or "money machines"; managers, for their part, represent the corporation almost as a human being, with a sacred right to life, or as a nation under siege from foreign attack. I am not taking sides in this dispute—this is not a book on the merits of mergers and acquisitions. Really, I am illustrating a fundamental schism in intention and in expression: the fact that business people in the same time and place talk about business in very different ways. This different use of language, especially the different use of metaphor, raises the questions that this book attempts to answer.

There is, first, the question of history: Have things always been so? Have the purposes of business always been in dispute, and have those purposes changed over time? Have the descriptive forms, the metaphors, changed? To answer these questions, I sampled the writings of business leaders from Wedgwood in the eighteenth century to Iacocca, Geneen, and others in our own day. The language of these business leaders will be a prime concern of this inquiry; in many ways, this is a book about language, and my principal source material is the speech of business leaders.

The plan of this work is as follows: Part I is concerned with metaphor, and the level of inquiry and critique is focused *inward* on a business—that is, how does metaphor structure a leader's concept of the business and how does it help him define his role? Part I begins with a general survey of metaphorical theory and a brief historical review of business thought (chapters 2 and 3). Then, chapters 4 through 9 study the most common business metaphors, seeking their sources in art, literature, and philosophy and developing the influence of each metaphor on business practices.

Part II shifts the emphasis from metaphor and business practice to an investigation of business purpose—the reason for business activity as articulated by business people. First, in chapter 10, the linkage of metaphor and purpose is given, following Kuhn's insight that a scientific paradigm suggests appropriate metaphors to express the paradigm. I argue that the different purposes of business can be analyzed in the context of Kuhn's model.

Chapters 11, 12, and 13 present the three historically important business purposes or paradigms: producing goods and services, maximizing wealth, and building an enduring institution. These paradigms are discussed in terms of their source in economics and culture; the business issues they create; the leaders who exemplify each paradigm; the impact of these purposes on our civilization; and, of course, the metaphors that are allied with these paradigms. The viewpoint in these chapters is quite different from that in part I; it is *outward* from the business—mainly a cultural and moral critique, rather than a critique of internal business practice.

Finally, chapters 14 and 15 present a review of the major paradigms of business, argue their ultimate failure in modern times, and explore the question of the legitimacy of a business in the context of these paradigms. New paradigms and metaphors are suggested, and their suitability is discussed.

In brief, this book essays answers to the following questions:

- What are the purposes of business that leaders have espoused over the years? Where did these ideas come from? How legitimate are they?

- What are the implications of these ideas for our society?

- What are the most common metaphors used by business people, and how has their use changed over the years? Where do these metaphors come from?

- What are the implications of metaphorical use to business leaders and to their corporations? What actions do the metaphors suggest? What roles do they define?

- How are metaphor and purpose related?

- Where is this all leading? What new purposes and metaphors are in the wind, and what do they portend?

Part I

Metaphor in Business

2
The Web of Language

Metaphor

In the first place, we must ask: Why is metaphor used at all in
business? Well, even a simple business, say a small manufacturing
concern, is appallingly complex. A company of a few hundred people is a tangle of interactions—among the employees themselves,
outsiders, materials, and machines. To complicate matters further,
no business—indeed, no human activity—is conducted with utmost rationality and objectivity; it is "saturated with subjectivity,
abstraction, guesses, making do, invention and arbitrariness."[2]
Various commentators have attempted to grasp the nub of a business organization. It has been described as "a structure of mutual
expectations" and "an identifiable social entity pursuing multiple
objectives through the coordinated activities and relations among
its members and objects."[3] Perhaps as useful as these is William
James's description of the world of sense data—"a buzzin', bloomin'
confusion."[4]

This endemic complexity really beggars description and has
launched an enormous number of mental and verbal constructs to
attempt a handhold on the nature of an organization. The mind is
driven to sort out the world and find a clue to its nature. It isolates
some "commonsense" areas and satisfies itself on the intelligibility
of that limited portion of experience, then attempts to understand

other aspects of the world in terms of this baseline. The original, simplified commonsense area of understanding then suggests the terms by which larger areas can be understood.[5] In most cases (some would argue all), the process of understanding and comprehending is therefore metaphorical in nature—the understanding and expression of one phenomenon in terms of another. This mapping of thought—the buildup of mental constructs from the simple, easily understood to the complex and problematical—this application of the concrete to wider circumstances can be helpful, but it can be dangerously wrong. Literature can illuminate this point; I think especially of Vonnegut's *Cat's Cradle,* in which Vonnegut defines a *karass* as a group of people united in some way for some transcendent purpose—a concept congenial to all of us from our immediate, concrete experience of family and loved ones. The common failing of thought is to apply this concept to false karasses or *grandfaloons*—that is, congeries of people who have no real common purpose or mission. Unhappily for the statesman and business leader, Vonnegut categorizes all governments and businesses as grandfaloons—entities that only exist as purposeful and meaningful, indeed only exist at all, in the minds of their participants.

What, then, do business leaders do to get their minds around this "bloomin' confusion," this immense array of processes and interactions? The first step has always been to conceptualize the organization as a thing. This, of course, could be a basic category error, as Vonnegut maintains—a reification of what in reality is a complex process of human and material interaction. This is a common problem; the very structure of our language conceals from us the extent to which the objects of our attention are not things, but relations extended in time.[6]

Businesses were first conceived of as things in the late Middle Ages, with the advent of double-entry bookkeeping. Before this technical innovation, a man's business, whether he was trader or artisan, was incommensurable with the other aspects of his life. Double-entry bookkeeping, first developed to check errors in accounts, became a technique to separate a man's business from his private life. The firm could then be seen as a separate entity, with an existence beyond the life of the operator/owner.[7]

Accounting provided a means to *value* an enterprise and thus make it available for sale, like any other commodity. In short, this breakthrough in a means to operate the concern paced the owner's conception of his business as a thing. The Venetian traders of the thirteenth century thus started the moderns on the road to metaphorical conception of a business enterprise—the mental construct of a vastly complex set of processes and activities seen in the light of a thing, an object, another commodity to be bought or sold.

Metaphor—not simply the metaphor of an object—has become pervasive in business thought and expression. The practice is so common that we scarcely recognize that metaphor is used; it seems to be simple, commonsense speech that is employed. We speak of the man at the helm, the business in troubled waters; we conceive of a business as growing, surviving, dying; we ask "Who has the ball?" "What is the game plan?"; we attack and destroy competition; we have a well-oiled operation or one in need of an overhaul. These are part and parcel of ordinary consciousness and expression, but a moment's thought clearly shows that we are awash in metaphor in almost all conceptions and articulations of business practices.

Most business metaphors are trite and obvious, but as I will try to show, they still conceal some fundamental ideas about business, its purposes, and its operations. Occasionally, one sees a striking and new metaphor, but unhappily for the aesthetic sense, these are quite rare; perhaps this rarity adds to their charm and appeal. For example, one of the first "modern" businessmen, Josiah Wedgwood, spoke of "fall[ing] in love with and mak[ing] a Mistress of my business."[8] And F. P. Sanford, Jr., CEO of a small contemporary insurance company, has used the analogy of a symphony orchestra—"simple themes repeated with growing force as new participants join in." Sanford also has used a highly extended description of his business as a river, "starting with a tiny trickle, sometimes blocked and in danger of drying up . . . finally a powerful stream sweeping obstacles before it."[9] The former chairman of ITT, Harold Geneen, has offered an original and powerful metaphor to describe the process of operating a business: It's like cooking outdoors on a wood-burning stove. You must pay constant attention. You cannot control the temperature very well, and you are subject to uncontrollable vagaries of wood type and wind shifts.[10]

There is hardly a thing, process, institution, or human activity to which a business has not been compared. Businesses have been likened to a structure, a variety show, a surgical operation, an excavation, a farm, a religion—even, as we have seen, to a mistress. Economic conditions themselves do not escape metaphorical expression. In the nineteenth century, poor business conditions were described as "panics," a not inappropriate extrapolation of the emotions of the participants, if a bit overstated. In the twentieth century, we find first "depression"—the reified economy becoming smaller—then the Great Crash, combining two rich and popular metaphors, those of "journey" and "machine."

In summary, metaphors have been widely used to structure the participants' understanding and articulation of their activities. To that extent, metaphors serve a very useful purpose that is, improving the understanding and, ultimately, the control of the processes in which the actors are engaged. The right metaphor can also substantially assist the manager in communicating his view of the business to those who must do the work. But we could take the view that this is nothing but lazy and careless thought and speech, that these metaphors add nothing to our understanding of an enterprise. George Orwell cautioned us:

> There is a huge dump of worn-out metaphors which have lost all evocative power and are merely used because they save some people the trouble of inventing phrases for themselves.[11]

And William Davis, in the *New York Times,* excoriates business jargon: "a blizzard of buzzwords burying thought."[12]

It is unarguable that few of us use original metaphor; virtually all of us are imprisoned by metaphors embedded in the language as cant and slang. But this is precisely the point. If, indeed, metaphor structures the way we think and see the world—a point I will develop later—then whether these expressions are original to us or handed down is really unimportant. What is important is that these expressions do, in fact, color our modes of perception and thought.

A better argument against metaphors, worn-out or original, is their ultimate insufficiency, their inability to help us grasp the total experience we wish to express. Being "like" something is fundamentally different from "being" something. A business is not a game, nor a river, nor a machine. Running a business is not cooking on a wood stove nor is it steering a ship. However much these analogies help us understand and illuminate new areas of the phenomenon, they necessarily hide other important features of the actual process.

With all these limitations and caveats, however, it is important to realize that metaphor is an integral part of our thought process. We use metaphor much as we breathe; we cannot avoid its use or its consequences. As Wittgenstein puts it, we cannot escape the web of language; it is an inherent human limitation, tantamount to not being able to jump out of one's skin.[13] And Heidegger said: "Language is the house of Being. Man dwells in this house."[14] I should add that this house is built on and of metaphor.

But what is the power of metaphor—the facility that places this verbal trick at the very center of comprehension and expression? Surely it is the ability to suggest a reality beyond ordinary, discursive thought.[15] In the face of impenetrable complexity, the right suggestion, the right analogy, can in a word or two lift our understanding beyond anything attainable by reams of prosaic speech. The experience of business, as I suggested earlier, is exceptionally complex, and metaphor has found a major role in helping the practitioners grasp the phenomenon, deal with the "buzzin' confusion" and articulate their comprehension for others.

For example, when Alfred Sloan faced the Great Depression at the head of General Motors, he did not speak of his declining sales and eroding balance sheet. He spoke of GM as a great ship in a fierce storm, immediately conveying to employees, suppliers, stockholders—and, not least, himself—the key idea: The business, though enormous and powerful, was in the grip of events beyond its control, was in peril, and required the highest degree of courage, skill, and leadership.

Our inquiry will be concerned with metaphor in business— more specifically, with the metaphors used by the actors themselves, the leaders of businesses. We will see how the expressions have changed over time, from the eighteenth through the twentieth centuries, and explore the source of these metaphors in art and philosophy. The world has changed a great deal in 200 years, both in material terms and in our conception of reality. These two factors are closely intertwined: Changes in material conditions surely affect our conception of things, but our view of the world, and that view's impact on economic actors, in turn affects our material reality.

Before we discuss these matters in detail, it will be helpful to look at a very brief history of business speech.

Historical Perspective

Business, as we know it today—or at least as we would recognize it today—is barely 200 years old. The first glimmerings of what would be considered modern business practice go back to the eighteenth century in Britain. Josiah Wedgwood (1730–95), usually recognized as the father of modern industrial practices, began the organization of his ceramics workshop in the 1760s. His extensive correspondence with his partner, Bentley, adumbrates many of the themes that we have grown familiar with in business practice and theory: mass production as a means to cover fixed overhead costs,[16] association (collusion) with competitors,[17] and the never-ending problems with a labor force.[18] Wedgwood found himself constantly embroiled with his workers over equitable compensation; during one of these periodic negotiations in 1772, he grasped the essentials of mass production economics: produce more, costs will be less, prices can decline, more demand will be created, so more can be sold. Wedgwood saw "the vast consequences in most manufacturers of making the greatest quantity possible in a given time."[19]

It is fair to say that Wedgwood operated his business for financial gain. All his actions—the mass production techniques, attempted price fixing, support for limiting the emigration of skilled potters[20]—were aimed at maximizing his personal and corporate wealth. However, in Wedgwood we first see the hints of another purpose for business. He speculated, in his correspondence with Bentley, about a more noble mission: the quest for fame and the good of manufacturing at large.[21] When the practical test came—releasing his designs to competitors—he followed Bentley's advice and put aside these dreams in favor of his self-described "degrading selfish chains, these mean selfish fears."[22] But this very early flirtation with another view of business—a purpose different from and more edifying than personal gain—is significant; Wedgwood can be counted a precursor to a view of business that eventually took root and dominated business thought for many years.

Wedgwood, typically for his era, used very few metaphors in describing his business. We have noted earlier his highly original comparison of his business to a mistress. He also spoke of the business as a farm:

> I saw the field was spacious and the soil so good, as to promise an *ample recompense* to any who should diligently labor in its cultivation.[23] (emphasis added)

I choose to emphasize "ample recompense" in line with my perception that Wedgwood saw his business venture as fundamentally a means to increase his own fortune. Of the more common business metaphors, Wedgwood chose the "machine" analogy, applying it to his work force, in a manner almost identical to that of Henry Ford: "to make such machines of men as cannot err."[24] Here again, Wedgwood is a precursor of a long tradition of business thought: mechanical analogies that reduced the business and the workers to machines at the service of the owner/operator.

Wedgwood and his followers, in this sense, earned the contumely of Freidrich Engels, who wrote: "They really believe that all human beings . . . have a real existence only if they make money or help to make it."[25]

Robert Owen (1771–1858) is much better known as a social theorist and activist, but he, like Wedgwood, was an active business owner and operator. Owen managed a number of textile mills from 1800 to 1828, before devoting the last thirty years of his life to social reform. He expressed his views on business at some length in his "Address to the Superintendent of Manufactories" (1813), taking as axiomatic that a manager's duty was "to produce the greatest pecuniary gain to the proprietors."[26] Owen's plea to the superintendent, and of course to the general population of industrialists, was for better treatment of their "vital machines"—the workers. He drew a direct comparison between these "machines" and the capital equipment employed in manufacturing, and he argued from a purely economic standpoint that clean, safe conditions and wholesome food would result in vastly improved profits—"a return exceeding 50%" was possible.

Owen needs no apologist for his attitudes toward the workers; he devoted thirty years of his life and his entire (and considerable) fortune to bettering the lot of the working class. We must assume that his polemic was a clever bit of salesmanship—convincing the management class that their hard-headed, pecuniary interests lay in the direction of better treatment of the workers. But the fact that he chose this line of argument, and his machine analogy, certainly indicates that this was the prevailing view of his time. He must have felt that the temper of the times was close to that described by Engels, thirty years later (1845): "Anything that yields no financial gain is dismissed as 'stupid,' 'impractical' or 'idealistic.' "[27] Owen, an idealist par excellence, was shrewd enough to couch his pleas in terms that the audience could understand and appreciate—economics, pure and simple.

The mechanical view of business continued in refinement and elaboration throughout the nineteenth century. Charles Babbage (1792–1871) established the basic principles of what became Frederick Taylor's scientific management: There are basic principles of management that can be broadly applied, and business management can be a science, not an art.[28]

Other thinkers contributed to this effort. Henry Metcalfe (1847–1917), the manager of U.S. Army arsenal, spoke for the careful measurement and recording of experiences as a precondition of applying scientific principles to business problems.[29] Henry Towne (1844–1924) prescribed the use of mechanical engineering techniques, not for the design of machines and products but for the design of the processes of work.[30]

This entire movement culminated in the towering figure of Frederick Winslow Taylor (1856–1915), the man most closely associated with scientific management. In fact, at present, "Taylorism" is a term of opprobrium—shorthand for old-fashioned and unfeeling management practices. The 1973 report to the U.S. Secretary of Health, Education and Welfare, *Work in America*, is basically a long philippic against Taylorism. One quotation will suffice:

> Industry is paying for its continued attachment to Taylorist prac-
> tices through low worker productivity and high rates of sabotage,
> absenteeism and turnover.[31]

In his heyday, Taylor enjoyed many successes, although he came
in for his share of the criticisms we have grown accustomed to.
Nevertheless, his contributions to business thought and practice
have been enormous. In contrast to Wedgwood, Taylor held as an
article of faith that a business existed to produce goods, not just
wealth. The key problem of business, in his view, was the appropriate distribution of the surplus wealth created by production, the
distribution between the owners and the workers. He believed he
could finesse this ancient problem, the division of the "pie," by
simply making the pie larger: "The object to be aimed at is high
wages with low labor cost."[32] All the controversial time-and-motion
studies and work-breakdown techniques were aimed at this fundamental result.

Taylor became a crusader for scientific management and saw
it as a revolutionary change in the workingman's attitude toward
his work and his employer.[33] Similarly, he saw the role of management in a new light, that of serving the men, rather than the reverse.[34] The manager had the duty to apply scientific methods in
order to make the worker more efficient, so that more could be
produced, at a lower unit rate but at a higher net wage for the
worker. In this vein, Taylor would agree with St. Augustine, writing 1400 years earlier:

> Even those who rule serve those whom they seem to command;
> for they rule not from a love of power, but from a sense of duty
> they owe to others.[35]

As we have noted, Taylor's underlying assumption was that a business existed to produce goods. This was the purpose that Wedgwood flirted with and Henry Ford brought to fruition—production.
Taylor approached lyricism in these remarks:

> There is hardly any worse crime to my mind than that of delib-
> erately restricting output, of failing to bring the only things into

the world which are of real use to the world, the products of men and soils.[36]

The production of goods as a transcendent goal later became a critically important idea in business; and machine analogies became allied with this purpose. Taylor's entire conception of business and the people in the business was mechanistic; in fact, his name is almost synonymous with this view of industry. In addition to this machine analogy, Taylor also employed sports metaphors, particularly football. He was one of the first to use this highly popular metaphor, and he saw, in the intricate team game, a good analogy to a successful business operation.

In Taylor, we see the culmination of the intellectual development that began with the industrial revolution. His basic belief was that business existed to produce beneficial goods, although he foreshadowed later lines of thought in recognizing that the workers had a stake in the business. Taylor also was typical of earlier figures, as well as his followers—Gantt, Gilbreth, and Follett—in viewing the job of management as fundamentally a job of *personnel* management: controlling, directing, rewarding, and disciplining the work force—not professionals and knowledge workers, but manual laborers and machine tenders. This exclusive focus on personnel matters seems quaint to us now, but it was the major concern of those times and certainly is consistent with the view of the business as a machine whose most complex and recalcitrant parts—the workers—needed the most attention.[37]

The late eighteenth- and nineteenth-century businesses were different in many ways from those familiar to us in the twentieth century. In general, they served a local market and had a small number of local suppliers. Government was a light burden, regulations were few, and taxes were not burdensome and were simple to compute. There were relatively few employees, and their jobs were relatively simple. The technology employed was also quite simple by current standards. Further, the employee population was generally homogeneous—culturally, racially, and economically. In every case, it is easy to see the differences between those times and the late twentieth century.[38]

The twentieth century has seen profound changes in business—

in its complexity and scope, but also in the attitudes of the participants. As we will see later, three major figures emerged who profoundly influenced business thinking in the twentieth century: Henry Ford, Alfred Sloan, and Reginald Jones.

Henry Ford is, of course, the archetypal twentieth-century industrialist. His creation, the Ford Motor Company, forever changed our concept of an industrial organization. Ford adopted Wedgwood's mass production techniques, but he also adopted the idea that Wedgwood ultimately rejected and that Taylor had articulated: A business exists, simply, to *produce*. Later, I will propose Ford as the exemplar of this paradigm of production.

Alfred Sloan, Ford's great rival, helped found General Motors. Sloan regressed in one sense to the nineteenth-century view that the firm exists principally to enrich the owners. His many contributions to modern business and its rationalization and efficiency were all based on this fundamental premise; his influence has been great. Sloan can be seen as the exemplar of the paradigm of wealth.

Reg Jones was not a founder or creator, like Ford and Sloan, but rather inherited the leadership of a major industrial firm, General Electric. Jones postulated a new view of a business, that of an institution whose purpose is to grow, excel, and endure. His success at GE and his influence as a public figure certainly made this a popular view among American businessmen, and I have selected him as the exemplar of the institution paradigm.

The University of Pennsylvania's Russell Ackoff, in his recent book, *Creating the Corporate Future*,[39] has also analyzed this 200-year record of business thought. In his view, during the early Industrial Revolution, organizations were typically viewed as machines whose function was to serve their creator by providing him with an adequate return on investment. The employees were treated as machines as well, with their tasks designed for mechanical performance. All this is familiar to us after our brief survey of this time, from Wedgwood to Taylor.

Ackoff states that this view of the organization, or at least this view as an efficacious concept, was only tenable so long as the owners held almost absolute power and the workers were unskilled, poorly educated, and faced destitution if they lost their jobs. These conditions changed dramatically around the time of

World War I. Widespread public ownership of corporations undid the power of the autocratic owner/operator. Social welfare legislation and union power reduced the specter of catastrophic unemployment. Increased mechanization and general technology improvements began to demand a higher-skilled and better-educated work force, and compulsory education began to meet this requirement.

Ackoff believes that after the Great War, the organization began to be conceived of as an organism, an entity with a life and purpose of its own. Its principal purposes became growth and survival; profit, like oxygen, became merely one of the necessities of survival, not an end in itself. The organic metaphor became quite popular (in Ackoff's view), and the ideas of management as the brains of the organism, workers as difficult to replace organs, and the like, became common. After World War II, Ackoff believes that this concept became passé; business people became more aware of the social role of the corporation as consumerism and environmentalism grew into strong movements. Considering the organization as an organism, with a life and purpose of its own, somehow misses the interdependencies that a real corporation faces in modern society. Ackoff's last metamorphosis of the corporation is a tautology: the organization as an organization. He means by this that an organization is a purposeful system, part of one or more other purposeful systems (the larger society) and composed of purposeful systems (suborganizations and people).

One could argue with Ackoff's timing for these shifts in view, or even for the empirical evidence for any of his analysis, but he has hit on some key points. As we shall see in the next chapter, in fact, metaphors used by business leaders have shifted over time, not as neatly and crisply as Ackoff imagines, but there are discernible shifts nonetheless. Ackoff also postulates that these metaphorical shifts are related mainly to exogenous factors: improved education, more complex technology, social legislation—all resulting in a differing level of complexity within the firm and in its relations with the larger society. This analysis has merit, but as I have already suggested and will demonstrate later, the metaphorical shifts are more likely associated with cultural movements and endogenous factors, particularly the fundamental sense of purpose—the paradigm—that the business leader brings to his organization.

But let us now return to metaphor—first a review of the theory, then the business use of metaphor itself.

3
The Bearer of Truth

As you see, the citizens of every age live subject to society
stuffed like geese at Christmas from beak to pinfeathers with
preposterous beliefs and spurious values, their minds netted by
philosophy or mystical illusions working to create false realities

—Evan Connell[1]

Theory of Metaphor

For a very long time, metaphor was a particular and exclusive
concern of literary analysis, especially the study of poetic expression and literary flourish. The link to poetry focused analysis and
discussion on the emotive effects of metaphor—its power to move
the soul through the play of words. The scholar and mythologist
Joseph Campbell[2] has shown that metaphor, myth, and symbols
are means of access to other forms of consciousness. They can
point us past those pairs of opposites that limit discursive thought—
for example, the logical dichotomies of man/God, life/death, man/
woman. The logical mind tends to structure reality into these pairs
of unbridgeable distinctness. But the message of most myths is that
ultimate reality is found not in these dichotomies, but rather in the
union of these apparent opposites. The figure of the Virgin Mother,
for example, suggests this union. Or consider the mandala symbol,
suggesting wholeness (the circle) but, at the same time, division
(the segments); it is a device that suggests to the mind a clear contradiction in logical thought—the union of opposites.

Beginning in the 1950s, linguists and philosophers began to
study the epistemological character of metaphor from the larger
viewpoint of all expression and thought. Paul de Man has spoken

of "the inescapable metaphorical quality of all human discourse."[3] Metaphor has emerged in modern analysis as no less than the bearer of truth.[4]

Perhaps the most concise definition of metaphor is that offered by the linguists Lakoff and Johnson: "understanding and experiencing one thing in terms of another."[5] A metaphor makes us conscious of some likeness, often a strikingly novel and surprising likeness, between two fundamentally different things or processes.[6] The philosopher Pepper[7] postulates that the mind first makes a fairly thorough mental description of an original, referring area— not just the characteristics but, more important, the structure of the original area, the manner in which the characteristics are related to one another. This structure becomes the basis for exploration and description of the original thing or process; from this base structure we then undertake to interpret all facts that relate to a new area.

Pepper introduces the concept of root metaphor—a set of characteristics from which all facts of the universe can be generated by certain processes of change. For example, in the sixth century B.C., Thales stated that all things are water. From this very global metaphor, and the structure of its characteristics, all facts could be explained.

Pepper's work is concerned with very large issues—fundamental ideas about the universe. (His relevant title is *World Hypotheses.*) His work, however, is consistent with the theory of metaphor I shall follow, that of Lakoff and Johnson, who wrote thirty-five years later. Lakoff and Johnson are concerned with the role of metaphor in everyday, commonplace experience. Their agreement with Pepper is fundamental: Our concepts, which are largely metaphorical, structure what we perceive, how we get around the world and relate to things and other people.[8] In brief, language and metaphor create our reality.

Whether there is a reality other than that we ourselves create is a subtle question, one that continues to occupy philosophers. William James has said that "collateral contemporaneous phenomena are 'the real-order' of the world"[9]—all other meaning is our own doing. The "real order" is a series of contemporaneous events— a birth in Alaska, a death in Bangladesh, a storm in the Pacific, and so forth. It is human consciousness, and that alone, that provides order, rules, structure—in short, reality.

As noted earlier, Lakoff and Johnson believe that this ordering and structuring of phenomena is largely metaphorical. We think this way because almost all of the concepts, processes, and things that are truly important to us are either abstract or poorly delineated—in a word, fuzzy. (Think of time—what is its nature? Or a mountain—where precisely does it begin and end?) To get a grasp on these vital concepts/processes/things, we use other entities that we understand much more clearly.[10]

Consider the metaphor "Time is money."[11] This is an all-pervasive concept in industrialized countries and may even be the best means to differentiate "the West" (including Japan) from traditional societies. The idea is so commonplace to us that we fail to see it as a cultural artifact and, in fact, a relatively new concept in human history. We are puzzled or irritated when we encounter others with a different sense of time. We tend to ascribe shiftlessness, even low intelligence, to those who do not share this view. But, in the West, time *is* money. The practice of payment by time units, begun in a general way with the Industrial Revolution, made it simple and obvious to conclude that time is a valuable commodity. Our lives are colored and shaped by this metaphor; we conceive of time as valuable, to be used appropriately; it is wrong to "waste" time.

Many of our values are shaped by such metaphorical expressions. For example, in our culture, "up" is a positive direction. Hence, "More is better" is derived from "More is up" and "Up is good". Similarly, "Bigger is better" is derived by way of the same reasoning. The future is also "up" for us, so the future will be better and there clearly will be "more" in the future. Since higher status is also "up," your future will bring a better lot. The future as bigger, better, and more prestigious is nothing less than the "idea of progress," perhaps the most fundamental tenet in the West since the Enlightenment and still an article of faith for millions, despite two catastrophic wars—and the pessimism of art and philosophy.

Lakoff and Johnson introduce the key concept of "ontological metaphor"—simply, our penchant for conceiving of events, activities, emotions, ideas, and so forth, as *things*.[12] (We saw earlier the role of double-entry bookkeeping as an impetus for reifying a business.) From childhood, our experience with physical objects provides a basis for understanding, a baseline to extrapolate to wider experience. Having secured our understanding of our personal experience with objects and the structure of that experience, we then pick out parts of our world, separate them from other phenomena, and begin to treat each experience as a discrete entity—in other words, a thing. Even when the experience is not clearly discrete or bounded, we still categorize it as a bounded entity, like an object. Lakoff and Johnson use the examples of mountains, street corners, and hedges—really "fuzzy" objects in a geometrical sense. I can add here the ambiguous nature of a business—still routinely treated as a thing.

The great intellectual danger of metaphorical use is its misapplication (think of Vonnegut's "grandfaloon"). Ontological metaphors really can serve only quite limited purposes, but our tendency is to conceptualize events as objects and activities as substances.[13] Take an event—a horse race. We say, and it is correct English, "Are you going to the race?" as though the race were an identifiable object. Or take any activity, any gerund in effect—say, washing windows. "*How much* window washing did you do?" In a very natural way, we also see some activities as persons:[14] "Life has cheated me," "This business is killing me," or, as we have seen, Wedgwood's conception of his business as a mistress. In personifying events and activities, we typically draw out certain aspects of a person; we see the activity as a friend, a hero, an adversary, and so forth.

I have noted how metaphor can lead one astray by its misapplication. Metaphor, through its very power to make the complex and fuzzy clear, or at least apparently clear, has another negative effect—limiting experience. Again, Lakoff and Johnson note:

> The very systematicity that allows us to comprehend one aspect of a concept in terms of another will necessarily hide other aspects of the concept.[15]

For example, we tend to think in terms like "Argument is war." This is mainly helpful; it structures our thought in terms of an adversary, an attack, a winning strategy, and so on, but it misses the idea of the cooperative nature of an argument. In reality, we argue to convince someone or, failing that, to learn something ourselves, not, in all but the rarest cases, to demolish an opponent. But our normal, metaphorical conception, "Argument is war," can obscure these positive aspects of the process. It is this failure of metaphor, if you will, that has been noted by Thomas Kuhn in a different context—the power that scientific theories have over us in obscuring data and events that simply don't fit the theory. I shall elaborate further on Kuhn's ideas in chapter 10.

Another difficulty with metaphor is that our defining concept is typically more concrete and more clearly delineated in our experience than the activity or process we wish to describe. Being more concrete, there is always more in the defining concept than is (or should be) carried over to the defined concept. My love may be "like a red, red rose," but surely I don't think that she is rooted in soil or fertilized by bees. Or, as the poet Malcolm Cowley has put it:

Love is the flower of a day,
Love is a rosebud—anyway,
When we propound its every feature,
We make it sound like horticulture.[16]

These twin dysfunctions of metaphor—its tendency to obscure important parts of experience and its countertendency to say too much in a mistaken way—have important consequences for thought. As I shall note later, a poor metaphor applied to business can have enormously harmful effects when actions are based on a mistaken analogy. For these are not mere fanciful and playful verbal tricks; these are ideas that ground our experience and determine our actions. We take a very concrete concept, with all of its implications, and apply it to something else that may resemble the original concept in some ways but surely is not identical with it.

This leads to one of the most important ideas that Lakoff and Johnson present: the idea of *entailments* of metaphors. It is the entailments of a metaphor—the relationships and concepts that the metaphor brings to mind—that determine its power and richness.

The lover thought of as a red, red rose conjures up the images of youth, beauty, fragility, and freshness. As I noted earlier, there are other entailments that are much less useful, but they are there nonetheless. The idea of entailments explains a puzzle: How can we use quite different metaphors—sensibly—to describe the same thing? We would all be comfortable with describing an argument as a journey (the argument is *proceeding*), a container (points *in* the argument), or a building (*constructing* an argument). We can do this because these quite different metaphors share a key entailment—in this case, the entailment of a surface. (A journey describes a surface along its path, and a container has surfaces, as does a building.) In this way, we find that complete consistency across metaphors is quite rare, but coherence, in the sense of shared entailments, is typical.[17] Our minds appear comfortable with this coherence and ignore the substantial inconsistencies. We shall find individual business leaders using a wide assortment of metaphors, but we shall also see coherence in their thought through shared entailments.

Let me summarize the key points on metaphor:

- Metaphor is a fundamental property of thought and expression.

- Metaphors actually create reality for us.

- Metaphors can obscure phenomena from our experience.

- Metaphors carry along with them entailments from the defining concept.

- The entailments of quite different metaphors can be the same and permit coherence among different metaphors.

- The entailments of metaphors can be dangerously inappropriate.

The Metaphor in Business

My principal assumption, based on the idea that metaphor shapes thought, is that the metaphorical usage of business leaders is both a reflection and a prime determinant of their intellectual framework and, hence, their actions. I have reviewed a fair sample of business writings, from those of Josiah Wedgwood in the eighteenth century to those of contemporary business leaders. The source material has been entirely primary—autobiographies, speeches, and published interviews with the prime actors—people who have founded and/or led business enterprises. I am aware of two methodological difficulties with this approach: the possibility of insincere speech and the strong probability, especially among the moderns, that the words are not their own; that is, they have been ghost-written. These objections would be more valid if the metaphors used were exceptional, highly extended, or literary, but in fact, these speakers use such commonplace expressions, as we shall see, that we can be reasonably certain that the metaphors are indicative of the speakers' mental "furniture." Also, I must note that, regardless of the source, the speakers have agreed with the metaphors sufficiently to associate their names with the remarks.

From the almost limitless (and mainly, drearily dull) literature of business speech, I have selected forty-three actors from the past 200 years. The actors and their use of metaphor are listed in table 3–1. I found that just six metaphors are by far the most commonly used (in order): journey, machine, organism, war, game and society. The choice of a journey as a favorite metaphor becomes clear when we look at a partial list of entailments for these metaphors (table 3–2). A journey, particularly a sea voyage, is an especially rich metaphor; there are few business circumstances or activities, or indeed metaphors, that do not share entailments with the figure of a voyage.

It is interesting to trace the shift in metaphorical use over time. I have made some rather arbitrary time divisions in the data, I believe with some rationale:

1770–1905: From the beginning through the maturing of the Industrial Revolution. This is the period that remade our world into an industrial civilization.

1905–1941: The period of World War I and the Great Depression. During this period, very large organizations such as Ford and General Motors were created.

Table 3–1
Actors and Metaphors

Actor	Year	Journey	Game	War	Machine	Organism	Society
							Metaphor
Wedgwood	1770			X	X	X	X
Owen	1813				X		
Towne	1866				X		
Crouch	1869			X			
McHenry	1869			X			
Gould	1870		X	X			
Carnegie	1870		X				
Metcalfe	1885				X		
Fayol	1890					X	X
Gantt	1901						X
Taylor	1903		X		X		
Ford	1908	X				X	
Robb	1910					X	
Gilbreth	1923		X		X		
Sheldon	1923	X			X		
Sloan	1923	X				X	X
Follett	1927	X			X		
Hopf	1936	X			X	X	
Chester	1936	X					
Nichol	1941	X					
Robertson	1946					X	
Petersen	1955						X
Jones	1970	X		X			X
Wriston	1970	X	X			X	X
MacGregor	1970	X	X				X
Hanley	1970	X	X				
Watson	1970		X			X	X
Geneen	1984		X			X	
Cook	1984	X			X		
Sanford	1984	X					
Sperlich	1984	X	X	X			
Harnischfeger	1984	X				X	X
Anderson	1984	X				X	
Frisbee	1984			X		X	
Azzato	1985	X					
Stone	1985	X					
Burr	1986			X			
Iacocca	1986	X	X	X		X	X
Perot	1986		X	X			
Olsen	1986		X				
Kissinger	1986					X	
Michaels	1986			X		X	
Borman	1986			X		X	

Table 3–2
Entailments

Entailment	Metaphor					
	Journey	Game	War	Machine	Organism	Society
Goal/purpose	X	X	X	X	X	X
Profit production	X	X	X	X	X	
Difficulty	X	X	X			
Unpredictability	X	X	X		X	X
Adventure	X	X	X	X	X	
Pleasure	X	X				
Team	X	X				
Cooperation	X	X				X
Gamble	X	X	X			
Tool	X			X	X	
Leadership	X	X	X			X
Serious	X		X			
Peril	X		X			
Nonserious	X	X				
Win/loss		X	X			
Destroy opponent			X			
Competition		X	X		X	X
Needs				X	X	X
Precision		X	X			
Transcendent purpose					X	X
Grow/evolve/die					X	X
Meaning						X
Loss of control			X		X	
Relate to other systems/ecology			X		X	X
Ambiguity					X	X
A course	X				X	X
Culture						X
Predictable		X		X		
Vehicle	X			X		
Breakdown	X			X	X	
Destruction	X		X	X		
Personality/spirit					X	X
Learning					X	

1941–1975: The post–World War II period up to the oil crisis. This period was marked by the dominance of U.S. industry, which stood largely without competitors after the war.

1975–present: From the oil crisis up to the present day. In this period, U.S. industry lost its preeminence and was forced to compete strenuously with foreign competitors.

Using these time periods, we can then look at table 3–1 in another way: metaphor usage by period. Table 3–3 shows the percentage of actors in a period who used each metaphor.

One particularly striking shift is the absence of the journey metaphor in the early days, then its rise to a place of favor. Also, the machine analogy has fallen from its strong early position to almost the status of disuse. The society metaphor—particularly associated with the idea of corporate culture—had its heyday in the postwar period and now has fallen from favor.

What can we make of all this? I will make an attempt at explanation in part II, where I will show the correlation of metaphorical use with the actors' basic purpose or paradigm. But there is at least one other possibility for the shift in usage—the external appearance of the business and its change over time. For example, take the predominant use of the machine analogy in the early Industrial Revolution. The work done and the technology employed were fairly simple and were easily grasped by the most casual observer. Further, the workers, with their simple tasks, appeared to be no more nor less than parts of the process machinery. Marketing, distribution, and finance were child's play by modern standards, so the overall *experience* of a business was the factory and the machinelike workers. It takes little imagination to see these

Table 3–3
Actors' Use of Metaphor
(percentage of actors using the metaphor)

Period	Metaphor					
	Journey	Machine	Organism	War	Game	Society
1770–1905	0	40	10	30	20	10
1905–41	64	45	36	0	18	18
1941–75	57	0	43	14	57	71
1975–present	50	6	50	38	25	13

Note: Totals exceed 100 percent because most actors use more than one metaphor.

actors conceiving of the entire business and all its activities as a machine.

Later, the idea of a business as an organism gained currency. Any observer would have noted that many businesses grew—that is, grew from a physical standpoint—more buildings, more machines, more workers. Others were seen to grow smaller in the same terms, and still others ceased operation, leaving abandoned buildings and equipment. Processes that grow, waste away, and die are all around us in the natural world, so the idea of businesses as organisms would be simple and compelling.

Business became much more complex after World War II. The workers' tasks became highly differentiated, many more knowledge workers were required, and hierarchical organizations with many levels of distinct skills and an enormous amount of human interaction—became common. A hierarchical organization, composed of heterogeneous individuals who must interact extensively—what could be a better metaphor for this than a society?

I believe that business metaphors are rooted in larger patterns of thought and in the actor's purpose, but it would seem that the external appearance of a business would make these metaphors quite congenial to the participants, especially when other ideas support these views.

We now turn to a thorough investigation of each of the prime metaphors used by business leaders. It should be noted here that these metaphors fall into two classes: descriptions of processes (journey, game, war) and descriptions of systems (machine, organism, society). That this is a real distinction can be demonstrated by another look at table 3–2: Of the thirty-three entailments listed in the table, twenty are shared exclusively by either process metaphors or system metaphors. The process metaphors convey some key business concepts: the ideas of difficulty, risk, winning and losing, and team effort. But these metaphors leave out other important ideas that the system metaphors suggest, particularly the concept of the needs of the system. The organism and society metaphors further suggest the facts of growth, evolution, and death; the ideas of a transcendent purpose and a unique spirit; and the key entailment of ambiguity.

In summary, this chapter has taught us:

- Metaphor is an all-pervasive form of language.

- Metaphor structures our view of reality, our basic thought processes.

- The power of a metaphor derives from its entailments, the concepts and images that the metaphor conjures up for us.

- The most popular business metaphors have been: journey, machine, organism, war, game, and society.

- The metaphorical use of businessmen has changed dramatically over the years.

4

The Journey

Leadership and le Voyage sans But

Tell me, O Muse, the story of that clever man who wandered far and wide after he had destroyed the sacred city of Troy. He had many painful and bitter experiences at sea while trying to get his men and himself safely home.

—Homer[1]

The Journey in Literature

From the very beginnings of literature, the journey has been a metaphor for the vicissitudes of human existence. One study describes the journey as "a basic and inextricable form of the imaginative life of man"[2]—that is, a fundamental metaphor structuring everyone's perception of his own life's experience.

Many of the great works of world literature are extended journey metaphors, from the preclassical *Odyssey* to Yeats's "Sailing to Byzantium" in the twentieth century. Every schoolboy could compile his own list of great journey tales: *The Aeneid, The Divine Comedy, The Canterbury Tales, Pilgrim's Progress, Gulliver's Travels.*

There are two separate themes in these journey works: an impulse toward renewal and rejuvenation and an impulse toward unity of knowledge—the need to make sense of the world, to order it in some way.[3]

The journey of renewal—best expressed in classical times in Virgil's *Aeneid*—took on a different light in the nineteenth-century Romantic movement. In Coleridge's "Ancient Mariner" and By-

ron's "Childe Harold," we find less rejuvenation than an aimless-
ness, *le voyage sans but*—the journey without a purpose, the journey as an end in itself.[4] The great French poet of the period, Charles
Baudelaire, summed up this image:

> *Mais les vrais voyageurs sont seux-la seuls qui partent*
> *pour partir . . .*
> *Et, sans savoir pourquoi, disent toujours:*
> *Allons!*[5]

> [The true voyagers are only those who part for the sake of part-
> ing—and, without knowing why, always say: Let's go!]

Conceivably, this treatment of the journey theme in the literature
of the time could account for the total absence of the metaphor in
the speech of contemporary business leaders. A journey without a
purpose could hardly appear congenial to men whose objective was
money-making—the prevailing view of the nineteenth-century
businessman. *Allons,* indeed!

However, this theme—*le voyage sans but*—has become important in modern times. The notion of business as a great, aimless
journey became associated with the business purposes of production and institution-building—production of goods as an end in
itself and the indefinite prolongation of a company's existence. We
shall explore this connection in part II.

The second theme—the search for order—has its roots in classical literature and was the impulse for some of the greatest
twentieth-century verse—Yeats's Byzantium poems. For Yeats, Byzantium—the capital of the Eastern Roman Empire—represented
the highest achievement of mankind: the harmonious blending of
all aspects of life—art, government, society—into a seamless whole.
Total harmony and order. In the first of these poems, "Sailing to
Byzantium," Yeats deplores the world of flesh and desire; he makes
his escape:

> And therefore I have sailed the seas and come
> To the holy city of Byzantium.

He asks of the Byzantine sages:

> Consume my heart away, sick with desire
> And fastened to a dying animal,
> I know not what it is; and gather me
> into the artifice of eternity.[6]

The later poem, "Byzantium," continues the poet's search for wholeness and his distaste for the complications of life:

> A star lit or a moon lit dome disdains
> All that man is,
> All mere complexities,
> The fury and the mire of human veins.[7]

The complexities of existence are disdained; the poet finds in By-zantium the meaning and coherence that he seeks. We shall find no business leaders with Yeats's power of expression, but many speak of journeys, and many seek meaning.

The Journey in Business

Clearly, the ties of business speech to literature could be tenuous in the extreme; but in fact, I found no use of the journey metaphor in my sample before the early twentieth century. As I have said, the early days of industrialization were contemporaneous with the Romantic movement in literature; the voyage without a purpose was unlikely to resonate with business leaders interested in generating wealth. Yeats's impulse to order, to make sense of the world, would be far more congenial.

Henry Ford, who used metaphor very sparingly in his 1923 autobiography, was the first business speaker whom I found employing this particular analogy. He spoke not of his business but of life as "not a location, but a journey."[8] The metaphor became quite popular thereafter in business speech. Alfred Sloan spoke of "the great adventure" at General Motors in the 1920s and 1930s;[9] but then, as the Depression approached:

> Before it was realized what was happening, this great ship of ours
> was in the midst of a terrific storm.[10]

Oliver Sheldon, a British businessman writing in 1923, saw himself "piloting the ship through the waters of change."[11] C.M. Chester, then chairman of General Foods, delivered a speech entitled "The Great Highway" on October 19, 1936. His highly extended metaphor pictures American business as journeying on the Great Highway, always making progress (this, recall, in the midst of the Great Depression). In his view:

> The road rapidly has been getting wider, straighter, smoother and brighter than ever.[12]

Journeys in general have been used often, but the most common metaphor has been a sea voyage. F.W. Nichol, the head of IBM in 1941, refers to "keeping one's head above water, staying afloat, swimming against the current, etc."[13] We find Citicorp's Wriston (mid-1970s) "sailing into waters [he] didn't know much about,"[14] joined by Monsanto's Hanley, of the same era, who wanted all to "get in the boat and row together."[15] Iacocca, writing in 1986, "jumped ship"[16] to Chrysler and found himself in "uncharted waters"[17] and, worse yet, "aboard a sinking ship."[18] His colleague Sperlich also saw "impending difficulty over the horizon" but knew his man would "remain at the helm."[19]

Enough. The journey analogy has become one of Orwell's worn-out metaphors as a description of life in general and of business activity. What is the peculiar attraction of this trope? Clearly, it stems from the very richness of the metaphor, the very large number of ideas that are associated with it. It is "perhaps the most complex and capacious in the history of literature."[20] Quite a number of entailments of the journey metaphor are useful for business description.

Entailments of the Journey

First, a journey normally has a goal, some objective or purpose to be attained; there is a natural carryover to any business—indeed, to any form of human endeavor. This is the entailment that Yeats expressed. And in business, we routinely talk about our goals and objectives as well as *milestones,* a direct reference to the journey trope. The voyage and business are also linked through the idea of a course to be traversed. Most business leaders think in terms of the "course" they and the business are on, either where events are "taking them" or where they "want to go."

A journey idea—particularly a sea voyage—can be a fairly good fit to the wealth-producing purpose of a business. We think of treasure ship or commercial cargo voyages—activities whose purpose is to produce wealth. Linked to this idea is the entailment of difficulty, even the peril of an undertaking. There is always the possibility of catastrophic failure: breakdown, shipwreck, and destruction. The "crash" of 1929 embodies this idea—a great journey come a cropper.

All the perils and trials of a sea voyage can really be subsumed under a key entailment: unpredictability. Life's uncertainty could not be better expressed than by an aphorism of the Italian humanist Guicciardini:

> When I consider the infinite ways in which human life is subject to accident, sickness, chance and violence, and when I consider how many things must combine during the year to produce a good harvest, nothing surprises me more than to see an old man, a good year.[21]

The radical contingency of all existence is vividly portrayed in the image of a sea voyage. We have all been riveted by Bligh's travail after the mutiny: the unlucky captain set adrift in the *Bounty* launch with eighteen loyal men, the mutineers exacting their revenge just short of outright slaughter. But for all his faults, Bligh was the consummate sailor and commander. In a 23-foot open boat, he managed a voyage of 3,600 miles through uncharted waters and brought his men to safety in the Dutch East Indies, seven weeks after the mutiny.[22]

In the plastic arts, we need only recall Géricault's *Raft of the Medusa,* a masterpiece of Romantic painting, to catch the concept of unpredictability, risk. The huge canvas—portraying the dead and dying, the pitiful survivors waving a rag to a tiny sail on the stormy horizon—still epitomizes "shipwreck" for every visitor to the Louvre.

Now a business is not subject to the whims of wind and tide, the fury of storms, the perils of reefs and shoals, and the depredations of (real) pirates and savages, but it is certainly unpredictable in the extreme. The entire scientific management movement, with Frederick Taylor in the vanguard, is largely an attempt to limit this endemic unpredictability of business.

But business is not, or does not have to be, all that grim. The journey analogy also conveys the adventure of engaging in a competitive business—the risks, the gamble, and, frankly, the sheer fun of it all. The perils and unpredictability are, to many, the spice that makes it all worthwhile as a life-long pursuit. This entailment is closely associated with *le voyage sans but* of the Romantic poets; there are many who *"partent pour partir."*

That said, the journey metaphor can also make us conscious of business as a serious undertaking. Many go to sea or embark on long, difficult journeys for the adventure, but in most cases there is a serious purpose as well—educational, scientific, political, or pecuniary. For example, *The Journals of Lewis and Clark*[23] shows the protagonists clearly enjoying the experience but also filled with a sense of mission and serous purpose.

Another key entailment of the voyage idea is the complex of ideas surrounding leadership. We immediately conjure up the idea of a strong, knowledgeable leader in whom we must put our trust, the related idea of a close-knit team, and the necessity for harmony and cooperation. These are all important features of a successful business and are a constant challenge to those less successful. The modern business concepts of teamwork and management leadership fit very comfortably with this entailment of the voyage metaphor.

Strengths and Weaknesses of the Metaphor

As noted, the journey metaphor, once it began to be employed, maintained a highly popular status. In all periods other than the early days, the analogy has been one of the most frequently used. The metaphor's main strength is its ability to capture the emotional intensity of operating a business. With a journey, especially a sea voyage, as our organizing principle, we can represent the spirit of business leadership and entrepreneurism: the adventure, the peril of the unknown, the need for the highest forms of leadership and team work, and perhaps most important, the sheer pleasure of it. This certainly accounts for its enduring power and utility in thought and expression. When "voyage" terms are used, the employees of a business are signaled several things. They clearly see the need for leadership—a ship's captain has had unthinking acceptance of his authority since the dawn of time. The employees—the crew—also grasp the need for cooperation and internal harmony; every ship is in peril with dissension aboard. And when managers use the language of a voyage, the employees intuitively grasp the risk of the enterprise but also the possibilities of adventure, the sense that they are part of an important undertaking.

But the metaphor has some very serious limitations, as we would expect, in the important areas that are left out. It totally misses the complexity of business, all the myriad interactions, the constant shifting from subject to subject—personnel management, marketing, production, R&D, materials management, finance, and so on. And a business doesn't come into port; the "journey" doesn't end. The day-in, day-out aspects of a business operation simply do not come through from this analogy.

A working definition of a good metaphor would have to be its efficacy: What can we *do* with this metaphor? How does it lead to action? One can express what it is *like* to run a business—what it feels like emotionally—but there are few guides to action, and those are very limited. There is one guide, however, for the business in trouble. Then, the CEO usually gets involved in all day-to-day decisions at almost all levels; we say that he "takes the helm when the ship is in a storm." These are very common expressions in business and, indeed, very common actions. So the sea voyage metaphor's strongest practical feature is its definition of the role of the leader. The captain of a ship, time out of mind, has had unlimited and unquestioned authority. He is the one who gives the orders, takes the risks, and reaps the rewards. The romantic notion of the man at the helm in a storm, the loneliness of command, the uniqueness of ultimate responsibility—these certainly are compelling images to any leader. (There is a bit of Odysseus in all of us.) But the journey idea doesn't give a clue about how to organize or how to deal with competition, shareholders, customers, capital markets, or virtually anything at all. Thus, it is a very rich, highly popular metaphor, but it is useful mainly for describing the actors' emotional state. This can be helpful, but when the idea conveyed is *le voyage sans but,* it can be quite pernicious. It can too easily slide into the romantic notion of a purposeless voyage, a ship of fools, and no business should be operated without some concern for the benefits to the larger society. This can happen if the metaphor's force guides the leader toward the purposeless voyage.

The metaphor's very weakness—that it is a problematical guide to action—as well as its richness can explain its long-term popularity. Since we can conceive of a business as something else entirely (either another process or another system) and still talk about it as a journey (because of shared entailments of these metaphors), then we can use both: the journey to describe the emotive state and other metaphors as guides to concrete action.

Summary

- The journey metaphor has been used extensively in literature since the dawn of time.

- There are two very different strains of thought in this trope: *le voyage sans but*—the journey without a purpose—popularized by the nineteenth-century Romantic movement in literature; and the journey to seek harmony and order in existence.

- The journey is a very rich metaphor; that is, there are numerous entailments that are useful for the business leader.

- The key entailments are a goal, difficulty, wealth production, unpredictability, adventure, the need for leadership, and the need for cooperation and teamwork.

- The metaphor is weak in that it misses the complexity of business—the multifaceted demands on the leader.

- The journey figure, in its *voyage sans but* variety, can be pernicious for the business leader, guiding him away from the serious purposes of business and toward the notion of an aimless enterprise, a ship of fools.

- The metaphor is strongest in representing the emotional state of a leader—his awareness of risk, adventure, and the call for leadership.

- The metaphor can be helpful to the leader of a troubled business, who must take personal command and must convey the risks to the employees. This is the key leader role that the metaphor supports.

- The voyage metaphor was never used in the early days of industrialization; it became very popular in the period from 1905 to 1941 (when it was dominant) and has remained highly popular. Today it is matched only by the organism trope in its frequency of use.

Let us now turn to another process metaphor—the idea of business as a game.

5
The Game

The Playing Fields of Business

Business is the greatest game in the world.

—Andrew Carnegie[1]

Early Examples

Andrew Carnegie (1835–1919) is now remembered principally as a humanitarian; his name is associated with hundreds of small-town Carnegie Libraries. In his lifetime, he gave away $350 million (those were pre–World War I dollars).[2] The metamorphosis of the memories of rapacious men like Carnegie and Henry Frick is an irony of history; Carnegie is now linked with the light of learning for small-town America, and Frick's name is associated with one of the best small museums in the world (New York's Frick Collection).

But Carnegie and Frick were both major participants in the rough-and-tumble of American industrialization, at a time when vast fortunes were made and the business leader exacted the utmost from both his workers and his less daring or more scrupulous competitors. One of Carnegies's biographers describes him as "the most cruel taskmaster American industry has ever known,"[3] whose "end was money and yet more money."[4] It is odd that despite these ferocious descriptions, Carnegie himself seemed to view business in terms of play, saying: "Business is the greatest game in the world."[5] He is reported to have scorned the technical details of his business (steel)—thinking instead in terms of surprise, competitive advantage, and winning. His statement upon entering the steel business in 1872 is revealing: "Let's build a steel plant as fast as we can and get into the game."[6]

Jay Gould (1836–92), another of the old "robber barons," appears to have had a similar view of business. In his lifetime, Gould was reviled as a master schemer and a money-mad speculator, and these characterizations have some merit. A recent biographer (Klein) attempts to restore Gould's reputation, but even he admits that his man had a view of ethical and legal niceties that bordered on the amoral. Gould routinely "employed bribery and other shady practices."[7] In Gould's defense, Klein shows that Gould was no worse than his contemporaries, and if he had a fault, it was simply that he was abler than his competitors and critics.

After a variety of business experiences, Gould built his fortune on speculation. He surprised everyone when, in 1883, he took control of the Erie Railroad and then actually seemed intent on operating the road, not just cashing in speculative profits as had been his custom. Speaking of that time, Gould said: "I didn't care about the money I made. I took the road more as a play thing to see what I could do with it."[8]

This aspect of Gould's thinking is highlighted by his biographer, who concludes that the game itself was the compelling attraction for Gould; money alone would not motivate a personality so complex. Gould was as much chess master as businessman, thriving on the challenge of intricate problems, stimulated by the clash of wits: "Wealth and power were markers of success, but it was the contest itself that animated him."[9]

The game analogy pervades Klein's study of Gould, with chess as the favorite metaphor. Gould is frequently described as a grand master—a player of such force and skill that he could make wholesale revisions in the rules.[10]

Taylor, Too

So this idea of business as a game—a notion that we mainly associate with today's sports-happy American executives—actually has its roots in much earlier times and is linked to such figures as

Carnegie and Gould, hardly playful types. The least likely figure for the game metaphor would have to be Frederick Taylor, that grim champion of mechanistic thought. However, Taylor himself used the analogy, although in a very characteristic way. Football was Taylor's chosen metaphor, and we can count him the first in a long line of business speakers to employ this particular analogy. Writing in 1911, Taylor thought football a "pretty good piece of Scientific Management"[11] and compared the game to a business enterprise. In his emphasis on the mechanistic aspects of the game, Taylor diverged from current usage, which stresses the game's leadership and competitive aspects.

Taylor focused more on the mechanical side of football, the intricate team effort—Gilbreth's "one best way"[12] to perform each of the game's tasks. Football is a game that places a premium on the division of labor—having specialists with highly differentiated skills at each position. Also, a football play requires the precise subordination of each player's actions to the objective of the play itself; there is little room for creativity, spontaneity, or individual judgment. In all these respects, the game was a fine analogy for Taylor's view of a business operation: precision, analysis, and optimization of each process and the workers' unthinking performance of regimented tasks. If there is a game that is not a game, play that is not play, with the focus on regimentation as opposed to spontaneity, it is the game of football.

Ken Olsen, founder and CEO of Digital Equipment Corporation, has used the game analogy to speak against the machine metaphor for his business. Olsen is in the habit of writing parables and sending them to his management team as guides to their thinking. In one of these, he contrasted the two ways to solve a jigsaw puzzle.[13] The first way, the implicitly mechanistic way, is to look at the puzzle and never make a move until you are convinced that all the parts fit together. This seems businesslike: "Do nothing until you see the whole problem through to the end"—that is, gather facts, analyze, plan, and so forth. For Olsen, this approach stifles all innovation; the proper way to solve the puzzle is to look at the pieces, and any time two seem to fit together, fit them together— that is, act, even on partial information. This is hardly scientific management, but it is a commonsense approach to problem solving and is probably a factor in the enormous success that Olsen's company has enjoyed.

Modern Usage

Game metaphors have become commonplace among modern business leaders—particularly in the sense of "winning." Walter Wriston, former chairman of Citicorp, speaks of "winning the game in the marketplace."[14] Ian MacGregor, who built AMAX, was not a speculator but nevertheless had the gambler's instinct and thought in terms of deals and coups.[15] He had the gambler's sense of the uncertainty and unpredictability of any action:

> Managing a company is a little like playing gin rummy. . . . You have to play your hand in accordance to what happens, how the cards turn up.[16]

Other leaders have stressed different aspects of play. Thomas Watson introduced the "penalty box"[17] into IBM. In hockey, a player who commits a miscue (foul), is removed from play for a fixed period. Similarly at IBM, the executive who had made a bad mistake was not fired (ejected from the game) but was moved to a less challenging assignment for a time, then reinstated if his performance and attitude were satisfactory.

Chrysler's Sperlich used a game analogy in a scornful manner, referencing cricket as a symbol of an effete, upper-class pastime. In his view, the Big Three auto makers "ran the game like a cricket match on Sunday afternoon."[18] His mentor, Lee Iacocca, is quite representative of modern American business in his penchant for the game metaphor. The following are samples of Iacocca's language from his autobiography:

> "Let them know the game plan"[19] (reference to football)

> "The speed of the boss is the speed of the team"[20] (race)

> "Pre-game sessions"[21] (football)

> "Nobody knew who was on first"[22] (baseball)

"Going down the tubes"[23] (surfing)

"Our battery and infield were in place"[24] (baseball)

". . . staggering from the first punch—the second almost knocked us out"[25] (boxing)

and, complaining about Japanese competition:

"[There is not] a level playing field for this game"[26] (football or baseball)

Ross Perot scoffs at the notion of a level playing field—now a fixture of American business thought. Referring to U.S. postwar domination, he says that the "level playing field" for the United States was one where we owned both teams and the stadium. How could we lose? Now, Perot advises America to beat the Japanese "on blocking and tackling" instead of buying new uniforms—that is, making cosmetic changes.[27]

Like many American businessmen, Iacocca is a great admirer of Vince Lombardi, the late coach of the Green Bay Packers football team. Iacocca thinks that Lombardi's principles of football are applicable to business: teach the fundamentals, enforce discipline, play as a team.[28]

Even the sober Harold Geneen succumbed to the prevalent game metaphor in American business. He speaks of his ITT associates as a "team," with a "game plan," that frequently "huddled" and occasionally needed "new players."[29]

Donaldson and Lorsch's 1983 book, *Decision Making at the Top,* studies contemporary American business leaders, concluding that these leaders are fundamentally gamesmen—motivated to win the game they are playing.[30] And game metaphors have become extremely common in modern times, especially, as I have noted, with the accent on winning. Although Iacocca does not cite this tenet of Lombardi's "philosophy," Lombardi's most popular aphorism is "Winning is not everything, it is the only thing." The phrase is nonsensical English (how is *everything* distinguishable from the *only* thing in this usage?), but this scarcely concerns the Lombardi cult. The words resonate with many businessmen's fundamental belief: The objective is to *win;* there is no other goal or purpose. Apparently, it was this that drove Jay Gould, rich beyond the dreams of Croesus, to ruin his health in the pursuit of ever more complex and challenging contests.

The Structure of Games

Games have a peculiar hold on most of us; perhaps it is our childhood throwing a long shadow over our adult years. The spontaneity, challenge, and joy of games are an integral part of most lives, from the middle-aged marathon runner to the sedentary bridge or chess player. Like so much of our culture and thinking, we owe the spirit of games to the classical Greeks. Edith Hamilton, the popularizer of Greek culture, tells us that the Greeks introduced adult play to the world; a careful study of Egyptian art and records shows nothing comparable. As Hamilton noted:

> The Greeks were the first people in the world to play, and they played on a great scale. All over Greece there were games, all sorts of games. . . . [They] strove for an honor so coveted as hardly anything else in Greece. An Olympic victor—triumphing generals would give him place.[31]

From the Greeks, we have inherited both this passion for games and the game as a metaphor for life. James Carse, professor of religion at New York University, has provided an analysis of the structure of games that illuminates the utility of the game metaphor for life and, I believe, for business as well. Carse, in *Finite and Infinite Games,* develops a number of highly useful definitions that can order our discussion of games. Carse's first distinction is between finite and infinite games. (The title of the work emphasizes the importance of this distinction for Carse.) Simply, finite games are played for the purpose of winning and thus ending the game; infinite games are played for the purpose of continuing the play.[32] I will focus first on finite games, since business speakers, in their analogies, appear to be concerned with such play—play that results in a clear-cut victory, as the sports analogies imply.

A finite game, if it is to be won by anyone, must have a definite end; in most games, the end of the game occurs when one side is victorious. (Ties are an obvious exception, and their peculiar unsatisfactoriness is explained by the violation of this principle. We abhor that ambiguity—a game completed without a victory.)

Also, there is no game unless the players freely choose to play; no one can be forced to play. Carse says, "Whoever *must* play, cannot *play*."[33] This is the commonsense notion of games and play—the freedom of the players to engage in the contest. Also, the term *game* implies that one cannot play alone; one must find an opponent—another who sees the activity as a game and agrees to the rules—and one usually needs teammates as well.

The idea of a game is closely tied to the idea of rules. It is by knowing the rules that we know what the game is. Rules also establish limitations on the players; rules are the contract among the players so that they can decide who has won. Rules, of course, cannot change in the course of play—at least for finite games, in Carse's terminology.

One last point is necessary on the nature of finite games: Such games are, in essence, murderous. The game is ended only when a terminal move is made, when one player is established as the winner and the opponent is dead as a player—dead in the sense of being incapable of further play.[34]

This brings out another point: the linkage of the game and war metaphors. In finite games, as in war, the objective is to eliminate the opponent. This implication of "game" may be a peculiarly American one—the assumption that playing implies that you have to be the best, that there is only one winner, and that losing is the same as dying. The spirit of the Greeks is lost—the sense of playing for the sheer joy of it, win or lose. The idea of play for play's sake is really embodied in Carse's other species of game—the infinite game.

But business people seem to prefer finite games—the types of games that spring to mind when we search for examples (football, baseball, bridge, chess, and so on), the games to which our business leaders endlessly compare their activities. Infinite games have an entirely different structure; their only similarity to finite games is that they, too, require a free choice from the player—whoever *must* play, cannot *play*. As mentioned earlier, infinite games are played for the purpose of continuing play, not ending it with a victory. In contrast to the fixed temporal and spatial nature of finite play, the infinite players cannot say when the game began, nor do they care; their purpose is to prevent the game from ending. To keep the game going, the rules must change:

> They are changed when the players agree they must or the game can't go on. . . . [They are] changed to prevent anyone from winning, and to bring as many people as possible into the game.[35]

As we examine the entailments of the game metaphor, I think it will become clear that the game is a good analogy for business, but that the particular analogies used by business leaders, because of their "finiteness," have serious limitations. I believe Carse's infinite game has a good deal more merit.

Goals and Difficulties

Any game—or at least any finite game—as we have seen from Carse, must have a purpose, an object. Even an infinite game is played for the curious purpose of continuing the play. This entailment of the metaphor is shared, of course, by most metaphors for business; we can see the coherence of this entailment with the voyage and organism tropes. As I have already noted, the purpose of the game of business, in the minds of business speakers, is highly focused on winning the game—a basic characteristic of finite games. This is not necessarily a poor implication of the game idea; businesses of any type naturally have objectives, and success in any terms is commonly associated with winning.

Another entailment of "game" that is shared by other business metaphors is the notion of a profit-producing activity. This may seem contradictory when we think of the free, spontaneous aspects of play. It was an idea quite foreign to the Greeks; the Olympic champion, regardless of the status and adulation, received only a crown of wild olives. But the modern businessman's fixation on sports and sports analogies really lies with professional sports—games that are played to be won but also to reward the participants in monetary terms, not mere glory.

References to amateur games are rare. Iacocca and others revere Lombardi—a professional coach. Baseball analogies are in terms of the major league, professional game. MacGregor speaks of gin rummy—a game, like poker, that is played for monetary stakes and loses meaning and interest if played for match-sticks. Perhaps this explains Sperlich's contemptuous reference to cricket; the game he describes on the "Sunday afternoon" is resolutely amateur—a gentleman's game.

For a game to be worth playing, there must also be some degree of difficulty. We learn at a very early age that tic-tac-toe is too easy, and few adults would spend time on it. Every tennis player plays to win, but who would continue to play an opponent if every set were won at love? A game holds our interest only if it presents an intellectual challenge, is played against an opponent of near-equal skills, or requires somewhat difficult physical exertions. This is a good match to the world of business in representing the challenge and difficulty of managing an enterprise.

Unpredictability

Games share with business, and with other business metaphors, the characteristic of unpredictability. There are two types of unpredictability in games, just as there are in business. First, there is the basic contingency of events, as we have seen in Guicciardini's aphorism (see chapter 4). Luck plays its part. Any game is subject to the bounce of the ball, the fall of the dice, the run of the cards.

The other source of unpredictability is the behavior of the opponent. Carse shows us that surprise is the key ingredient in winning. And by the same token, a good player is one who can anticipate the moves of his opponent:

The Master Player who already knows what moves are to be made has a decisive advantage over the unprepared player. . . .

A finite player is trained to anticipate every future possibility, to control the future.[36]

In business, this is no more than Taylor's scientific management. Business schools teach the aspiring business player the tools of analysis and prediction. The objective is to remove most, if not all, unpredictability from the game and give the manager a decisive advantage in his "play." As we have seen, the root purpose of scientific management is to remove ambiguity from business, reduce the complexity, and permit a degree of predictability—much like Carse's "Master Player."

If there is one focus of modern business education, it is to train students for the analysis of typical business situations; they are really armed only to avoid surprise, rather than to have a mental attitude that seeks unusual connections—the font of creativity. As Carse puts it: "To be prepared against surprise is to be *trained*. To be prepared for surprise is to be *educated*.[37]

Fun

Calling an activity a game implies, of course, that the activity is undertaken for pleasure; the most common definition of *game* is "an amusement" or "a pastime." This is both a helpful concept and a potentially pernicious one for the business leader. The entailment does capture the adventure and enjoyment of operating a business—the challenge and the rewards for success. On the other hand, the concept could minimize the seriousness of the undertaking—managing a business is certainly more than a pastime. As Carse has noted, players must be free to play, or there is no game. But Carse also warns that players must veil this freedom from themselves; they must "forget" the voluntary aspect, or the competitive spirit will desert them.[38] In short, players must act seriously. This is a very wise caution; the operator of any business has a responsibility for the careers and well-being of any number of people—employees, suppliers, customers, stockholders. Only the solitary speculator "plays" alone. All other business people carry many hopes and fortunes with them, and if they are or consider themselves gamesmen, they must veil this, even from themselves, and act seriously and responsibly.

The Team and the Risk

There are very few games that are played alone—that is, alone against a single competitor—and these games, such as tennis and boxing, are chosen infrequently by business speakers in their use of metaphor. "Game," then, usually implies a team, with the concomitants of cooperation and leadership. We are all familiar with teams that are unsuccessful, even though they have superior talent. The players either cannot cooperate or have lacked the time to gather to learn smooth team play. All-star games in most highly integrated team sports, such as football and basketball, are rarely well played, although the talent on the field is definitively the best. Most sports watchers would agree that a reasonably good team that has been built over the years and has practiced together for some time would defeat any transient assemblage of all-stars. This illustrates the vital need for cooperation—the meshing of individual talents into an effective whole—and it also illustrates the role of leadership. Like an organism, a good team has a spirit that animates it, sparked either by a key player who inspires the team or a charismatic coach or manager.

All look to the team leader for the key play, but more often for the word or gesture that solidifies and motivates. Superior coaches also have this talent; coaching or teaching skills are necessary, but not sufficient, for a winning coach. The leader must also, somehow, make the players *believe*—believe that their victory is inevitable, that they will carry all before them, regardless of the opponent, situation, or score. Clearly, these entailments of teamwork and leadership are highly useful for a business.

The last entailment that I will touch on is the idea of risk. As mentioned earlier, Ian MacGregor chose a card game, the gambling man's game of gin rummy, as a metaphor for business. Any game entails risk; it would hardly be a game if it did not. Unless something of value is at stake—if only prestige—no one would bother playing. That business is a risky proposition goes without saying.

Strengths of the Metaphor

I have already covered most of the strengths of the metaphor—the entailments that make "game" a good fit with business activity. Like business, a game is almost by definition a goal-oriented activity, a process that is directed toward success. The analogy also conveys the sense of the adventure and pleasure that can be derived from business—a sense that is totally missing from the system metaphors (machine, organism, society) but is shared with the voyage idea.

As I have noted, games also involve risk or gamble—a very close fit with business activity. But the metaphor's greatest practical strengths for a businessman are probably the related entailments of cooperation and teamwork—again, ideas that are shared with the voyage metaphor but are brought into sharper focus for us moderns by the notion of a game. Few of us have had the experience of a risky ocean voyage, but virtually all male adults have played team sports and can relate directly to the spirit of a team and the impact of superior leadership. We can share Bligh and his crew's experiences only vicariously, but most of us have had the direct, concrete experience of executing a complex team maneuver in football or basketball and can feel at a visceral level the pride and satisfaction of those activities. Similarly, we have all directly experienced the pound on the back from the team captain, the highly charged words of a coach, and we can associate these experiences with the game metaphor. (Incidentally, it has been said that women of a certain age, not having had boys' routine experience of team sports, have difficulty with the requirements of team play in business—a requirement that seems like second nature to men. In recent years, however, team sports of all types have been heavily emphasized for young girls, and any later handicap for them in business should disappear quickly.) In business, many seem to harken back to these experiences and feel comfort in the game metaphor as they cope with the difficulties of coordination and cooperation in a business environment.

Leadership is also a very apt entailment of the game metaphor; again, our own direct experience in team sports provides a model for business activity. Whether we have exercised leadership personally or have only been directly affected by it, the process, the essential feel of leadership, is familiar to us and has a certain fitness about it. No business can function without leadership at many levels, and the use of game metaphors makes the idea of leadership compelling and natural and actively promotes the need for and the exercise of leadership.

Weaknesses of the Metaphor

The game metaphor is not without some serious limitations. The metaphor is simply too pat; it entirely misses the complexity and ambiguity of business. Games—even the most complex, such as chess or football—have very rigid boundaries: rules, playing field, time constraints. Very little of this is applicable to the operation of a business, which is a process that extends out in time with no fixed end and involves frequent changes in scope and activities. In fact, an overreliance on game metaphors could probably account for the American fixation on quarter-by-quarter performance. We all tend to think in these terms now in business—the artificial time boundaries of a quarter as a time to show results, to "win" or "lose." The Japanese—at least in modern American business folklore—do not share these concerns. Apparently, their view of the "game," if they view it as a game at all, is much closer to Carse's *infinite* game—a process whose aim is to continue play. We are told that their time horizon is radically different—decades and centuries, not quarters. They share with Carse's infinite players the aim of participating in a process that will endure beyond their individual lives.

Fundamentally, the connotation of winning and losing is a weak match with actual business experience. Everyone has received contracts in competitive situations, and that could be construed as winning, but rarely does it end the process; there are always other orders and, in fact, other competitors. The definitive win—the move that ends the game—is a very rare experience in business. Companies do go bankrupt—exit the game, if you will—but rarely from one bold stroke of a competitor; and almost always, the fallen "player" is replaced by another competitor.

The concept of "winning," although highly popular and well ingrained in us from sports analogies, is not a particularly useful idea. Business, in its essence, is raising capital, designing and producing a product or service, finding a customer for it, and servicing that customer. What that has to do with winning and losing is really rather obscure.

The other harmful aspect of the game metaphor is the connotation of an amusement, a pastime, a nonserious activity. Even if the "game" chosen is not a physical sport but an intellectual exercise like chess, the analogy is potentially harmful. Because games *are* pastimes—sterile activities (except as recreation) in the serious business of living and providing a livelihood for human beings. The idea of managing a business for the purpose of intellectual stimulation is a particularly pernicious notion.

Herman Hesse has explored perfect gamesmen in his novel *Magister Ludi.*[39] The original German title is *Das Glasperlinspiel*—"The Glass-Bead Game"—a highly complex, elaborate activity that is played according to the strictest rules by monklike mandarins who live in an intellectual paradise, Castalia. The province of Castalia is devoted exclusively to affairs of the mind—the playing of the glass-bead game; the players devote all their time and energy to the game.

The speculator Jay Gould bears a certain resemblance to the Castalians in his sterile exercise of intellectual powers in a great, complex game, with money only a means to keep score. Nothing is created in those worlds—Gould's or Hesse's; nothing is produced, and there is no gain for the nation or society. It is a game played only for the player's sake.

The Team Leader

The obvious guide for a business leader in the game metaphor is to act as a captain or a coach. The distinction between the two is a real one, both in sports and in business. The captain is an active player—quarterback, play-making guard, catcher. He is the player who is responsible for on-field coordination, and he has generally been given the role for his leadership qualities as well as his technical skills. In business, this is the familiar figure of the day-to-day "hands-on" manager—the one who makes assignments, reviews results, and motivates—even drives—people. A game of any complexity requires a "field general"; and every business needs technically competent managers with administrative skills and leadership qualities.

The coach plays a different but equally important role. "Coach" carries the connotation of teaching, and teaching is a vital part of a team coach's role. Every great coach has been a great teacher— surprisingly, perhaps, even in professional sports whose athletes have played the game since they were small children. But a great teaching coach has the intimate knowledge of the game's techniques that can benefit players at any level of experience. Lombardi is remembered as an inspirational leader, but he was a master technician as well—an expert in every aspect of the game. In the very same way, a business leader must continually coach his subordinates in the variegated aspects of their jobs. And in business at the higher levels, the required skill set is very broad: personnel management, decision making, financial analysis, technical grasp, strategic thinking, and so forth.

In sports, the coach is also the chief motivator. Styles vary enormously, and truly charismatic leaders are rare, but any successful coach must inspire confidence, even a feeling of invincibility, among the players. The connection between teaching and motivating is really very close; players gain confidence in their abilities and their team when they know that they are in the hands of a master of the game. (This probably explains why most successful coaches were very competent players themselves—even stars—in their own time.)

In business, exactly the same conditions apply. The leader must inspire confidence and trust. If the business is to succeed, the people in the organization must believe that they are competently led. The leader gains the organization's confidence first and most critically by the display of his own knowledge and competence—his technical ability to do his own job. His detailed knowledge of others' jobs—even in only one area, such as sales, marketing, or engineering—lends further credibility to his leadership. But a purely technical master is never sufficient. Like a great coach, the business leader must also be able to inspire his organization to the maximum efforts required. This is most important when things get difficult and the leader must take firm, even drastic action. An executive who has not inspired confidence will demoralize—perhaps destroy—an organization when difficult measures are taken. A great leader will carry the organization with him, even when the most Draconian steps have to be taken. He will rally the organization around him, just as a great coach will, by an acute, usually instinctive grasp of human psychology and by an adroit use of words, symbols, and actions that strike a deep chord in people's being.

The Infinite Players

Let us recall the salient features of Carse's infinite game:

- The game is not played to be won, since winning ends the game. Rather, the game is played with the objective of keeping play going.

- The game is not time-bounded; players don't know when the game began, nor do they care.

- A specific objective is to get as many people as possible into the game.

I think a moment's reflection will convince you that this type of game should be the one that the best business leaders play. If the organization is to thrive over the long run, the leader should not be concerned with the short-sighted, even naive, notion of "winning"; rather, he should be concerned with building an organization that has a future. In the same way, the leader should be interested in expansion (more people in the game) to improve his own business and the general economic well-being.

Another key condition of Carse's infinite game is rule changes. Recall that in an infinite game, the rules will change when the players agree that they must change, or the game will end. What are the "rules" with which a business leader must deal? A commonsense definition of game rules would be the establishment and the limitation of the scope of activities—the things that must be done and the manner in which they must be done. In a business, the application of this idea would yield rather broad consequences. It would not be stretching a point to say that "rule changes" for a business leader could entail:

- New products

- New markets

- New channels of distribution

- New process technology

- New organizational forms

- New methods of financing

- New configurations (acquisitions and/or divestitures)

In this sense, then, changing the rules is nothing more than a key function of the chief executive: strategic planning and strategic management. Strategic thinking must encompass all of these areas that will have a profound and, most important, a long-term effect on the business. These are the "rules" that must be constantly changed, or the business will fail—the game will end. For the business leader to ensure long-term success—get more people into the game—he must change the rules, in the sense of changing what is done and how it is done in his business.

In reading Carse's book, which is really a book about culture, the parallels between his infinite game and superior business leadership become quite striking. The problem, however, with this metaphor of an infinite game is very simple: No one seems to be using it explicitly. The game metaphors used in business, as I have tried to show, are "finite" games—time-bounded and win-oriented activities.

I have also tried to show that such finite games are rather limited models for business, except as an aid to teamwork and the acceptance of leadership. The infinite game seems a much better fit but has not been specifically employed to date. Perhaps wider exposure to Carse's ideas will change all this, and businessmen will use the language of the infinite game more explicitly.

Summary

- The game metaphor was used as early as the mid-nineteenth century by Andrew Carnegie and Jay Gould, who were not notably playful people.

- The metaphor is still used extensively by modern businessmen, particularly with the connotation of winning—particularly winning in professional sports. It achieved its most frequent use in the period from 1941 to 1975, but it remains a significant figure of speech.

- The work of James Carse provides a morphology of games. In particular, he cites two types: "finite" games—games played with the objective of eliminating the opponent; and "infinite" games—games played with the objective of continuing the play and attracting more players.

- The useful business entailments of games are goals, difficulty, unpredictability, fun, teamwork, and leadership.

- The metaphor is weak in conveying the complexity and ambiguity of business—its open-ended nature. It is also weak in its naive stress on winning.

- The metaphor provides good guides for the leader in modeling himself on coaches and captains, especially in clarifying his need for technical expertise as well as personal leadership.

- Carse's "infinite" game could be a very good metaphor for business, but it is not currently used explicitly.

6
War

Soldiers in Pinstripes

All things come to pass in accordance with conflict. War is father of
all and king of all.

—Heraclitus[1]

Historical Background

As this chapter's epigraph shows, war as a metaphor for life dates
back at least to preclassical times. Heraclitus (521–487 B.C.) saw
conflict and strife as the creative force behind all processes—human, animal, even inanimate nature. Many other voices throughout the ages have preached the preeminence of war. For example,
Thomas Hobbes (1588–1679), in a very characteristic pronouncement, wrote: "The condition of men . . . is a condition of everyone against everyone."[2]

The idea became a key ingredient of Western thought in the
latter half of the nineteenth century, when Social Darwinism became the conventional wisdom. War became the symbol, the image, the inducement for most thinkers and actors. Jacques Barzun,
reviewing the writings of the period from 1870 to 1914, says:

> [It] is one long call for blood . . . [from] a variety of parties,
> classes, nations and races whose blood was separately and con-
> tradictorily clamored for by the enlightened citizens of the ancient
> civilizations of Europe.[3]

Social Darwinism embroidered on Darwinian biology by incorporating the idea of force into Darwin's notions of struggle and

survival. It was a simple matter for men to use these revelations of "science" to justify their own behavior. Worse than the justification of antisocial acts, war itself became glorified—real war, not just the metaphor for life and action. Barzun tells us that in this time, people "poetized war and luxuriated in the prospect of it."[4] Byron, writing before the time of Darwin, nevertheless perfectly represented the Romantic spirit in these lines from "The Destruction of Sennacherib":

The Assyrian came down like the wolf on the fold,
And his cohorts were gleaming in purple and gold;
And the sheen of their spears was like stars on the sea,
When the blue wave rolls nightly on deep Galilee.[5]

The beauty of the poetic expression reinforces the beauty of the scene; war is portrayed as a marvelous, glittering pageantry, comparable to the glories of nature. In a directly analogous manner, the French Romantic painters, particularly Géricault, depicted the color and dash of war—cavalry officers in splendid uniforms astride magnificent chargers.

The European militarists, of course, rhapsodized on war during the long peace between the Franco-Prussian War and World War I. Marshall von Moltke, chief of the German General Staff, described as a "sensitive and cultivated man," nonetheless could write, in words that echo Heraclitus twenty-five centuries earlier: "Perpetual peace is a dream. . . . War is an element of the order of the world established by God."[6]

Friedrich Nietzsche (1844–90), whom we often consider *sui generis,* was not immune to the prevailing thought of the late nineteenth century. He has his Zarathusthra proclaim: "War and courage have done more great things than mother-love."[7]

The glorification of war itself, and the use of the metaphor as a description for all human activities, did not go unchallenged in this period. Tolstoy's *War and Peace,* published in 1866, starkly portrays the horror and misery of war and conveys a powerful message about the senseless slaughter and destruction. Stephen Crane's *Red Badge of Courage* is similarly an indictment of war, vividly picturing the catastrophic experiences of a Civil War soldier.

After the debacle of World War I—millions dead, economies shattered, countrysides ravaged—the glory of war lost much of its appeal. Erich Maria Remarque's *All Quiet on the Westerm Front* spoke to the heart of a war-weary world. Similarly, after World War II, realistic novels such as Norman Mailer's *The Naked and the Dead* portrayed war as an ugly, brutal, and unredeeming business. But each generation must learn these lessons anew. Along with the knowledge of its horrors, something deep in the human spirit still resonates to the attraction of war. The metaphor of war, highly popular in the late nineteenth century, has returned, as we shall see, to respectability in contemporary business usage.

Business Usage

The war metaphor was not a popular idea among business speakers until the late nineteenth century, the heyday of Social Darwinism. Clearly, these business speakers caught the prevailing spirit of the times. The only earlier example I can find is Josiah Wedgwood, who in 1772 wrote about his business as a series of battles and fights.[8] But this was pretty tame stuff compared to the later speakers.

The era of Jay Gould (1836–92) furnishes some splendid examples of the war metaphor. Gould himself, as I have shown previously, was principally a gamesman and generally expressed himself in those terms. But in a statement that could have been made by Tolstoy's old Marshal Kuzutov, Gould said: "I avoid bad luck by being patient. When I get into a fight, I always want to let the other fellow get tired first."[9]

Gould's contemporaries were much more sanguineous. The American newspapers of the time were particularly bloodthirsty in describing business transactions. Every contest for control of a company was routinely described as a "war." For example, the "Great Erie War" of 1868 was a stock market struggle between Gould and Commodore Vanderbilt.[10] And when Gould tried to corner the gold market in 1869, a *New York Times* reporter wrote:

> As the roar of battle and the screams of the victims resounded through New Street, it seemed as though human natures were

undergoing torments worse than any Dante had witnessed in Hell.[11]

Reading this, it is difficult to imagine the actual events: middle-aged businessmen, sitting in comfortable offices, reading and writing various pages, conferring with colleagues, buying and selling stock, and routinely going home at night to wives and children.

The struggle for the Atlantic railroad pitted Gould against James McHenry, a British financier. McHenry took this transaction rather seriously:

> We have moved against the enemy in three columns. One . . .
> has been threatening a flanking movement, and a third under
> yours truly . . . has succeeded in undermining the very citadel
> of the Erie. In order to cover my mining operations, I kept up an
> incessant bombardment through the press.[12]

McHenry's associate (I guess I must say "lieutenant"), George Crouch, wired his chief: "Eve of battle. Victory certain."[13] And Gould's partner, Jim Fisk, described the affair this way: "It was each man drag out his own corpse."[14] Remember, this was really all about some complex stockmarket manipulations.

In line with the general revulsion against combat after the world wars, I could find no business use of the metaphor in the twentieth century until the 1970s, but then the violence of expression began to pick up appreciably. Donaldson and Lorsch, in their 1983 study of CEOs, *Decision Making at the Top,* quote one business leader as follows: "This business is war games. We don't mind losing the battle, but we hate to lose the war."[15] And Clifford and Cavanagh, in their 1985 book, *The Winning Performance,* state that "mid-sized growth companies have become masters of guerilla war."[16]

The recent competitive struggles of the American airline companies have produced a rash of violent language. Donald Burr of People Express said that his company "got locked into a cut-throat fare war with Continental and United"; and, echoing Clifford and Cavanagh's words: "I'd rather be a guerilla fighter and stay alive than have an army and be destroyed."[17] And Frank Borman, Burr's rival at Eastern Airlines, saw industry competition as a "dog-fight" in which "upstarts will be squashed."[18]

And, of course, the metaphor consumer *par excellence,* Lee Iacocca, caught the bloody-minded mood of the 1980s. He saw himself as "the ruthless commander" who "liked to be in the trenches."[19] But the ruthless commander also had compassion for his men. Speaking of the massive layoffs at Chrysler, Iacocca mourned: "It's like a war: we won, but my son didn't come back."[20] Such expressions have become so common that I must again remind you of the actual events. Thousands of people lost their jobs and had to seek a living elsewhere or go on public assistance; there are no reports of death or dismemberment as a result of Iacocca's actions at Chrysler.

Even the cerebral software business can succumb to the call for blood. Oracle's CEO, Lawrence Ellison, "takes no prisoners" according to an industry watcher. Ellison himself says that his ideal sales vice-president would be Genghis Khan, and he adds: "It is not sufficient that I succeed—all else must fail."[21]

Modern business's penchant for war has been summed up in a recent book by Reis and Trout, *Marketing Warfare.* The work, dedicated to Karl von Clausewitz, is a primer for the business leader as he approaches his task in the spirit of warfare. One quote sums it up:

> The true nature of marketing today involves the conflict between corps, not the satisfying of human needs and wants.[22]

Sad.

The Good Side of War

A number of entailments of the war metaphor are fairly appropriate for business. These "good" entailments, not unexpectedly, are mainly shared with the other popular business metaphors. First, war almost always has some goal, some purpose for the activity. It is common for warring nations to establish war aims in a highly formal way. Both the combatants and the nations at large expect that their leaders will proclaim some important, even noble, purpose for the sacrifices expended. The common distrust and scorn of mercenaries is probably explained by this. Most of us simply cannot believe that the need to earn a living is sufficient grounds for the deadly profession of war. But mercenaries aside, the war metaphor evokes in many minds the idea of a high purpose for the business enterprise.

Another entailment shared with other metaphors is the notion of difficulty. War is a highly demanding process, calling for the highest degrees of discipline, courage, and skill. Its difficulty is embodied in our image of the ideal warrior: strong, self-reliant, a match for any opponent, ready to undergo any hardship in the pursuit of his goal. Closely related to this idea of difficulty is the inherent riskiness and unpredictability of war. The "fortunes of war" is a commonplace. The fate of kingdoms and nations is staked on a single battle; the outcome is considered so uncertain that it has long been believed, from Homer's *Iliad* to modern times, that the gods intervene directly in the clash of arms. Like the other process metaphors (voyage and game), the war metaphor speaks to the business leader in the language of risk and uncertainty.

But strategy is the key entailment that war brings to business. The idea of business strategy—actually a rather recent notion—is a direct, literal transposition from war to business. Reis and Trout, whom I cited earlier, were not the first to draw upon the teachings of von Clausewitz. The very word *strategy* has been taken from the military arts. And there is actually a rather close fit between the strategy considerations of an army or a nation at war and those of a business enterprise. Just as in war, the business leader assesses his own situation, his strengths and weaknesses; he judges the enemy's (competition's) position, strengths, and weaknesses; and then he thinks through the opportunities that are presented and the threats that must be dealt with.

It is accepted nowadays in business that a company without a strategy, a firm that has not done this type of thinking, is probably heading for serious trouble—like a nation at war that has no long-run plan for ending the conflict.

Consider one example from the history of warfare: the Union in the American Civil War. After a few sharp defeats that destroyed the illusion of a quick, cheap victory, Lincoln adopted General Scott's Anaconda Plan. The plan was to split the South in two:

seize the lower Mississippi, then slowly strangle the separate halves. The Union leaders knew, from an assessment of strengths and weaknesses, that a prolonged war of attrition, a war that would put a premium on superior manpower and industrial capacity, was a war they would very likely win. The Confederacy, on the other hand, had no clear-cut strategy. Their hope was that superior generalship and superior soldiering would win the great battles, and the Union would sue for peace after some battlefield losses. Clearly, it was a highly risky strategy, if a strategy at all.

Many firms have benefited from the emphasis on strategy, and certainly a great deal of time and effort has gone into strategy considerations. Critics have complained about this effort and the sterile results in some cases, but on balance, the strategic orientation is a good one for business. For this, we are indebted to the metaphor of war.

The Janus Face of War

The war metaphor has a number of key entailments that are highly ambivalent—both excellent associations for a business and potentially very damaging. Take the entailment of a serious purpose for either war or business. As I noted in the game metaphor discussion, business *is* serious, and the leaders must take a serious attitude toward their actions. Viewing a business as a game is simply not a helpful frame of mind. But just how serious is it? The nineteenth century *New York Times* report that we saw earlier is comical; clearly, the seriousness of the affair has been highly exaggerated.

And the same type of problem, the problem of degree, arises with another entailment: leadership. War requires the highest level of dedication and competence in a leader, and virtually every successful company has had outstanding leadership, so the fit between war and business is a good one—mostly. The trouble comes when war entailments extend further—for example, into Iacocca's reference to the "ruthless commander," a very natural description of a war leader but hardly appropriate for business.

The competitive entailment of war has its strong points in focusing the mind on the realities of true competition in a marketplace and the need to "win" in the sense of succeeding as a business. But so many negative associations are linked with the competitive idea. "All's fair in love and war" is a popular notion; when survival or simply winning the war is at stake, most nations resort to almost anything. Clearly, this is a poor match for ordinary business practice. Is all fair in love, war, and business?

This last point raises another, again ambivalent, entailment: the idea of rules. I covered rules in a broader sense in the game discussion; here, I want to focus more on rules of behavior. It is really odd that the murderous destruction of war could in any way be associated with rules; but in fact, formal warfare has been governed by rules for centuries. We are all familiar with the Geneva Convention and its provisions that ban chemical and biological weapons, regulate treatment of prisoners, and so forth. Warfare had its rules, though, long before that. On August 13, 1649, Oliver Cromwell and his "Ironsides" refused quarter and killed 2,000 people at Drogheda, near Dublin. (The date and the place are still remembered in the Republic.) Was this a crime comparable to the Nazis' slaughter of the innocents at Babi Yar or a dozen other places? Well, not exactly. Two thousand people were massacred, but Cromwell acted in a tradition accepted for centuries: the defenders of a fortress, who failed to surrender after the walls had been breached, had no claim to quarter.[23] Cromwell was within the rules.

There was a very similar set of circumstances during the Hundred Years War, circumstances immortalized by Rodin.[24] Rodin's sculpture *The Burghers of Calais* was commissioned in the nineteenth century to honor the six town leaders who sacrificed themselves in 1347 to spare the general populace from the sword. The work exudes pathos: the men in shrouds, wearing rope halters—some resigned, some hiding their faces in anguish as they walk to their dooms. Rodin's genius portrays the agony of this moment and naturally evokes contempt for the perpetrator—Edward III of England. But Edward was actually acting magnanimously. As a resisting besieged town, Calais had lost all rights, and all the defenders could be put to the sword, just as at Drogheda 300 years later. Edward had generously settled for the death of the burghers alone and ordered their appearance, as Rodin showed, ready for execution.

So there are definite rules for warfare, and there have been for a very long time. They are harsh rules, but rules nonetheless. This could be somewhat comforting to the businessman who often feels heavily encumbered by rules: laws, regulations, industry conventions, standards, and so forth.

But there is another type of warfare, warfare that really has no rules: the guerrilla. By definition, this type of war is "no holds barred." Guerrillas resort to any tactic—civilian murder, random sabotage, armed robbery. The opposing forces—rule-bound if they were engaged against a "regular" enemy—also lose all constraint and resort to summary executions, reprisals, hostage-taking, and the like. The bitter experience of a guerrilla war was perfectly captured by Goya in his *3rd of May,* painted in 1814 as an account of the Napoleonic War in Spain—the war that gave us the word *guerrilla.* The viewer is confronted by guerrillas being executed by a firing squad of regular French troops. Our eyes are drawn to the central figure—white-shirted, arms thrust out in a final and hopeless gesture.[25] All the agony, bitterness, brutality, and tragic waste of all guerrilla wars, up to the present day, are captured in Goya's painting.

Recall that this is the type of warfare that some of our business leaders have spoken of in positive terms; Clifford and Cavanagh, for example, praise executives who are masters of guerrilla war. I believe that they use the metaphor to suggest innovation, flexibility, and creativity in business—all positive things. But the true face of guerrilla warfare is so bleak and the entailments of random destructiveness and lack of any convention are so negative that I must rate it very inappropriate for business.

Take another look at Goya's *3rd of May.*

The Dogs of War

Shakespeare has Marc Antony say, "Cry havoc, and let slip the dogs of war";[26] and we realize the havoc and destruction, the loss of control that warfare brings. It is an old saying that it is easier to start a war than end one. War seems to imply naturally that those in charge will lose complete control of events. War, by its nature, is immoderate; the leader must force things beyond the limit, throw everything into it, if he is to succeed. Macaulay wrote approvingly of Lord Nugent: "He knew that the essence of war is violence, and that moderation is war is imbecility."[27]

It is this extremism that is particularly disturbing about the war metaphor—the idea that all is taken to extremes. The competitor not just bested, but destroyed, every action pushed to its farthest possible limit, the all-out nature of the struggle—these associations are not especially helpful for business situations. Business is fundamentally a peaceful economic enterprise, providing employment, products, and services for the community at large. The idea of a life-and-death struggle, without limits or constraints, is a highly dangerous signal to the business leader. Business is a serious, demanding undertaking, certainly—but a battle to the death? Surely this is a perilous overstatement.

The War Leader

Businessmen who employ the war metaphor must, of course, view themselves in the role of the commander. There are some positive aspects to this role. The image of a great war leader conjures up associations of high competence, moral strength, and the ability to inspire and lead men.

And the hierarchial nature of an army permits a variety of roles for the leader. He can be "in the trenches," as Iacocca has placed himself; he can also be Iacocca's "ruthless commander," sacrificing his men to achieve his purposes. The idea of strategy—a good one for business—can also be conveyed through the war leader role. The business leader can conceive of himself in the great tradition of the master strategist—perhaps the American Chief of Staff George Marshall, at his desk in Washington, thinking through the immense complexities of a world war and dispatching fleets and armies around the globe. This is certainly a compelling image for a leader of a multinational corporation, and the metaphor has a great deal of merit in this context.

On the other end of the scale is the figure of the guerrilla leader. As I have noted, this role can help stress the need for innovative tactics and creative approaches; it is in the nature of a guerrilla leader to take the bold stroke. But it is also in his nature to operate in a spirit of primitive lawlessness. His cause is so noble or his situation so desperate that no action is too frightful.

But the war leader idea seems to have taken a firm hold on contemporary business people. Many have admired the flamboyant portrayal of George Patton in a recent film. His courage, determination, bravado, and inspirational qualities have provided a model for business managers at all levels. Patton's will to fight through all obstacles to success has definitely struck a chord. It is unsettling, however, that most seem to favor the macho figure of George Patton over a far greater patriot and general, George Marshall, who was chief of staff, secretary of defense, and secretary of state.

Strengths and Weaknesses of the Metaphor

I have already touched on the strengths and most of the weaknesses of the war metaphor. The positive aspects of the metaphor are its entailments of risk and difficulty and the need for outstanding leadership. These are all good fits to the experience of business. The need for and the process of strategy development have also been helpful ideas that business has generally adopted from warfare.

The weaknesses of the metaphor have also been mainly identified—in particular, the extremism of the language and actions associated with combat. Henry Ford spoke against the "delusion that life is a battlefield."[28] Russell Robb, writing in 1910, also cautioned that the military model is seriously limiting because it fails to account for the division of labor; a business needs specialists, whereas our ordinary picture of an army is an indiscriminate collection of replaceable soldiers.[29] Robb also pointed out that an army is assembled for an emergency, a one-time effort. Clearly, a business must plan for the long run and cannot operate in the style or with the organization of a military force. Even a "long" war is over in four or five years.

Weick has taken dead aim (forgive the choice of words) at the military model in his work on organizational psychology.[30] He makes a number of telling points. First, the war metaphor can be a self-fulfilling prophecy. If we assume that our competitors (or even suppliers, customers, employees) are hostile, they will surely be hostile when we are hostile. Weick also finds fault with the attitudes that the metaphor inspires—the tough, macho stances. This can be appealing and exciting for the participants, but it is out of place in a serious business environment. The metaphor can also shield true problems from the businessman. War, by its nature, is wasteful and disorderly—characteristics that a business simply cannot have. But the idea that one is in the midst of combat can be a fine excuse for a sloppy operation. The metaphor, like any metaphor, can also limit the options that a leader thinks he can command. The tendency will be to discharge people automatically, even brutally, in times of trouble; to tighten controls; to enforce discipline. Military thinking can also enshrine the notion of the chain of command and the necessity of organizing in hierarchies. Although any of these things can be necessary or desirable under the right circumstances, the military mind-set would tend to force extreme actions.

And that brings us back to the innate extremism of the military metaphor—the notion that "anything goes" in a fight for survival. Hobbes summed it up: "Force and fraud are in war the two cardinal virtues."[31]

On balance, war is a very poor metaphor for business. I must agree with the psalmist, who petitioned the Almighty: "Scatter Thou the people that delight in war."[32]

Summary

- War as a metaphor for life is preclassical in its origin.

- The war metaphor became popular in business only in the late nineteenth century, no doubt influenced by Social Darwinism. In the twentieth century, the experience of true warfare dampened the use of the metaphor, but it has revived in the 1970s and 1980s.

- The useful entailments of war are a goal; difficulty; the need for strong, skilled, and courageous leadership; risk; and probably most important, the notion of strategy.

- The weakness of the metaphor stems from the inherent extremism of war. The metaphor suggests attitudes and actions that are not appropriate for business: "It is not sufficient that I succeed—all else must fail."

- The metaphor suggests a variety of leader roles: the global commander and his strategic emphasis; the tactical manager "in the trenches"; or the guerrilla leader, for whom no course is too bold nor too frightful.

We move on now to the system metaphors—the analogies to machines, organisms, and societies.

7
The Machine

Taylor and Positivism

The fair test of business administration . . . is whether you have a
business with all its parts so coordinated . . . so interlocking . . .
that they make a working unit.

—Mary Parker Follett[1]

Background

The business as machine is the earliest metaphor for a business and
the most maligned in modern times. We find it employed by our
first industrialist, Josiah Wedgwood (circa 1770). He wanted to
"make such machines of men as cannot err."[2] Fifty years later,
Robert Owen, as we have noted, also spoke of factory workers as
"living machines."[3] This view of business is commonly attributed
to Frederick Taylor, and with good reason. Taylor's entire approach—scientific management—rested on the assumption that a
business was a great, complex machine, amenable to analysis, prediction, and control. Taylor's disciple, Frank Gilbreth, stated it
best: "The best results come only when everything is standardized
down to . . . the most insignificant level of detail."[4]

In modern times, William Cook, CEO of the Union Pacific
Corporation, could still see his company as a "powerful engine of
progress," a "vigorous and innovative force in our economy"; and
of course he could not escape the railroader's sense that he was
"running" the business.[5]

This concept of business is actually a subset of a strong current
in modern thought. Galileo's and Newton's tremendous successes

in the field of mechanics in the seventeenth century caused a general optimism in many minds about man's ability to understand and predict the workings of the universe. This line of thought culminated in the work of Laplace (1749–1827), who held that the universe is entirely mechanistic and predictable—a giant clockworks, if you will.[6] Laplace boasted that if he knew the velocity and position of every particle in the universe, he could predict the future. We see here a radical shift from Guicciardini's pessimism, his sense of the world's inherent randomness and unpredictability.

The mechanical construct for reality has been aided significantly by Auguste Comte's positivist philosophy. Comte's positivism is really a methodology for scientists and philosophers, an approach to these fields that stresses observation and experimentation and shuns conclusions about the substantive nature of reality. But behind this methodology, most have found an assumption about reality—dry, mechanical, unmetaphysical—in short, "positivistic." In a major way, positivism is the credo of twentieth-century business civilization. The historian Stromberg puts this very well:

> In the broadest sense it might be said that modern Western civilization is positivistic in that metaphysical or religious modes are not congenial to it. Everyday life is so conditioned to mechanical models and explanations. . . . What grows on the world is a certain matter-of-factness.[7]

Comte's influence first took hold during France's Second Empire (1851–71), but as Stromberg has indicated, his weight is still felt today.

Another rather late entrant into the mechanical view of reality appeared with Italian Futurism, a movement mainly concerned with the plastic arts. The first Futurist Manifesto (they dealt in manifestos as much as in painting and sculpture) is remembered chiefly for Marinetti's provocative words: "A roaring motor-car which seems to run on machine-gun fire is more beautiful than the Victory of Samothrace."[8]

Futurism was a rogue movement in many ways, calling for the contemporary artists (literally) to burn down the museums, and ending with a solid Futurist phalanx in Mussolini's Fascist Academy. The machine/animal—principally, machine/human—analogy was a strong and recurrent theme in Futurism, but with an entirely different stress from that of the contemporary artists in France and Germany, who used mechanistic imagery for satire and irony. The Italians, who had come very late to the Industrial Revolution, saw only glory and power in the machinelike attributes of man and his creations. The Futurist masterpiece, by any measure, is Umberto Boccioni's *Unique Forms of Continuity in Space*. Despite the abstract and mechanical title, the work, a magnificent bronze, is clearly a humanlike creature, lunging forward with a more than human stride. The head appears as a machined artifact, the feet in seven league boots. As a Tate Gallery publication says:

> There is something both awe-inspiring and a little frightening about the vision of the Futurist demi-god striding sightlessly through space.[9]

It is all there in this one splendid work: the danger of the machine-man "sightlessly" pursuing his ends, the glory and exultation of mankind with its Faustian machine powers, and perhaps most frightening, the sheer, arresting beauty of the concept and the execution.

Entailments

Pepper saw the mechanical current of thought as one of his "root-metaphors," used extensively—and unconsciously—by many in their view of the world.[10] Pepper particularly notes the following implications of this metaphor:

- It implies that things can be ultimately expressed in exact, quantitative terms.

- There is an effective relationship, or law, that obtains among the parts.

- The *qualities* of the parts (e.g., color, texture) are irrelevant to the machine's efficacy.

These are, of course, the essential axioms of the scientific management school in business thought. The last point, the irrelevance of the qualities of the parts, has definitely carried over into the machine metaphor for business, particularly in the assumption about people. In this view, the people in a business, especially the production workers, are no more nor less than interchangeable parts—complex and demanding, of course, but nonetheless interchangeable parts.

Henry Ford took issue with the mechanistic concept of a business, stating flatly: "A business . . . is not a machine."[11] Ford seemed sincere in this, insofar as the *entire* business is concerned; his conception of it was more subtle than a mere machine analogy. However, he was also explicit in his view of the production workers, endorsing the idea that management should reduce the necessity for the workers to think.[12] Max Weber (1864–1920), the great German sociologist, agreed with Ford to the extent that a business *should* not be a machine, but a strong tendency existed toward that state. He wrote of a constant process of rationalization, a tendency of matters to be organized and subjected to rules and orderly processes; in other words, bureaucracy is almost inevitable. He was among the first to see that the result was loss of spontaneity, disenchantment, and the pedantic triumph over the free spirit.[13]

James Carse has explored the causal link between machines (or bureaucracy) and the deadening of initiative:

> To operate a machine one must operate like a machine. . . .
> Machinery does not steal our spontaneity from us; we set it aside ourselves, we deny our originality.[14]

But a number of entailments of the machine metaphor have proved highly useful to business. The analogy shares with "journey" the important suggestion of a profit-producing entity. With very rare exceptions, machines have been created to improve productivity and to create wealth. The capital equipment of any manufacturing firm is clearly there to produce profits for the organization. By the same token, a commercial vessel or treasure ship is in fact a machine artifact, a tool, with the express function of generating wealth—hence one of the links between the machine and voyage metaphors. With the idea of profit production in mind, it is a simple and obvious step to see the entire business under the construct of a machine.

Perhaps the most useful and powerful entailment of the machine idea has been its connotation of predictability. Harkening back to Laplace's view of the universe, it is in the nature of an actual machine, from the very fact of its human creation, that it is totally analyzable and comprehensible. Knowing its separate parts and their interconnection, and drawing on the findings of physical science, one can compute any machine's workings, now and in the future, to virtually any degree of accuracy. Faced with the complexity of any business, this surely makes a powerful appeal to those who must lead. We can see in the triumphs of industrial engineering (Taylorism, if you will) a manifestation of that strong streak of rationality in the Western mind. Viewing the business as a machine, one can focus on inputs of raw materials and supplies, outputs of finished goods, the operations of material handling and processing, and so forth—all as orderly, predictable events.

Even the flow of information and the vagaries of markets can, in principle, be analyzed, designed, improved—in a word, rationalized. The pervasiveness of the rational (i.e., machine) model in contemporary business thought has been cited by the organizational theorist Pfeffer: "There is no norm so central to the existing practice and ideology of management as the norm of rationality."[15]

The machine as a profit-producing tool, as having a serious purpose, and particularly as a surrogate for predictability—these are the positive aspects of the metaphor as it relates to business. But as Peters and Waterman have said, the model is "right enough to be dangerously wrong."[16] A number of negative associations come to mind when we think of machines. For one, in the popular mind at least, we can see a certain loss of human control when machines are employed extensively. Industrial automation has long carried the specter of electronic control of processes—machines that make decisions with a speed that is beyond human capability, with a real potential for mischief. This connotation is contained, as well, in the idea of the destructive nature of machinery. Machines can go awry with most serious consequences—we think of runaway locomotives and aircraft disasters. (Again, there is a linkage of entailments with the journey metaphor.)

Machines are also subject to breakdown. This can be a matter of inconvenience—a halt in productive work and extensive repairs—or, potentially, real disaster. We think of the computer HAL, in the film *2001*, which in fact is in control of the mission. Its breakdown, akin to human madness, has disastrous effects on the mission. The entire first half of the film is pervaded by the trapped feeling of the human crew in the power of a renegade machine intelligence.

Orwell's *1984* is likewise a nightmare of technology and machinery gone mad. In the novel, the use of technology for social control has produced a brutal society in which the human members are reduced to a mechanical state. We are all familiar with Big Brother—a mechanical, and malevolent, intelligence.

All these connotations of breakdown and loss of control—clearly antithetical to the other idea of a machine's predictability—are alive in our consciousness when we conceive of a business in this manner. Social critics have certainly focused on this danger of machine control of key processes and institutions; most business leaders also feel a certain unease about the loss of human decision making and its replacement by computers and other mechanical devices.

The Machine's Impact

The ramifications of the mechanical way of thinking about a business can be profound. When a business leader conceives of his organization in these terms, he tends to organize and manage in a mechanical way.[17] The impulse is to routinize all functions and processes, as Weber has pointed out. A telling fault with this approach has been the expectations that it creates. Having conceived of and designed the organization as a giant clockworks, it is mystifying when the "machine" simply doesn't operate as it "should."

Typically, the diagnosis then is either that the design is wrong or that additional controls, routines, and mechanical-style governing are required.

If, in fact, the real issue is the leader's fundamental concept, if he is in thrall of a basic category error, we could predict a downward spiral: more controls, routinizing, and rationality—which further chokes off spontaneity and innovation. More than one business has succumbed to this fateful prescription.

On the other hand, it is unarguable that a degree of rationalization has been highly successful for many businesses. Planning, budgeting, and good financial controls have been the salvation of many enterprises. It is these factors that we normally have in mind when we speak of a business being well managed—that is, successful—and it is the loss of the knowledge and control of costs that unerringly points to poor or lax management.

Many companies have also attempted, with mixed success, to rationalize the management process itself. Management by objective (MBO) programs are a means to link top management's objectives down through the hierarchial management pyramid to the lowest level of decision making. The objectives of the lower levels are established as more detailed subsets of the superior's goals. If properly implemented and tied to compensation, MBO can lend coherence to the entire management process and can also move the organization along by clarifying each manager's tasks and setting specific targets for progress and improvement. Like any program based on the machine analogy, the MBO system works best in a highly predictable and stable environment—for example, the telephone companies, or at least those we knew before divestiture.

Mechanical, rationalized approaches have also had good success with the production aspects of a manufacturing concern. Materials requirements planning (MRP) systems have been developed to rationalize the scheduling of finished-goods production, the procurement of materials, and the production of subassemblies. Inventory control systems, either in isolation or with MRP, have improved many balance sheets. Modern statistical process control, based on careful observations and recording of experience—as prescribed by Metcalfe in the nineteenth century[18]—have been highly successful in many manufacturing companies. The technique is used to zero in on the "significant few" areas of the shop that are limiting productivity and output.

The entire field of operations research grew out of mathematical techniques developed during World War II. These are powerful methods to optimize the output of complex phenomena through mathematical modeling. Great gains have been realized by this mechanical approach when it has been applied to such thorny problems as the optimal location of plants and distribution centers or the best product mix from petroleum refining. We find here a triumph for mechanical thinking in the replacement of hunch and guesswork by careful mathematical analysis of highly complex problems.

It would be a mistake to underestimate the efficacy of the machine analogy. Many facets of a business have an orderly, analyzable, and potentially predictable form; the use of mathematics, science, and logic has been, and will be, extremely successful in many areas. The fact that a business is highly complex and that certain aspects are not accessible to logic and science is hardly reason to abandon faith in the power of reason. Guicciardini, who well knew the complexity and intractability of the world, still could say: "We must not surrender, like animals, a prey to fortune; rather, we must follow reason, like men."[19]

The machine analogy works well for routine and repetitive aspects of a business—one might say, in those areas of a business where a machine itself would work well.[20] If the tasks to be performed are straightforward, the environment stable, the product mass-produced, then a mechanical analogy can be quite apt and useful. The fast-food business, for example, is a model of mechanical design. The processes of food preparation, order taking, and customer delivery have been routinized to the last detail. Not for the fast-food industry is the *angst* of modern personnel management: the employees are eager teenagers, paid the minimum wage; and when they become bored or disillusioned, their replacement is assured by the relentless logic of birthrate statistics. The high turnover ensures that the minimum wage is the going wage, and everyone involved seems happy with the outcome—the management with its low-paid and docile work force, the kids with their simple, machinelike jobs and the resultant spending money.

The Soulless Machine

The fast-food industry has few labor problems because of high turnover, minimal training requirements, and an inexhaustible supply of teenagers. But for most businesses, it is in the area of personnel management that the machine metaphor has had its real failings. The metaphor simply underestimates the human element in business—the quirky, intuitive, emotional human beings who consistently fail to act as one would expect—fail to act, that is, like machines.

Most managers now realize that people just don't work well when they are treated like machines, but many still persist in designing organizational forms that ape machinery. We have all grown familiar with organizations that have been designed for perfect rationality—that is, rational behavior from their operators as well as the outside world. All should work smoothly, because the work flow, information flow, and external environment have been analyzed, controlled, and optimized. What is precisely wrong with this approach is that nothing is left to chance; there is no field for innovation, and human ingenuity and intuitive genius are given no rein. There have been few organizations, at any time and in any field, that have not needed innovation to prosper—indeed, to survive.

This deadening of initiative is the prognosis—accurate, we must agree—of Weber. In the same way, the growth of such a bureaucracy has a curious effect on the attitudes of the employees. The power of the routine begins to suggest to the workers that the enterprise *is* a giant machine, and their role in it is of the smallest kind. Imperceptibly, the interests of the employees begin to take precedence over the goals for which the organization was initially created.[21] Economists define this as "agency costs"—the necessary costs involved when the shareholder entrusts his capital to others (his agents). Businesses conceived and organized as machines are highly vulnerable to unacceptably high agency costs. These agency costs can come to be accepted as a way of life, and the mechanical-minded manager tends to ignore potentially useful social controls—controls that are suggested by the metaphors of game, voyage, organism, or society.

The loss of spontaneity can prove dangerous for the management function as well. As I noted earlier, MBO systems can have beneficially cohesive effects on a management team. The MBO system is normally linked with an annual planning and budgeting process as well as annual compensation. If the mechanical analogy has too firm a grip on a manager's mind, planning seems to become reality; the entire process of conducting business—from R&D through production and the vagaries of distribution to new-found customers—becomes, in the plan, knowable, calculable, and predictable.

Naturally, the world is not so benign, and every performance misses the plan, in one way or another, through internal inadequacies or through the fluctuations of market and economic conditions. But an MBO system—particularly one that is tied to compensation—can keep managers marching in lockstep toward unattainable goals or even, in light of external factors, toward goals that no longer make sense or are clearly counterproductive.

The Machine Gone Awry

Mechanical analogies are also often applied to predicting market behavior, using survey information and statistical techniques. Electronic order entry and inventory control have also become commonplace and are generally very useful. But the combination of market predictions and automated order management and inventory control systems can prove disastrous. Let me describe one scenario.

Manufacturers of fad teen wear do test marketing, learn enough to produce some level of goods, and push the goods through the distribution channels. When they reach the retail store, if the items sell well, the retailer knows from past experience that he'll get only half of his needs, so he doubles his order. The wholesaler may add his own doubling. The manufacturer's order entry and inventory systems sense this ground swell of demand, now augmented by the channel's hedging. If the demand is, in fact, reasonably good, the retailers face back-ordering and redouble their orders to get anything at all. The order system sees gigantic market acceptance at this stage; enormous production, even new plant capacity, is ordered. By a logical process, real demand has been misinterpreted by an order of magnitude, and no one has taken account of another factor: the demand is ephemeral, the fad has passed, and all the ordering and production are for nought.

Such mechanical systems simply do not account for the human factor—the human sagacity (or greed) of the retailers and the unpredictability of the buyers. It is a common error to think of "markets" as impersonal, predictable, abstract economic units. But people, not markets, buy. And people are ambivalent and unpredictable in the extreme—all of us, not just fad-happy teenagers.

The shortcomings of the mechanical model have been well summarized by Peters and Waterman.[22] In their view, the model fails in several ways.

- It leads to an abstract, heartless philosophy—a focus on things rather than people.

- It devalues experimentation and creates a climate in which mistakes are abhorred.

- It denigrates the importance of values.

The Leader

Let us explore the role of the leader—the actions and attitudes that the machine metaphor brings to his consciousness. As we have discussed, for certain aspects of a business, the concept is very useful, and the best managers have mastered the techniques of scientific management and apply them where they are appropriate. But the worst failing of this construct, summed up in the word *Taylorism*, stems from the manager's assumption that his workers are machines. This was a crude assumption by the early business figures, culminating in Taylor, but the moderns have not escaped this cast of mind. The entire human relations school, sparked by Elton Mayo's work on the Hawthorne experiments, can be interpreted as simply a more sophisticated machine analogy for human beings. Various psychological theories have been advanced, gen-

erally aimed at understanding and ultimately manipulating the behavior of the work force. The underlying assumption must be that
these people are machines, albeit extremely complex and sophisticated machines. But I would argue that no generally accepted theory of human motivation has been devised, despite the Freudian
revolution and three-quarters of a century of subsequent research
effort. Heraclitus's caution is as valid today as it was 2,500 years
ago: "You will not find out the limits of the soul, even if you travel
every way, so deep is its measure."[23]

Every human being is *sui generis;* attempts to mold him, rationalize him, or in any way make a machine of him will never
succeed. The leader as machine tender, in complete control of machinelike workers, will rarely be a successful role.

I think the most interesting role for a business leader under the
machine metaphor is designer/creator. If he holds his business to
be a machine, he is the creator of all this and can ascribe godlike
power to himself within this creation. There is definitely this sense
in the writings of some of the business leaders, particularly those
in the early days. One would expect the natural feeling of ownership and proprietariness, but in Wedgwood and, later, Ford, the
sense of the business as the result of a pure act of creation comes
through strongly. Ford, in fact, said: "There is something sacred
about a big business. . . . Its continuance is a holy trust."[24]

This entailment—an object created by the leader—is unique to
the machine metaphor; it is not logically connected with the other
common metaphors: journey, organism, game, war, and society.
There are obvious dangers in this view, however; no company is
well served by a leader who believes himself omniscient.

Summary

- The machine metaphor was the first used by a business
  speaker—Josiah Wedgwood, circa 1770. It remained highly
  popular until 1941 but has subsequently fallen into disuse as
  an explicit description. Its spirit remains, though, in the techniques of Frederick Taylor's scientific management.

- The metaphor has its roots in a strong current of modern

thought: the idea that the world itself is machinelike in its ultimate nature—that is, ultimately predictable. This idea is incorporated in the philosophical doctrine of positivism, and it achieved an artistic manifestation in Italian Futurism.

- The useful entailments of the metaphor for a business include a wealth-producing tool, a serious purpose, calculability, and predictability (up to a point).

- The harmful associations of the idea are mainly the unfeeling treatment of people, the overemphasis on rationality, and the attendant neglect of ambiguity and intuition.

- The metaphor can suggest to the leader that his employees are literally cogs in a machine and that his task is simply to keep the machinery running.

- Further, the founder of an organization can conceive of himself as the designer of this engine, who has full knowledge of all its operations and all its potential. This presumed omniscience could be very dangerous.

8
The Organism

Evolution and the Good Shepherd

"Biophilia," the innate tendency to focus on life and life-like processes
... our existence depends on this propensity, our spirit is woven from
it.

—Edward O. Wilson[1]

Background

The organizational scholar Morgan has provided us with an excellent working definition of the organism metaphor in business.
The organization is conceived of as: "a living system, existing in a
wider environment on which it depends for the satisfaction of various needs."[2]

Let me elaborate on the sense of this definition by examining
the key words. *Living* can only refer to an entity that is born,
matures, and dies; the key idea of evolution is also naturally associated with living things. The term *environment* makes us conscious of the interdependence of the organization with the
surrounding society. *Needs* is an extremely important entailment
of the organism idea. The metaphor tells us that an organization
has needs of its own that are independent of, even in conflict with,
those of the owner or the larger society. This entailment of the
organism metaphor is in the starkest contrast to the machine trope.
Machines do not have needs, despite our everyday language to the
contrary. We speak of machines as requiring "feeding," as being
"patient servants" or even "recalcitrant," but it is patently obvious

that these are metaphorical expressions that attribute organic, even anthropomorphic, characteristics to inert matter.

The organism metaphor, applied to the world at large, is one of the most ancient ideas in human consciousness. The basic stream of thought has two main channels: *anthropomorphism*—that is, the concept of the universe as fundamentally humanlike; and *domestication*—the idea that the universe exists exclusively to serve mankind.

Anthropomorphism really begins with animism—the belief, common among primitive peoples, that the world is ruled by humanlike spirits. All events that we moderns would call natural are considered the work of spirits—living beings with the human characteristics of emotion, rationality, benevolence, and often malevolence. There are cultures, for example, that do not believe in death as a natural event; always, it is the work of a malefic spirit.

Pepper has characterized animism as one of the root metaphors that drives human consciousness.[3] In the larger view, animism is the idea that the human being—his type of body, structure of mind, and emotional makeup—is the prototype for all reality. Put as primitive animism—thunder as the gods playing ninepins—the idea is distasteful, even comical, to us. But in its highly developed forms, this root metaphor is congenial to most moderns. Western religions, for example, are imbued with the idea of a benevolent creator, an intelligence who rules the world and is conscious of our destiny. Even those without a religious sense are still comfortable with the idea that the ultimate reality is spiritual (or at least mental), that the world is more than dead matter. Even if we cannot believe in the God of Genesis or the World Spirit of Hegel, who has not sensed in the marvelous progress of evolution some guiding force, some intelligence? At bottom, who really believes that the world is only matter and electricity and that our own consciousness is some epiphenomenon?

But these are all animistic ways of structuring the world, modeling the universe on the forms with which we are most familiar: our own minds and bodies. For this reason, the organism metaphor is probably the most appealing to the great mass of people. Pepper, in fact, claims that it is the only root metaphor with which man feels completely at home.

Domestication—the idea that the world exists to serve us, that it is all one great domesticated animal—is a concept related to animism but more developed and more restricted, in that a *role,* not just a structure, is assigned to the world outside ourselves. This way of thinking is deeply engraved in our consciousness; it is a habit of thought that is congenial to most of us, despite the progress of environmentalism. As with all deep, cultural concepts, we find it difficult to believe that it is not a feature of ultimate reality—that it is not a universal belief but really a cultural artifact. The idea is mainly a Western one, mainly Judeo-Christian, in fact. The Greeks saw man more as a part of the world, with superior powers, of course, but a part of a greater whole. Eastern thought, from its beginnings to the present day, sees man as indistinguishable from the universe as a whole—the world is one.

We can find the source for the Western view in the first chapter of Genesis, God's charge to Adam:

> "Be fruitful and multiply, and replenish the earth and subdue it:
> and have dominion over the fish of the sea, and over the fowl of
> the air, and over every living thing that moveth upon the earth."[4]

Here we have the Western ethos starkly portrayed—all of nature, "every living thing," is an instrument for man's use.

The thought of late antiquity and the Middle Ages is saturated with this idea of nature as merely a field for human action and exploitation. Augustine saw man as a pilgrim in this backdrop of nature and even saw man's own material body as simply a servant of his soul.[5] From St. Francis to Thomas à Kempis, we find the root concept to be man's exile and pilgrimage in this world—importantly, man's radical distinctiveness from the world of matter. This whole line of thought can be seen as culminating in Goethe's *Faust,* who has become for us the quintessential Western man—striving for godlike powers, bending the world of nature to his will. Frederick Taylor was hardly Faust, but he could say: "Very ordinary men with ordinary equipment can solve . . . any problem."[6]

Business Usage

Because these ideas are so deeply rooted in our culture and language, we seldom think of them as metaphorical constructs. But business speech is saturated with such words as *health, grow, die, survive, evolve, tire, age, disease,* and the like—all expressions of "organic" thinking. In business, the use of the metaphor goes back to Wedgwood, as I noted earlier, who spoke of his business as a "mistress."

Russel Robb, writing in 1910, was the first I found who clearly articulated the idea of a business as an organism:

> An organization is much looked upon as a machine, [but] if it is to be a sort of organism, we must recognize . . . *esprit de corps* [which] gives life and power.[7]

Here we have a self-conscious rejection of the old idea of business *qua* machine and a new awareness that "organism" is a concept that may have more merit.

Other managers/thinkers also began to come to this conclusion. Henri Fayol (1841–1925) was an experienced managing director as well as an important thinker in the field of organizational design. Fayol proposed fifteen principles of organization that are still largely valid today—principles that are permeated with the metaphors of an organism or a society. Regarding his first principle—division of work—he says: "Specialization belongs to the natural order. . . . The more highly developed the animal, the more highly differentiated its organs."[8] His eighth principle—centralization—is argued as follows: "In every organism, animal or social, sensations converge towards the brain or directive part."[9]

Alfred Sloan of General Motors, the major business figure of the 1920s and 1930s, made extensive use of the organism metaphor. He spoke of the evolution of his enterprise—that it must respond or die. He saw this as basic:

> An organization must grow—growth, or the striving for it, is essential to the health of an organization. . . . Deliberately to stop growing is to suffocate.[10]

The use of such terms has continued to the present. Normally, this usage is unconscious and is taken as commonsense speech. Occasionally, however, we find a deliberate attempt to embroider the metaphor. In a 1946 speech, the president of Westinghouse, A.W. Robertson, saw business as comparable to the California sequoia. His short speech is replete with gems of organic metaphor:

> The giant sequoias of business grew big and strong because of the economic climate. . . . The organizations that do survive usually have the knack of fitting into their environment, which is another word for giving the public what it wants. Such organizations grow big and have vitality comparable to the big trees of California that neither fire nor storm can kill . . . [but] if the climate becomes adverse, they would die.

and

> Casualties in business are always terrifying—there is always an epidemic ravaging business.

and

> The disease of business is the same as old age for the human body . . . [compared to] the vigor of its early youth and sturdy manhood.[11]

Wonderful stuff. Our close contemporaries have not adopted this baroque style, but the pervasive use of the organism metaphor continues nonetheless.

Harold Geneen saw business as a "fluid, ever-changing, living thing"[12]—a far cry from the machine analogy. Citicorp's Walter Wriston spoke of companies dying for the lack of the right atmosphere.[13] The favorite expression of IBM's T.J. Watson, Jr., was "galvanized into action."[14] (I can't resist the picture of a very large, very dead frog, electrodes attached to the nerves, and IBM management throwing a switch to revive the creature.)

Robert Anderson, chairman of Rockwell International, said in 1984 that his objective was to forge the disparate parts of his company into "an entity deeper and broader than any of those constituent parts."[15] The trite expression "greater than the sum of its parts" and the overused word *synergy* are in a way defining concepts for an organism—an entity that realizes its full potential, or any potential whatever, only when all the parts are subsumed in the whole.

And last, but hardly least, we have the most prolific metaphor user, Lee Iacocca. The organism metaphor seemed to have a strong hold on Iacocca, particularly in its pathological aspects. Some examples from a rich seam in his autobiographical descriptions of life at Chrysler: "survived its brush with death," "bleeding," "hemorrhaging," "cancer," "survival," "radical surgery," "triage."[16] When he was not taking up arms against a sea of troubles or suffering the proud man's contumely (Henry Ford II), Iacocca was subject to the thousand natural shocks that flesh is heir to.

Romanticism and Complexity

There are two major entailments of the organism metaphor, both rooted in nineteenth-century thought and, more specifically, the Romantic movement. I refer to the idea of the endemic complexity and ambiguity of living things and the idea of evolution—the fact that organisms grow and die but the species evolves toward higher things.

The Romantic movement in the nineteenth century affected all the higher spheres of human activity: history, art, politics, economics, religion, and philosophy. Romanticism was in many ways a reaction to the seventeenth- and eighteenth-century Enlightenment; the rationalism and mechanistic materialism of Laplace and Descartes in philosophy, the artistic classicism of David, and the rationalized politics of the Directory. In its place, the Romantics espoused a basically spiritual view of reality. The tenets of Romanticism were (and are):

- The expression of personal emotion as good, even wise
- Intuition, as opposed to rational thought, as a source of truth
- The value of personal experience

and most important for us,

- The view of society as an organism rather than a machine[17]

In literature, we find the emotionally charged and personally oriented Rousseau as a precursor of Byron, Coleridge, and Blake; these writers supplanted the cool rationalism of Corneille's classical theater. In the plastic arts, the precise classicism of David is replaced by the color, movement, and exoticism of Géricault, Delacroix, and again Blake, who particularly drew upon personal vision and intuition in both his poetry and his paintings. But it is in political thought and philosophy that Romanticism has left an indelible mark on business thinking.

The great conservative political theorist of the Romantic period was Edmund Burke (1729–97), the bitter enemy of the French revolutionary leaders. Burke saw in the thinking of Saint-Just and Robespierre a fundamental misreading of the nature of man and the nature of society. The revolutionaries were attempting to reform French society overnight on the basis of schemes of the utmost rationality. Burke, from the standpoint of English thought and its long reverence for tradition, piled polemic on polemic against the French leaders, culminating in his *Reflection on the Revolution in France* (1790).

> The leading idea emerging from [Burke's] eloquence and subtlety was that society is a vast and historical product that may not be tinkered with at will like a machine.[18]

Later, in philosophy, Hegel (1770–1831) developed his system of thought, with the stress on process, development, and evolution as the underpinnings to reality.[19] In his system, the spirit of God lives in the historical process.

In both Burke and Hegel, we find the basic assumption that society—any assemblage of human beings—is a highly complex, organismlike structure that is a historical product and is subtle to the point that the analysis and synthesis techniques of the Enlightenment are useless. There is a spirit of some sort at work in these assemblages that no amount of analysis can discern; one cannot take it apart and reassemble it for the better, like a machine. The entity is akin to a living thing—an organism—and analysis (i.e., disassembly) is a death sentence. Many business people have heard this message.

Darwin and Evolution

The second key idea associated with the organism metaphor is evolution. The Hegelian stress on process and development as a clue to the explanation of reality had its impact on scientific thought. Darwin's *The Origin of Species,* which appeared in 1858, demonstrated that the world of nature we see around us is the result of a slow process of evolution—a gradual change in the form of living things and the extinction of forms that are ill suited to their environment.

Herbert Spencer (1820–1903), the Victorian philosopher, took Darwin's biological ideas and applied them to sociology—to human societies. (The phrase most commonly associated with Darwin, "survival of the fittest," is actually Spencer's.)[20] In its crudest form, Social Darwinism equated the poor of the industrialized world to Darwin's unfit species—those that had lost or will lose the evolutionary struggle because they are ill adapted to the demands of modern life. The key concept, similar to biological evolution, is that the competitive economic struggle for existence is the engine for progress. This is a long way from the belief in the advance of culture and the tenets of Christian charity; Yeats disdainfully commented:

> We pieced our thoughts into philosophy.
> And planned to bring the world under a rule,
> Who are but weasels fighting in a hole.[21]

Social Darwinism is an important idea in business and has entered the thinking of most practitioners and theorists. (Andrew Carnegie's biographer tells us that Spencer and Darwin were Carnegie's intellectual heroes.[22]) And it is commonsense business thinking to believe that companies fail because of their ill adaptation and that the strong must, and will, succeed. Unfettered—and unforgiving—competition is the royal road to progress. The public outcry over the Lockheed and Chrysler loans demonstrates that this idea has entered the consciousness of the general public as well.

The organism metaphor, with its associations of spirit, process, and evolution, was the conventional wisdom of the nineteenth century in many realms of thought; the metaphor's hold on the twentieth-century business mind is still strong.

Other Entailments

I have already touched on some important entailments of the organism metaphor: the notion of the needs of an organism, quite distinct from a machine's "inputs"; the idea that an organism depends on a relationship with an exterior environment for its well-being; and, of central importance, the essential complexity of living things—Burke's concept of society as something that cannot be tinkered with at will, as a machine can be. There are a number of other important entailments that relate to business. For the explanation of these, it is useful to recall the distinction between the two types of organic thinking: anthropomorphism and domestication.

Some of the entailments apply to any organism, human or not. First among these, we find the key idea of a goal or purpose, with perhaps the distinction that in our culture, we tend to think that human beings have a goal for their existence, whereas the rest of nature has only a purpose, as I have described. This entailment provides an obvious linkage to the metaphors of journey and machine and provides adequate coverage for an important business idea. Another tie to these metaphors is provided by the notion of "breakdown." Organisms are subject to breakdown, at least in everyday parlance, although this is rather patently a machine metaphor applied to an organism.

We can see a further linkage in the idea of loss of control, which may not seem to fit an organism, but think of runaway horses, nature run wild, slave revolts, madmen. There is something unpredictable about all living things, most especially humans, and this unsettling idea carries over to business with the organism metaphor. Clark, writing in 1923, commented on the economic structures that men had built: "[They] appear with the force of living things, with purposes foreign to mankind . . . . If we do not tame them, they will devour us."[23]

Much more important for business purposes, organisms grow and die. These are entailments of the metaphor that are often involved in business speech and thought—the idea, as expressed by Sloan, for example, that growth is the iron law for any business. And all business leaders know the real potential for catastrophic loss, dissolution of the enterprise, bankruptcy—death in almost any commonsense usage of the term.

The last entailment, which applies both to humans and to domesticated animals, is associated with evolution. Two important ideas are subsumed under this general notion: competition and adaptation. I have already discussed how the ideas of Social Darwinism have become deeply ingrained in business thought—even popular thought—in the United States. Competition is almost universally viewed as right—its outcome just and its free expression the sole path to economic improvement.

Adaptation is a related idea, but it places more emphasis on the total surrounding *milieu,* not simply the struggle against competing species or one's fellows. With this model in mind, a business leader sees his organization as a product of countless adaptations to an environment; he must conclude that hasty change would be a mistake (tinkering with it, again, as with a machine) and he must also be constantly aware of changes in the environment or opportunities for successful niches—like Darwin's finches in the Galápagos.

Only one entailment that relates solely to domesticated animals need occupy us here, and that is the notion of a tool for profit-making—another tie to the voyage and machine analogies. As I have said, from the time of Genesis, it has been a deeply held belief that the world of nature exists to serve man; it is a tool in his hands. We in the West believe that all domesticated animals exist for our purposes alone, to make our lives easier, richer, or more entertaining. Wild animals, the Faustian mentality would say, are not domesticated simply because it wouldn't be worth the trouble—there would be no profit in it, or clearly we would have done it by now.

The entailments of the idea of business as a human being—the anthropomorphic models—are by far the most interesting. Although other animals can be unpredictable, this is a human trait that almost defines the species. Every human being is complex to the point of unfathomability; and each one is different—radical uniqueness characterizes the species. The objective of most art, particularly that of the novel, is to plumb the depths of human nature in its awesome complexity and variability.

In *The White Hotel,* D.M. Thomas has attempted to sketch the complex interior life of one person as a means to illuminate the Holocaust for the reader. All of us have difficulty comprehending the outrageous statistics: 6 million people tortured and murdered. What could a number like that possibly mean? Thomas's approach is to portray just one victim—a fairly ordinary woman, Lisa Erdman-Berenstein—who has been analyzed by Sigmund Freud and has had an unusually close relationship with him through visits and correspondence. She and 250,000 others were slaughtered by the Nazis at Babi Yar, just outside Kiev.

We are all familiar with—in fact, benumbed by—newsreels, still photos, survivors' accounts, statistics, analyses, and so on, of the Holocaust. But Thomas's words are surely the most meaningful and the most poignant:

> The soul of man is a far country that cannot be approached or explored. Most of the dead were poor and illiterate. But every single one of them had dreamed dreams, seen visions and had amazing experiences, even the babes in arms (perhaps especially the babes in arms). Though most of them had never left the Podral slum, their lives and histories were as rich and complex as Lisa Erdman-Berenstein's. If a Sigmund Freud had been listening and taking notes from the time of Adam, he would still not fully have explored even a single group, even a single person. And this was only the first day.[24]

And Freud, in the novel, completely missed the point of Lisa's life and troubles. And there were 250,000 at Babi Yar. And the Holocaust consumed 6 million unfathomable, irreplaceable, unique human beings.

Human beings (and to a lesser extent the lower animals) also have distinct personalities—some unique spirit that seizes our attention when we are in the presence of a fellow creature. In a like manner, some organizations have also achieved "personalities" of sorts—ways of doing things, people's dress, speech, jokes that unfailingly identify them with a particular organization. I am thinking particularly of AT&T, IBM, Citicorp, and Bechtel in this context.

We can also see a human association in business references to "health." Although health (or illness) is a characteristic of all living things, the use of this entailment in business usually has a human context. I have already quoted Lee Iacocca in this regard, noting his penchant for an important element of this notion—pathology. Business leaders typically make a direct connection between the status of their business and the idea of a person's health; "healthy," "sick," "bleeding," "cancerous," etc. and the like, are very common usages.

Probably the most important entailment of the human being metaphor is the idea of the value of a business organization. In virtually all cultures, a human being has transcendent value; his life and well-being are not negotiable commodities, not things to be traded off against other principles or values. The exceptions are obvious—warfare, capital punishment, abortion—but the fact that these are exceptions, and are considered unacceptable exceptions by many, really makes the point. People are not *there* for any purpose; they are a purpose unto themselves. In short, their value transcends any other values.

Transcendent value is a very appealing idea to many business leaders. It is very common to hear management speak of the needs of the business as senior to any individual's needs or desires—a clear application of this notion. And when the troubles come, not a few leaders have resorted to any means, fair or foul, legal or not, to ensure the continued existence of their enterprises—exactly as we would expect a human being to act when his survival is at stake.

Guides to Action

The organism metaphor has a good deal of merit as a guide to management action. The various entailments lead the manager to conceive of the organization as unique and highly complex, the product of some historical process; he sees it embodied with some spirit, almost independent of the physical and human components.

Peters and Waterman, in their stunningly successful best-seller

In Search of Excellence, have provided a number of guidelines for managers. In all respects, the authors have turned away from the old machine analog and embrace both a society and an organism metaphor. They prescribe eight actions for the modern manager, four of which are clearly organically based, as follows:[25]

A Bias for Action: Do It, Fix It, Try It. There are several ideas here.[26] First is the notion of flexibility in an organization—rapid and radical change and decision making—an idea closely associated with the behavior of an organism. The stress on "do it," as opposed to "analyze it," is related to the Zen insight on the workings of the human body and mind. The novice in Zen archery, for example, is encouraged to remove his ego consciousness from the task, "see" himself performing the act, and then let the body (and lower forms of mental activity) perform. In short, "do it, fix it, try it."

Get Close to the Customer. The idea of knowing the customer's business—spending a great deal of time observing and listening to him—is quite analogous to primitive hunting. To survive, hunters have always known their prey to an astonishing degree; every nuance of behavior and habitat is ingrained in the hunter's thinking and language.

Stick to Your Knitting. The idea here is to do what the company has done well historically; do not venture into businesses that are unfamiliar. This is an organic idea in that it speaks to the fundamental limitations of any organism. The genes determine the ultimate capability of any organism: fish don't fly, humans do not leap 20 feet into the air, and so forth.

Here is an example of this type of thinking:

> To tell declining steel companies to emulate the management practices of the booming Silicon Valley may be to suggest to prickly pears to try harder to become avocadoes.[26]

Simple Form, Lean Staff. This is the concept, basically, that form should follow function, that the working parts of an organization should relate simply (Peters and Waterman say "elegantly") to one another. I think the organic basis for this notion is clear.

Strategy

Organic thinking has also been embraced by today's best strategic thinkers. Harvard's brilliant theorist of corporate strategy, Michael Porter, has derived a model of corporate competition that is organic at its base.[27] Porter stresses one factor that most affects a company's ability to be profitable: the industry in which the company exists. This could be called the "speciation" of industry—every company placed in its proper species, the triumph of Linnaeus's biological classification applied to business. Once classified, a firm's fortunes are determined by the fortunes of its species/industry, which in turn are determined by five fundamental factors.

First, in his model, Porter cites the intensity of internal competition within an industry. This will vary with the number of firms in the industry, the resources they can bring to bear on these markets, and the sheer competence and will of the managers—their determination to succeed. The computer business, for example, has a different competitive milieu from the legal profession. This "internal" competition is entirely analogous to Darwinian intraspecies competition—the "survival of the fittest"—transformed by Spencer into Social Darwinism—the war of man against man.

Porter sees the threat of new entrants into an industry as the second force driving the profitability of the industry participants. An example would be IBM's entrance into the personal computer business. This can be seen as analogous, in biological terms, to new populations of the same species invading the environmental niche of an original group. Newly introduced populations, with particular skills to gain prey or other food sources, can drive the aboriginal inhabitants to the wall. In the same way, most industry participants are wary of new entrants, with substantial resources, entering into their markets and making life difficult, even impossible, for them.

Porter's third factor in determining an industry's success is the threat of substitute products—that is, the entrance of new companies with new technology, new solutions to customer's requirements, even new ways of doing business. In product technology, we have witnessed the transistor's total replacement of the vacuum tube. In the world of nature, examples abound of newly arrived forms supplanting an aboriginal species. The original environmental participants had established niches of habitat, prey, and food supply and enjoyed stable population levels. The new arrivals, more competent in prey acquisition, for example, are able after a time to drive the aborigines from the niche and push them to extinction or, at best, a precarious subsistence living.

The bargaining power of customers is Porter's fourth factor that can determine an industry's profitability. Large customers, especially when demand is soft and suppliers numerous, enjoy a buyer's market and strongly reduce the suppliers' profitability. This is essentially the case in today's (1987) computer business. (Porter's factors can clearly aggregate. In the computer business, the level of internal competition is very high, with both a large number of companies and many resource-rich firms that are determined to succeed.) In blunt biological terms, this can be expressed as the power of the prey. If a species is adapted to make a living from a difficult prey, its survival chances are slim. And with the inexorable forces of evolution, the prey naturally becomes more difficult; it devises new defenses of muscle, fang, or talon; it may become more evasive through sheer speed or agility or even with passive resistance, such as a highly offensive odor or taste.

Finally, Porter cites the power of suppliers as a factor in industry profitability. If a supplier or group of suppliers has virtual monopoly power, the suppliers' success is at the expense of the buyers—there is a sellers' market. We saw this dynamic clearly in the 1970s, when OPEC was strong and unified and the international oil industry (and downstream industries) suffered severely. Those with control of vital supplies, raw materials, technology, or what have you, can control—depress, in fact—the profitability of dependent industries.

The biological analogy is to symbiotic or parasitic creatures— those whose success depends on the success, or even tolerance, of a host species. The cattle herons of the West Indies ride on the backs of cattle and are tolerated because they feed on insects that torment their hosts—a happy arrangement for all but the insects. Clearly, parasitic creatures of all types fit this analogy to those who are dependent on "suppliers"; their survival and well-being is dependent on the survival of the host as well as the host's tolerance of their existence.

It is not my purpose to denigrate Porter's work by showing this biological basis; on the contrary, I believe his inquiry is deep and very much to the point for current business. Rather, I mean to show the pervasiveness of this metaphor as well as its real power to elucidate certain areas of business.

Strengths and Weaknesses of the Metaphor

The organism metaphor has many strengths, not just for such theorists as Porter and Peters, but for the practical business person. Perhaps most important, it highlights what the voyage and machine tropes ignore—the complexity and ambiguity of business life. I repeat myself to stress the point again: A business is a terribly complex set of relations, and even if the relations were ultimately fathomable by scientific management, the ambiguity would remain. There is simply no way to pin down the ultimate workings of a business in all its variegated aspects, not least because it is composed of human beings, whose motivation, emotions, and predictability simply escape us.

Once having accepted this complexity and ambiguity and the view of the organization as a product of countless adaptations, it behooves the manager to approach change with a good deal of caution. He should tend to think of change in terms more like raising children or training dogs than like rearranging a machine. In the former case, principles are required, of course, but they are general ones, not step-by-step procedures—not a blueprint to start with, but rather the knowledge that we are entering into a *process* of change and that the particular steps will be determined by where actual experience leads. Also, the parent or teacher must change as well. As Carse puts it: "True parents do not see to it that their children grow in a particular way. . . . They grow with their children."[28]

The metaphor is also very helpful in focusing the manager on the *needs* of an organization[29]—the fact that a business is more than a blind tool, but has needs that vary from sufficient capital to the emotional needs of its human members.

The metaphor also forces one to think of the organization as a delicate assemblage of suborganizations that must all work in harmony for the "health" of the whole. Further, the manager gains a sensitivity to the surrounding environment, the play of forces that can affect his firm and the need to understand them and adapt his organization to them. Much more than the machine analogy, the organism metaphor stresses change and adaptation as a way of life—albeit careful, "evolutionary" change, not root and branch.

Closely related to the notion of evolutionary change is the necessity for innovation. Organisms that do not continually create new solutions to the problems presented by a shifting environment pass from the scene. Peters and Waterman are very explicit about this entailment:

> We believe that the truly adaptive organization evolves in a very Darwinian way. . . . [It] fosters its own mutations by experimenting, making the right mistakes . . . [and] killing off the dumb mutations.[30]

This is perhaps the metaphor's greatest practical strength—its power to focus the manager's mind on the constant need for innovative behavior. Weber's bureaucracy and Taylor's machine fail this critical test.

The idea of an organism has some major shortcomings, however, as a description for business. The metaphor's power and innate appeal should not deceive us—a business, it goes without saying, is *not*, in fact, an organism. Real organisms are much more fragile, much more limited in organizational form than business organizations.[31] Organisms are limited in many ways; the form of an individual organism is determined by its genes, and can vary only within very narrow limits as a result of environmental factors. Organisms also follow an inexorable life course—birth, youth, maturity, age, and death. Rejuvenation belongs to the spiritual realm; all organisms are clocks that are running down—fragile, time-bound creatures.

Business organizations, on the other hand, depend for their success on infinitely renewable human energy and creativity, not biological functions. Change in structure and purpose, even radical change, can be made to organizations, and that is often the right prescription, but it could be hampered by overreliance on an organism metaphor. For example, many modern hi-tech companies employ an "ad-hocracy" organizational practice whereby teams of people are assembled from many disciplines and organizational "homes" to serve a particular short-term need. It is difficult to find an organism analogy for this type of organization. In a similar way as I have noted, Peters and Waterman's prescription, "Stick to your knitting," is really a statement of limitations—the idea that fish don't fly; each organism has its proper place and function.

But many organizations *have* changed their basic lines of business very successfully; many have become quite different from their original form. Would W.R. Grace still exist as a shipping line, or would UMC exist if it only made matches? The focus on fundamental limits of an organization, while lending an air of healthy caution, can more often lead to groupthink—the death of innovative thought.

As we have seen in Porter's work, the organism model is terribly deterministic: you are what you are, just as a man is a man and can never be a bird or a fish. Your "species," the industry you are in, your origins, and so forth—these determine what you can be. These beliefs can clearly be very limiting to the business leader. Success may depend on radical departures from past lines of business and past practices. Harold Geneen saw no reason for ITT not to engage in almost any business. He saw business as the management of countless transactions and relationships, not as a being with its fate written in its genes.

The limitations of organic thinking have been illustrated perfectly by the experience of People Express Airline. The line built its early success on an unorthodox, highly decentralized form of management. Job changing was encouraged; for example, a pilot could become a computer programmer for a while, then a reservations clerk. The chief financial officer was a certified flight attendant and insisted on flying weekly. This "happy anarchy" spurred People's early success but created chaos when the line grew. An analyst reported on his attempts to suggest change to People's management: "They'd tell you: 'This is our philosophy. We can't change it. It's us.' "[32]

Holding on to outworn practices that management believed to be the company's essence, People Express found itself in serious financial trouble and was forced to sell out to Texas Air Corporation.

The idea of evolution itself can lead a business leader badly astray, especially if he follows orthodox Darwinian thinking. The biologist Stephen Jay Gould has illustrated this point for us in his analysis of the New Zealand kiwi.[33] The kiwi egg is by far the largest of all bird eggs relative to body size—up to 25 percent of the female's weight: "so large that females must waddle, legs spread far apart, for several days before laying."

Why such a large egg? As Gould notes, evolutionary biologists have a traditional approach to riddles of this sort. They assume that the trait must provide some benefit to the creature, that natural selection has worked to provide this advantageous element.

In business, it is very common to think that the current technologies, market positioning, products, practices, organization, even specific people, are there because they are the result of a long, successful adaptation to conditions—that they are "the things that got us this far."

Gould believes that this style of Darwinian reasoning—in biology—embodies a crucial flaw. He cites "the easy slide from current function to reason for origin" as a major fallacy. The fact that something works well is not necessarily a clue to its origin. Natural selection cannot explain every feature in the simplistic terms of benefits to survival.

There is an alternative: Good function may have evolved for another reason, or for no reason at all, and may have simply been co-opted for its present use. Gould compares orthodox Darwinian reasoning to the view of Voltaire's Pangloss, who proclaimed that our noses were made for spectacles and our legs for pants.

Gould's explanation for the huge egg is simply that kiwi evolution entailed a substantial decrease in overall body size, and the egg size did not keep pace. This is a very substantial difference in explanation from the orthodox—the crucial difference between the idea that the big eggs are good for something now so natural selection favored them and the idea that the feature was retained from an ancestral species and proved merely nonfatal.

Every company of any longevity has its oversized kiwi egg and its orthodox Darwinians who have taken the "easy slide from current function to reason for origin."

Ambiguity Overdone

I have dwelt upon the organism trope's overconcentration on limitations; it can also be pernicious by an overstress on the ambiguity and complexity of a business. Again, my belief is that the complexity entailment has a good deal of merit for business, but there is the danger of overstatement. If the manager totally accepts this view, he is unlikely to do the necessary analytical work of management; he is much more likely to rely on instinct and "gut" feelings for his decisions. Plainly put: the metaphor can be a good excuse for avoiding a lot of hard work and difficult thinking.

Another problem can arise from the organism metaphor if it is taken too literally. Real organisms have interdependent parts that must work together. This idea can be a valuable one for business, but in fact, all parts of an organization need not necessarily work together in closest harmony. There are organizational forms—for example, "federal decentralization," as described by Drucker[34]—in which the company is broken into autonomous pieces that have virtually no interdependence or communication with one another. Sloan's General Motors was the prototype for this highly successful organizational form. But the organism metaphor would suggest that there is something wrong with this type of organization, that there is not sufficient interaction and interdependence.[35]

The Leader

The leader's role under the organism metaphor will vary, depending on the type of organism postulated—that is, human or non-human—as well as on the part the leader plays—that is, active or passive, either part of the organism himself or an outside agent.

In the case of the human model, if the leader conceives of himself as a part of the organism, he must, of course, be the brains. As Fayol has pointed out, every natural organism has a central, guiding agent. This model of leadership is familiar to all of us in the person of the entrepreneur—the manager who is involved in every aspect of the business and makes all the decisions. Actually, I believe that Fayol's analogy is far too limited. In almost any organism, and certainly in the more highly developed ones, the higher brain does *not* make all the decisions; the nervous system is structured as a hierarchy of delegated decision making, very much like a large corporation.

The conscious human mind does not get involved in the chemical composition of the blood nor in the secretion of hormones; those tasks are delegated to much lower levels in the nervous system. This more expansive analogy of the nervous system to business can be useful in showing the leader that he *is* the brains, in the sense of guiding, planning, and ultimate decision making, but also showing him the value, the "naturalness" of delegation of authority. Also, if the natural organism is to function well, it is vital that the network of decision functions communicate with each other; the brain must be notified if the parts are malfunctioning, and the like. This entailment is a good guide for the leader: He must foster excellent communication up and down the organizational hierarchy of decision making.

In many cases, the leader conceives of the organization as a human being, but he doesn't see himself as a part of the "person"; rather, he stands in some relationship to the organization. We have already seen Wedgwood and his business *qua* mistress. Wedgwood's feeling, although unusual, provides a clue to the sensibility of the founder of a business. Founders seem naturally to develop a warm fondness for their business—a type of parent relationship, in fact. A human parent is naturally fond of his child, ready to make sacrifices for him, and also ready to discipline, scold, punish, and so forth—all for the child's own good. With very little translation required, I have described the typical paternalistic founder/manager—Henry Ford, for example. Peters and Waterman make

the point explicitly in describing Watson (IBM), Kroc (Mac-
Donald's), and Marriott: "Like good parents they cared a lot and
expected a lot."[36] Also, we all know that some parents let the grown
child go—let him make his own decisions—and some parents never
tire of trying to control every aspect of an adult child's life. And
we are likewise familiar with the founder/manager like Ford, who
made all the decisions in a large organization, or the founder like
Ken Olsen of Digital Equipment Corporation, who is still much
involved in his creation but delegates many decisions.

If the business leader is not the founder, he is more likely to
see himself as the mentor of an organization. "Mentor" describes
a relationship as meaningful as "parent." The mentor has an emotional bond with the pupil, he is conscious that he is responsible
for a unique spirit that must be molded and guided. Whether "parent" or "mentor," the leader who sees his organization as a person
and himself as responsible for that person has formed an emotional
attachment. This relationship can be most clearly seen when "raiders" attempt to take control of an organization. An observer of
these battles can see two mutually incompatible views of business
in full clash—a classic case of conflicting paradigms in the sense
of Kuhn's theory, which we will discuss later.

Fundamentally, the raiders have a mechanical view or, at best,
a domesticated animal view of business. To them, the business really
is nothing but assets—economic units that are wealth-producing
and can produce more wealth if managed by the right people (hence
their willingness to outbid the market). Alternatively, the raider
believes—in a radically antiorganism view—that the parts of an
organization are worth *more* than the whole, that units can be sold
and the net proceeds will be worth more than the purchase price
for the whole (again, the reason that the raider will outbid the
market).

That is the raider's side; his metaphors are a money machine
or a cash cow. The parent/mentor, of course, does not even begin
to see this. When corporate managers try to defend themselves
against raiders, the press often derides them for making insincere
defenses simply to save their jobs. Certainly this happens, but I
believe that the truth usually lies elsewhere. The "parent" feels
deeply about his organization as a living, breathing thing that

somehow has transcendent value. It is not a piece of machinery nor a hunk of meat, not something to be bought and sold like a beast or dismembered for the sake of some transient financial gain by a stranger who neither knows nor cares about its history and spirit. Listen to Walter Kissinger, former CEO of the Allen Group, and note both his implied organic metaphor and the obvious sincerity of his feelings:

> The victims may range from well-known consumer names to our leading defense contractors. . . . None is sacred or immune from the onslaught of the financial wizards who move companies like pieces of paper and casually trade their "Boardwalk" and "Park Place" with junk bonds as payment. . . . It is of no interest or concern to these individuals that they touch the lives of a ms of thousands of workers who may become unemployed; that they destroy the careers of dedicated individuals who have devoted their lives to building a company; that they frequently destroy communities, that they undermine the vitality and creativity of a company.[37]

For now, the raiders appear to have the law and academia on their side. The law tends to look out for the stockholder to ensure that he will receive the best price for his ownership. This enshrines in the law the mechanical/domesticated animal view of a firm—a money machine, a mere economic unit. Similarly, most academics go back to economic efficiency and the laws of supply and demand: In sum, productive assets should be in the hands of those who will make them most productive, as evidenced by their willingness to pay the highest price. But the law and theory to one side, a leader whose firm has been "raided" and dismembered knows that some wrong has been done, some sacrilege committed, some unique spirit extinguished.

The role of the leader will be quite different if he conceives of his firm as a domesticated animal rather than a human being. The simplest analogy for this leader is a shepherd. The good shepherd has, of course, an emotional bond with his flock—even, in the Scriptures, prepared in the extreme "to lay down his life for his sheep." That is surely an exaggeration; no shepherd who is not a madman would do that. A shepherd may be fond of his sheep, but fundamentally he exploits them—they have an economic purpose for him. The "good shepherd" in business will care for the organization, perhaps be paternalistic, and certainly ensure the proper care and feeding—for example, capital and human resources. The indifferent shepherd will be more short-sighted and will provide minimum care, perhaps even sell off assets in a bad season—like slaughtering or selling the brood ewes. But both view the organization as exploitable.

The best example of this domesticated animal way of thinking is the Boston Consulting Group's methodology for corporate planning. The technique is called portfolio planning, because the corporate leader is encouraged to think of himself as managing a portfolio of assets; he is guided by BCG's technique in his investment/divestment decisions. Assets (product lines, business units, subsidiaries) are categorized into dogs, cash cows, stars, and problem children. It's easy: You sell or kill the dogs, milk the cash cows, feed the stars, and either solve the children's problems or sell the children. It all has the air of a menagerie, and it's all based on the concept of a business as a domesticated animal.

But regardless of whether the metaphor speaks to the leader in the image of a human being or a domesticated animal, it tells him something important. It tells him that the business is complex, difficult to change, the product of an historical evolution—and probably most important, it tells him that his business is something special, has some unique spirit, some extraordinary value.

Summary

- The idea of the world itself as an organism is very ancient. This idea—animism—is one of the root metaphors of human consciousness.

- As a business metaphor, the idea has become increasingly popular and is currently, along with the journey metaphor, the most frequently used.

- The idea has two strains: anthropomorphism—the world as humanlike; and domestication—the world of nature as a field for human exploitation. Both ideas are represented in business: the business as a unique being with purposes that transcend all other considerations and the business as a domesticated animal, an organism to be exploited.

- Some key entailments of the metaphor—complexity, ambiguity, and evolution—are rooted in nineteenth-century Romantic thought.

- Innate complexity and ambiguity are good matches for actual business experience and are an excellent tonic for those bred on scientific management.

- Evolution—more particularly, the complex of ideas called Social Darwinism—has had a major impact on business thinking. The notions of competition, a struggle for survival, innovation, and change as the keys to success—all stem from Darwinian thought.

- The idea of the business as humanlike suggests that the business's survival and goals are superior to any other purposes, including society's. Also, the idea suggests that the business has some unique spirit that must be preserved and is complex and ambiguous to the point of ultimate unfathomability—like a person.

- Many of Peters and Waterman's ideas are seen to have an underlying bias toward an organic metaphor. The excellent strategic work of Michael Porter also shows the influence of organic thinking.

- The metaphor's weakness is principally in its assumption of rigid determinism; in this regard, it is similar to the machine metaphor. An organism has its form and its fate written in its genes. Radical change is simply not possible—a perilous limitation for a business. Also, the idea can help perpetuate outmoded practices by supporting the view that these practices have evolved over time for a good reason. Recall Stephen Jay Gould's kiwi egg.

- The metaphor suggests several leader roles: as the brains of the organism, directing all activity; as the parent or mentor, the guardian of this unique being; or as the shepherd of a flock, who cares for his sheep but, in the final analysis, exploits them.

9
The Society

Shamans and Statesmen

It is not the consciousness of men that determines their being, but on the contrary, their social being that determines their consciousness.
—Karl Marx[1]

Background

Society is one of those phenomena, like art or our own language, that is so pervasive that it is taken for a natural feature of the world. Aristotle, in fact, provided that central insight—that society is part and parcel of the world:

The state belongs to the class of objects which exist by nature and man is by nature a political animal. Anyone, who by his nature and not simply by ill luck has no state is either too bad or too good, either sub-human or super-human.[2]

Aristotle speaks to the nature of society and also to the nature of man: A man is only truly human when he is part of a society; the stateless man is hardly a human being. Man attains his true humanity only in the context of a society of his fellows.

The naturalness of society, its place in the order of creation, was deduced by Aristotle from his experience of the Greek *polis*, but the insight has been confirmed by later experience and research. There does not appear to have been a time when men lived without society—contrary to the political theories of Hobbes and Rousseau, who postulated a primeval "state of nature," a time before men coalesced into social forms. Even our remote ancestors, the Paleolithic hunters of Western Europe (35000–8000 B.C.), appear to have lived in an organized society. The great cave art of that time not only indicates a high degree of technical expertise but also suggests an organized communal life. The location and the profusion of the cave paintings at Lascaux and Altamira contradict the notion that the art was reserved for the few or for the painter alone. The technical requirements alone would have demanded a fair degree of organization; the effort required to cut trees for scaffolding and to gather materials for the painting would necessitate a community of some sort.[3]

The evidence of comparative ethology also supports the view that man is a "political animal" in his very nature. The animal stocks we are closest to, the anthropoid apes, are mostly communal by nature, living in small bands for mutual protection, food gathering, and rearing of the young. It seems clear that even before man was man, before the big-brained *homo sapiens* emerged, our animal ancestors lived in a species of society. So modern evidence seems to conclude that Aristotle was right: Society is an "object" that exists by nature.

As we have seen, Burke defended this same idea—that a society is a natural, organism-like thing—but Burke extended the idea, perhaps unjustifiably. His contention, and the contention of all conservatives at all times and in all places, was that an era's particular *form* of society was part of the natural order. In contrast, we have the Neapolitan thinker Giambattista Vico, writing in the early eighteenth century and virtually ignored in his own time. Vico proposed one of history's great revolutionary ideas—a radical idea then, but a commonplace in modern thought: History and forms of society are man-made "objects," not features of the natural landscape; men can make their own history and devise their own type of social organization.

> The world of human society has certainly been made by men, and its principles are therefore to be found within the modifications of our own human mind.[4]

This idea was central to the very opponents of Burke, the French revolutionaries, who tried to remake the society of the *ancien ré-*

gime in a few years. The heirs of Robespierre and Saint-Just are with us still in social revolutionaries the world over and, as we shall see, in the advocates of radical "cultural" change in modern business.

From our vantage point in the modern world, it is sometimes difficult to understand the basis of this debate. It seems clear and obvious to us today that Vico was right: A society is a creature of men's minds and actions. But nothing could be less obvious to medieval man, who believed that God had created lord and bishop in their places as certainly as He had created men with two hands and two feet. Even the eighteenth-century opponents of revolution, like Burke, who held no brief for the excesses of the Bourbons, still were convinced that a society was a creation of centuries of life and thought and that is could not be taken apart and reassembled like a machine. The debate continues today in business thought between the proponents of "cultural" change in business and their conservative foes.

It has become commonplace now in business theory and practice to consider a business organization a kind of society. Today's conventional wisdom has been well stated by the scholar Morgan: "Organizations are socially constructed realities."[5] As early as 1957, another scholar, Selznick, had analyzed organizations in the light of social structure, mapping the features of a society into the structure of an organization. Selznick showed the close relationships, the essential similarities. Both a society and an organization exhibit certain features:

- Assigned roles
- Internal interest groups
- Social stratification
- Shared beliefs
- Participation and communication
- Dependencies[6]

So, for some time now, the rather odd idea of business as a society has grown familiar to us. Let us see where this notion has taken us.

Types of Societies

We shall look shortly at our business leaders' use of the society metaphor, but first it will help to put their remarks in context by outlining the various forms of society. Even at present, mankind displays a wide range of societal types, each potentially a model for a business organization and each implicitly employed by business speakers. First, I shall make the distinction between traditional and modern societies.

Traditional societies are characterized by a very high degree of social cohesiveness and also a very high degree of social *stasis;* each member shares a number of basic assumptions with his fellows, and one of these assumptions is his immutable place in the society. Such societies are also marked, as an almost necessary condition for their continuance, by a thoroughgoing homogeneity: one language, one racial stock.

The clearest example of such a society is the primitive tribe, an example used extensively by William Ouchi as a prescription for modern business organizations. Ouchi emphasizes the cohesion, the shared values and unspoken assumptions that a tribe maintains and that a business should strive for.

But we need not look so far from modern industrial society as a tribe to find traditional societies. Medieval society was in all respects traditional—universal acceptance of one faith, one order of society, and an unchangeable social standing for each member. This sounds oppressive to us moderns, but apparently these societies gave a great deal of assurance and spiritual comfort to their members.

Even in the modern world we find such societies. The thrust of present-day Moslem fundamentalism is nothing less than a return to a truly traditional society—a reaction against such pernicious modern ideas as democracy, free-thinking, and women's rights, which they believe have undermined the cohesion and values of the old civilization. There are numerous other examples. Britain before World War II was largely a traditional society with a rigid class system but also a high degree of social integration; each member knew his station but drew comfort from the success and the values of British society. The sacrifices of the war—unrewarded by gains for the lower classes—coupled with massive immigration of alien peoples from the Old Empire, wore down the cohesiveness of British society. Today, although more traditional than the United States, Britain, for good or ill, has moved into the modern world.

It may seem that I have presented an odd grouping of societies: primitive tribes, feudal Europe, and twentieth-century Britain. The constant in all these—what characterizes them as "traditional"— is the great degree of immutable social stratification and, closely related, a strong social cohesiveness. It would be mistaken to say that these people are "resigned" to their social status, for they implicitly believe in the rightness of their station and draw meaning and comfort from their place in a larger social entity. Although there is obvious social differentiation, at the same time there is a substantial degree of shared values, customs, beliefs, and ritual that hold the society together and provide meaning for even the lowest members.

Modern societies are all heirs to revolutionary France, when the irrationality of privilege was first unmasked, when Vico's lesson was first put to use. The Jacobins saw only the dark side of privilege and social stratification—the death of human aspirations, the inequities and cruelties of the *ancien régime*. They did not understand what we now see clearly in retrospect: the value and spiritual comfort of the traditional society. But the genie is out of the bottle, and most of us now live in "open," modern societies.

Modern states vary considerably in their form and in the degree of freedom enjoyed by their inhabitants. We are all familiar with totalitarian societies, in which the interests of the state are senior to the rights, privileges, even well-being of the citizens. On the other end of the scale, we have constitutional forms of government, in which the rights of the citizens are protected and, in theory at least, take precedence over the demands of the society as a whole. The U.S. constitutional form is the most familiar example of this type of society. It is characterized by a system of separation of powers, as originally prescribed by Montesquieu, to prevent the government from obtaining too much power over its citizens.

But totalitarian or open, constitutional or tyrannical, all modern societies have left something behind. Friedrich Tönnies, the pioneering German sociologist, saw this in the 1880s. The effects of capitalism, urbanization, and an overly rationalized set of norms had produced a general malaise in the modern world, a sense of *anomie* (the word is his colleague Durkheim's) in its citizens. Tönnies made the key distinction between *Gesellschaft* (society) and *Gemeinschaft* (community), to contrast the anonymity and value-lessness of modern life with the tightly integrated cohesive communities of an earlier time.[7]

In many cases, the metaphor of business speakers harkens back to traditional societies and focuses on the rich meaning and strong values that such communities afford. It must be said, again, that traditional societies are rare in the modern world, and business leaders who propose such forms are either searching for a lost world or are suggesting that New Guinea jungle dwellers or the medieval world are apt models for modern-day business organizations.

Business Usage

Henry Gantt is the first business speaker that I have found who used the society metaphor, although his use was implicit and he only alluded to the idea. Writing in 1901, Gantt referred to the beneficial nature of obstacles: "They force everyone to do his duty" and lend "a moral tonic to the community."[8] Henri Fayol was more explicit in his use of the metaphor; his tract on management is largely based on organic (as we have seen) and societal analogies. Among his fourteen principles of management, I find six that seem to be society-based:

- Authority and responsibility
- Discipline
- Unity of command
- Unity of direction
- Subordination of the individual
- Equity[9]

It can be seen that with the single exception of the last principle—equity—Fayol was referring to an authoritarian regime—not an open society, but a society of strict rules of behavior, with the saving grace of equity for the members. It is also clear that Fayol was in no way conceiving of a primitive tribe, but more likely was referring to the largely traditional, hierarchical forms of his time—the Third Republic and Victorian England—socially stratified societies, but constitutional, in that the citizens had fundamental rights.

Henry Ford explicitly rejected the society metaphor in his words, as we shall see later; but in some of his actions, he made it clear that he conceived of his business and his staff as a society of some sort. Ford is remembered for his revolutionary idea of the five-dollar day—roughly double the prevailing rate at the time of its introduction in 1913. But Ford also established the "Ford Sociology Department" at that time and employed 30 investigators (150 by 1919) to visit the workers' homes and determine whether there were family problems or whether the workers drank or gambled. Those who received a bad report had their wages halved.[10] Ford's reasoning parallels that of the French revolutionaries: Virtue is the key for a great society; private virtue is as important as public virtue and is an appropriate concern of the state.

Alfred Sloan also put his society metaphor into action. When he became president of General Motors in 1923, he was convinced that decentralization was analogous to the freeman's way of life:

> Centralization, to his way of thinking, smacked of regimentation and dictatorship. . . . His profound conviction [became] that decentralization most nearly corresponded to what he believed should be the model of a Free Society in general—the wide distribution of responsibility.[11]

Sloan's principles for the new organization were:

- The chief executive of each operating unit should have complete responsibility for the unit.

- Each unit should be self-contained; that is, it should contain every necessary function.

- Certain central organizations, such as law, are absolutely essential.

Peter Drucker has called Sloan's GM organization "federal decentralization," in an obvious reference to the U.S. form of shared state and federal powers. The GM organization, however, is modeled more on the *theory* of states rights than on its present-day realization. Actually, Sloan's model is much closer to feudalism—self-contained economic and political units, with the feudal lord bearing all responsibility and only tenuously linked to a central authority. Only in time of crisis was the central authority recognized and able to exercise its fundamental power.

We find a very explicit analogy to the U.S. government in a 1955 speech by Petersen, then CEO of Standard Oil. (The speech was delivered to a group of Japanese businessmen. How the world has changed in thirty years—an American lecturing the Japanese on business practices!) Petersen saw the organization in the same terms as Montesquieu and the framers of the U.S. Constitution—that is, as a system of conflicting interests that serve as mutual checks and balances. The interests that Petersen noted were the familiar players in the stakeholder view of the firm: stockholders, employees, customers, government, and the general public. (Usually, suppliers would be included in this list.) The job of management is to balance these interests and maximize the benefits to all.[12]

Culture is naturally associated with the idea of society. Reg Jones of General Electric was the first I found who spoke of a corporate culture. The strength of GE was derived from its "value system, shared knowledge, traditions, history and self-image."[13]

One of Jones's favorite expressions was "working with the grain,"[14] a recognition that all his actions must be sensitive to an existing set of practices and traditions—in short, a culture. As the leader of a "society," Jones found himself preoccupied with the question of succession from the very beginning of his term—not a concept that would readily come to mind from any other business metaphor but society.

Walter Wriston had a clear idea of the style he wished to create at Citicorp. He sought the clash of ideas in an open environment and repeatedly used societal images—speaking of "revolution" and "changing the world." Wriston explicitly advocated "a participative society at Citicorp."[15] He clearly had in mind an organization modeled on one of the American ideal forms—an open society in which all shades of opinion are voiced and all are free to participate in debates on public policy. It is a basic tenet of American political theory that the best ideas will win out in the marketplace of public opinion. Wriston said: "The way you change the world—you launch an idea into the marketplace."[16] No business or nation actually operates in as freewheeling a manner as Wriston—or the American Civil Liberties Union—proposes, but the ideal of full participation by all employees has grown in appeal and is not an altogether foolish notion.

Ian MacGregor represented, at least in his choice of words, a more conservative approach: "It is better to evolve things than go in for revolution."[17] In these words, MacGregor represents yet another ideal of American political life—the conservative, traditional idea (back to Burke) that there is some inchoate wisdom in the societal form we have and that changes should be gradual, piecemeal, and carefully considered. And MacGregor stayed within the mainstream with this pronouncement: "[My] basic principle—the consent of the governed."[18]

Others have spoken to another strain in American history—the revolutionary ideal. Henry Harnischfeger (Harnischfeger Corporation) has emphasized the progressive streak in American politics, harkening back to a revolutionary heritage now 200 years old: "No company reaches the century mark by worshipping its ancestors and embalming its tradition."[19] Here we have an explicit rejection of traditional society, particularly the tribal form—the most conservative of any form of communal life, in which ancestors are literally worshipped and tradition is much more important than the brief lives of the transient individuals.

Lee Iacocca found yet another type of society in the Ford Motor Company of Henry Ford II—an absolute monarchy. Iacocca makes continual reference to Ford as a "king" who operated from a "palace" and expected to be treated as "royalty." But there are kings and there are kings; Henry II, in Iacocca's mind "held the power of life and death over all of us."[20]

Things were much worse, though, at Chrysler. Iacocca found what every social thinker fears most: "The place was in a state of anarchy."[21] The dread of anarchy is a recognition of the soundness of Aristotle's insight: A man cannot achieve his human potential without a society. Iacocca also chose another societal form; he compares Chrysler to the Italy of the *Risorgimento:*

> [Chrysler] was like Italy in the 1860s—the company consisted of little duchies, each one run by a *prima donna* in his mini-empire.[22]

Iacocca's concept of Italian history is inexact—the House of Savoy, the Hapsburg Empire, and the Papal States were hardly "little duchies"—but he makes his point clearly and vividly. And we are all familiar with this organizational pathology and the harm that "empire-builders"—managers concerned only with their own power and influence—can do.

Current business scholars have also adopted the society metaphor, apparently as a reflection of their subjects' thinking. Donaldson and Lorsch, in their 1983 study of CEOs, found strong concurrence with Reg Jones's concern about succession—the legacy left to the next generation is a major worry.[23]

In their book on midsized companies, Clifford and Cavanagh agreed: "CEO's—what they're after, what they do need, is the satisfaction of leaving a legacy."[24] They also discovered the CEOs' concern for some form of written "constitution" for their companies:

> Most of the business leaders talked about corporate credos and philosophy—literate, concise statements of values, guiding principles.[25]

But it is to Peters and Waterman that we owe the current vogue of the society metaphor in business. We have already seen their use of the organic image in their discussion of "excellent" companies. Their attributes of excellence that are related to a society metaphor are as follows:[26]

Autonomy and Entrepreneurism. The idea here is one of freedom— an entirely open society with no social stratification, a society in which individuals have autonomy and are not held back by social standing or hierarchy.

Productivity through People. This is an allusion to the single most important asset of any society—its people. This recognition of the primacy of the people is a characteristic of modern societies, sparked by the preamble of the U.S. Constitution—"We the people of the United States"—and the favored sobriquet of revolutionary France—*citoyen.*

Values. This is the attribute that Peters and Waterman seem to stress beyond everything else. I shall postpone a discussion of this for a later section.

Loose-Tight. This somewhat awkward phrasing actually refers to a form of management that gives wide latitude to the employee in most things, but imposes very specific restrictions in a few key areas. The idea is familiar to us as a particular type of constitutional government in a free society—a society that values liberty. The word *liberty* seems to have a definite meaning to us, but its meanings can vary. Recall that the Soviet and other Marxist societies are self-proclaimed democracies with free citizens. Is this simply hypocrisy and newspeak? Not entirely. The philosopher Isaiah Berlin has explored the different notions of liberty and has elucidated this point.[27] He has defined, first, *positive liberty*—autonomy, but in association with a state's purposes, such as unity, harmony, justice, order, virtue. But the state, to achieve these purposes, can and will interfere with the individual in all aspects of his private life. It is this type of liberty that Rousseau espoused in *The Social Contract,* the type of liberty enjoyed by Ford's "$5 per day" man—the freedom to join the organization but then lose all control of both his public (work) life and his private life. It was the type of freedom that the citizens "enjoyed" under the Directory in Revolutionary France, the freedom of the citizens in contemporary Marxist societies. But it is a species of liberty nonetheless.

    Berlin's *negative liberty* is closer to the Western norm and also to Peters and Waterman's "loose-tight." Negative liberty is simply the right of the individual to be restrained only within rigidly defined areas of his existence. The state reserves to itself certain rights and imposes certain duties; all else is open to individual choice. This is analogous to a management style that specifies the levels of

authority for certain very specific transactions and permits autonomy in everything outside these limits.

Our last business writer is O'Toole, who reinforces Peters and
Waterman's "society" bias. O'Toole writes of "vanguard management"; his ideals are very close to Peters and Waterman's and those
of their "excellent" companies. He tells us: "This book is about
reform, not about revolution."[28]

O'Toole's society metaphor is apparent in his description of
the "vanguard" philosophy of management, using such words as
justice, harmony, integrity, balance. O'Toole also betrays a "society" bias in his prescription for successful companies:

- People-oriented
- Visible leadership
- Plan for employment stability
- Provide a sense of ownership

The Entailment of Meaning

The notion of a meaningful existence has been bound up with the
notion of society since time out of mind—recall Aristotle's comment on man's dependence on society for his very humanity. But
one of the bargains we seem to have made for industrial progress
is a diminution of meaning in individual lives. O'Toole remarks
that "the search for meaning has become the *leitmotiv* of modern
times";[29] and O'Toole is not a social philosopher—he writes about
business. Ernest Becker, a true social philosopher, has charted this
same malaise in modern life:

> Man wants to know that his life has somehow counted, if not for
> himself, then at least in a larger scheme of things, that it has left
> a trace, a trace that has meaning.[30]

This theme is expressed consistently in modern thought. The psy-
chologist Bruno Bettelheim wrote:

> If we hope to live not just for the moment, but in true conscious-
> ness of our existence, then our greatest need and most difficult
> achievement is to find meaning in our lives.[31]

But if Aristotle was right, meaning should not be an issue for modern man any more than for his ancestors, for after all, we all live in organized societies and should find our meaning in this social context. Clearly, many have not. The positivistic flavor of industrial society erodes the comfortable feelings of belonging and security in our lives. As we have seen in Stromberg, metaphysical and religious modes are not congenial to industrial society, and "what grows upon the world is a certain matter-of-factness."[32] It is this "matter-of-factness" that is at the center of Tönnies's notion that we have achieved "society" at the expense of "community"—that we have gained the material benefits, the physical security of society, but have lost the sense of community and fellow-feeling that is at the heart of a humanity in the embrace of a true society.

The Irish poet John Montague has expressed this modern dilemma beautifully in his work "Process." Note the absence of metaphysical or religious themes but the central place he gives to "love or friendship"—that is, community. The second verse begins:

Each close in his own
world of sense and memory,
races, nations, locked
in their dream of history,
only love or friendship,
an absorbing discipline
(the healing harmony
of music, painting, poem)
as swaying rope-ladders
across fuming oblivion.[33]

The right kind of society gives us those "swaying rope-ladders across fuming oblivion"—the human warmth and comfort, the "absorbing discipline" and the consolations of art. But the right business environment does as well—perhaps not the "healing harmony" of art, but quite definitely the human relationships and the challenge and satisfaction of exacting work. It is precisely this insight of Montague's that is at work in the contemporary emphasis on business as a society—an entirely nonmetaphysical foundation for true meaning in people's lives, but a foundation nonetheless.

Contemporary business theorists share the vision that work in a modern company can provide meaning for people, even without the support of metaphysical or religious faith. Peters and Waterman's "excellent" companies and O'Toole's "vanguard management" purportedly fill this central need—meaning for the employees. In this ideal environment, people find the satisfaction of service, the challenge of "an absorbing discipline," the comradeship of fellow strivers, and—the concomitant of any good society—the belief that they are a part of something greater than themselves, that their lives, in Becker's phrase, will leave a trace that has meaning.

Culture

In contemporary business, it has become as common to speak of a company's "culture" as its balance sheet. Both business leaders and business theorists have taken for granted that a corporation has a culture that must be understood, nourished, perpetuated, even changed for the better. McKinsey and Company, the management consultants, prescribe an analysis of culture—along with corporate structure, skills, technology, and so forth—as a necessary precondition to strategic planning. The notion of corporate culture has entered the mainstream of business thinking; the idea appears natural and sensible to most business leaders; the queerness of this idea—the comparison of prosaic business practices to exotic rites—has largely escaped us.

With little fear of contradiction, Peters and Waterman state flatly that the dominance and coherence of a particular culture are largely responsible for the success of "excellent" companies.[34] Their book stresses, above all else, the climate of the excellent companies, their establishment and preservation of a "strong" culture. O'Toole's "vanguard" management teams are also well aware of this: "For any social organization to function . . . it is necessary for all its members to share a world view."[35]

It is this feature of a "strong culture"—the shared world view— that seems to be the most appealing. If the organization's members have common ideas, they share the basic precepts and assumptions of the company; then the principles of operation are engrained in their minds, much as the superego of Freudian psychology enshrines parental strictures. In these excellent or vanguard companies, it is seldom necessary for management to give detailed instructions—everyone knows pretty much what is expected of him in a variety of circumstances. And it may work; Johnson & Johnson management attribute their success in handling the Tylenol crisis to the corporate culture: Managers at all levels understood the "right" response, and hundreds of good decisions were made, almost instinctively, throughout the chain of command.

This complex of unspoken assumptions, this spontaneity of culture, is a key feature of the idea. Carse has made the distinction between culture and society:[36] Society is defined as the sum of relations that are under some form of public constraint; these would be the normal rules and regulations of a company, probably embodied in a manager's handbook or company rules. Culture, on the other hand, is whatever is done by *undirected* choice—whatever the employees at all levels actually do in the performance of their duties. Everyone knows that a management handbook is almost a rare book—a fixture of the manager's bookshelf, not his everyday work life. His true guide is the set of practices and assumptions that he appears to have breathed in with the air of the company, the result of the nuances he has picked up from a thousand transactions with scores of people. In this sense, the analogy with a tribal culture is sound. No one "learns" a culture; it is absorbed by countless experiences in the social milieu.

Smircich, a student of organizations who has analyzed the cultural aspects of corporations, has concluded that the metaphor is a good one for understanding organizational behavior. She defines culture in words that would closely fit the Johnson & Johnson Tylenol experience: "A fairly stable set of taken-for-granted assumptions; meanings and values that form a backdrop for action."[37]

The "backdrop for action" is a critical feature of the cultural idea. If a strong culture did nothing else but make the employees feel good about themselves and their company, the notion would have received much less serious attention. But the efficacious feature of the idea is that the process of business is enhanced, strengthened, if the employees share a common view and, in essence, know what to do without being told.

This, curiously, was the goal of Frederick Taylor for his scientific management. Taylor sought a revolution in the minds of the workers,[38] a realization that their increased output would serve themselves as well as their masters. If he could introduce this "unspoken assumption" into the workers' thought processes, Taylor was convinced that all would benefit: The management would no longer need to drive the workers, and the workers would work both more productively and with a much improved attitude.

Smircich has provided us with a morphology of culture that will be useful in exploring its applications to business.[39] Any culture exhibits artifacts, perspectives, and values. Let us look at each of these factors in turn.

Artifacts are the tangible aspects of a culture—the verbal, behavioral, and physical language, the stories, myths, ceremonies, technology, and art of the society. The idea of a specialized language is a good fit for business; every company has shorthand, jargon terms that are unique to it; they are a source of cohesiveness to the employees and usually an irritant to outsiders. Even the physical appearance of a firm's property—the plants, mills, and offices—often acquires a distinctive signature and could be construed as a cultural artifact. For example, there was a time when one could clearly fix the status of an IBM executive anywhere in the United States by the items of furniture he was permitted in his office—not just a generic lamp, table, or sofa, but the *identical* lamp, table, or sofa, whether he sat in Poughkeepsie or San Jose.

Smircich speaks of the "socially shared rules and norms, solutions to common problems, how situations are defined and interpreted, what is acceptable behavior." These are familiar ideas to us—the mind-set, the *perspective* of the employees of a particular firm. One very interesting outcome of a common perspective is the usual approach to problems—"how situations are defined and interpreted." Many companies have a "distinctive professional skill"; for example, IBM executives are commonly business school graduates, most aerospace executives are engineers, American Express favors financial people, Procter and Gamble prefers marketing types, and so on. An educational background very often determines our approach to problems and their solution. In fact, the very conception of a problem—the categorization of it as a problem at all—is largely determined by the problem solver's type of education. Engineers tend to be problem-oriented; they tend to see the world as a set of problems awaiting their analysis and solution, and they take pride in the appellation "problem solvers." Marketing-trained people see the world more in terms of opportunities—as a rich vein of untapped potential for the right combination of product, price, promotion, and channel of distribution.

Business literature and experience are filled with stories of clashes among the separate visions of marketing, engineering, and financial executives—each with his vision of reality and his notion of what the problem/opportunity is really all about. The benefit of a shared view—a management team sharing the same perspective on issues—is obvious.

Smircich describes *values* as "the evaluational basis for judging situations, acts, people and objects." Values reflect the real goals, ideals, standards, and even sins of an organization. Selznick has also commented on this key concomitant of culture:

> The formation of an institution is marked by the making of value commitments, that is, choices which fix the assumptions of policy-makers as to the nature of the enterprise—its distinctive aims, methods and role in the community.[40]

A set of coherent values will color all aspects of organizational life and will produce other benefits: social integration, cohesiveness— in fact, meaning for the participants.

I believe there is some merit in the concept of culture; in particular, the idea has great explanatory value for the environment and operations of a company. However, it is an easy step, although almost certainly unwarranted, to the conclusion that the royal road to success is the *invention* of an appropriate culture. Culture, by its very nature, is a spontaneous, unconscious creation of many minds and many generations. The philosopher Susanne Langer, who has speculated on the origins of a culture, has emphasized the slow, even haphazard, process of cultural evolution: Tribal ways are handed down as unconscious mannerisms that become ritualized over many generations.[41]

Although the idea of changing a culture in a self-conscious way has become popular in modern business, I believe it ignores the hazards and difficulties that the natural evolution of culture would seem to imply. The histories of the French Revolution and post-1917 Russia speak to the risk of this undertaking. An authentic culture always spills over the boundaries of a society. Some societies have attempted to initiate a culture—Soviet art and the revolutionary Cult of Reason are examples. But if the aim is only societal interests, the results are false, even ludicrous.[42]

I will return to this point later, but is should be emphasized here that a self-conscious construction of a culture runs the risk of insincerity and artificiality and will ultimately fail to realize the benefits of an "improved" culture.

Myth, Rituals, Symbols

Every society has its prevailing myths, its prescribed rituals, and its set of powerful symbols. We ordinarily think of these features of society in terms of preindustrial, "primitive" groups, with their outlandish creation stories, exotic rites, and curious symbolism. But societies closer to us in material progress and social organization exhibit the same features. For example, medieval Christendom had its all-embracing creation and redemption myth, its church ritual attuned to the cycle of the seasons, and its all-encompassing symbol of the cross. These examples are clear to us because we stand outside these societies in time.

But modern industrial civilization also has its "tribal" culture—even in the most irreligious and seemingly rational societies. It could be said that the modern belief in rationality—what Weber calls "the specific and peculiar rationalization of western culture"[43]—is itself a prevalent myth. Our culture cherishes the belief that man's mental powers are capable of—have, in fact, accomplished—the explanation and understanding of the world. Modern rituals are as prosaic as the cycle of Olympic sports, as personal as the ceremonies for marriage and death, as solemn as the inauguration of presidents and the coronation of kings. And just as the cross symbolized (and symbolizes) for the believer the irrelevance of this world and his ultimate redemption in Christ, the modern computer terminal—the ubiquitous CRT—symbolizes for modern man the power of the information age and its fundamental rationality.

That real societies are sustained by symbolism is unarguable; that business organization exhibit the same behavior is a rather new conception, inspired by the metaphor of a business *qua* society. Peters and Waterman are uncompromising in this belief, asserting that "excellent companies take advantage of the emotional, more primitive side of human nature."[44] These authors cite the "dominant use of story, slogan, legend" and the "rich tapestries of anecdote, myth, fairy tale."[45] The examples they give bear some family resemblance to the cultural artifacts familiar to us from anthropological studies: ceremonies of celebration, such as the Silicon Valley "beer-busts" sponsored by companies after a successful year; the prevalence of stories about the founders of Hewlett-Packard, repeated by employees too young to have known "Dave" or "Walt"; and appealing corporate logos or slogans.

Virtually every company has routine ceremonies that could be interpreted as ritualistic: shareholder meetings, retirement parties, the celebration of service dates, and so forth. Even buildings can become symbols of the company; for example, Digital Equipment Corporation is still headquartered in the old mill where the company was founded twenty-five years ago, and this appears to give the employees a sense of their origins as well as a sense of the distance they have traveled.

Many employees in many companies are proud to wear company hats, pins, tie clasps, and the like, that display the company logo and symbolize their attachment to the company fortunes. The point is made—if these are "symbols," "rites," and "myths," the list is virtually endless.

What is this all about, for either a company or a "real" society? The thrust of this behavior seems to be man's search for meaning, whether in the workplace or in the larger society. Ernest Becker focuses on man's innate need to transcend his creatureliness, to believe that his time on earth is more than an animal existence:

> Man is not just a blind glob of idling protoplasm, but a creature with a name who lives in a world of symbols and dreams and not merely matter. His sense of self-worth is constituted symbol-

ically. . . . Man erected symbols which do not age or decay to
quiet his fears of his ultimate end.[46]

Or, as Evan Connell has put it:

> Things that remain and are not
> diminished by time are whichever live
> in men's hearts; or have fallen or
> have been thrown into the sea.[47]

The things that live in a man's heart and shield him from the
abyss of meaningless and creatureliness are precisely these rituals
and myths, these practices that point him beyond his own limited
life and show him some meaning for his existence. This seems a
tall order for a business to fill, but common experience yields some
confirmation; for example, the boredom and disaffection of many
retirees indicates that the work experience provides some degree of
fulfillment.

Symbolism, myth, and ritual can also provide another benefit
for a business, beyond the emotional and transcendental functions
that I have been describing: the simple function of understanding,
comprehension. Susanne Langer has said:

> An idea that contains too many minute yet closely-related parts,
> too many relations with relations, cannot be projected into dis-
> cursive form; it is too subtle for speech.[48]

But it is not too subtle for myth and symbol.

Langer's comment was directed at society and culture, but its
application to a business seems quite apt. Speech and, by extension,
rational thought, are discursive in nature—that is, serial. Processes
and situations are rarely well conceived in this form; they are much
more clearly represented in presentational form, in the form of
images. Symbols or rites are much more capable of presenting processes than the linear language of speech or discursive thought. The
operations of a business are inherently complex and interrelated,
and the appropriate rites and symbols could provide a good guide
to ultimate understanding.

Another helpful attribute of symbolism in a company, as well as in a society, is its aid to social cohesiveness. Langer, in describing ritual, has said:

> The ultimate product of . . . [ritual] is not a single emotion, but a permanent attitude. . . . It yields a strong sense of tribal or congregational unity, of rightness and security.[49]

Every business leader, from Frederick Taylor and his search for the "revolution in men's minds" to the contemporary executive, seeks this "permanent attitude" in his employees—this sense of belongingness that will ultimately further the organization's ends.

Peters and Waterman have noted the prevalence of "stories" in their excellent companies, particularly the "Dave" and "Walt" stories at Hewlett-Packard. The function of such stories is not just to create a sense of belonging in the new employees but also to convey the founder's views on right action. Bruno Bettelheim has written on this function of fairy tales:

> [Fairy tales] embodied the cumulative experience of a society as men wished to recall past wisdom for themselves and transmit it to future generations. These tales are the purveyors of deep insights that have sustained mankind through the long vicissitudes of its existence.[50]

This seems to have been the function of the Hewlett-Packard stories—not, perhaps, sustenance for the vicissitudes of life at Hewlett-Packard, but almost certainly a direct and effortless means to pass on to the new employees the sense of purpose and the appropriate means of operation that had inspired the founders.

Phillip Selznick wrote a sober, prosaic book about organizational leadership well before the recent "culture" fad. But Selznick, writing in 1957, presented the same themes that have become very familiar to us—in particular, the notion of organizational myth. Note his emphasis on the use of myth to create meaning and cohesiveness:

> To create an institution, we rely on many techniques for infusing day-to-day behavior with long run meaning and purpose. One of

the most important of these techniques is the elaboration of socially integrating myth. These are efforts to state, in the language
of uplift and idealism, what is distinctive about the aims and
methods of the enterprise.[51]

Selznick speaks not only to the efficacy of myth and other symbolism but to the duty of the leader to *create* these symbolisms. As
I will detail later, this is a tall order for any executive—the self-
conscious creation of useful symbolic forms, however necessary it
may be. In any event, this entailment of the society metaphor—
corporate culture and its attendant symbolism—has gained a firm
hold on modern business thinking. Many silly things have been
done in the name of "useful" ritual, symbolism, and myth, but on
the whole, the knowledge that these things are important has probably been beneficial.

The Ills of Society

One of the important benefits of the society metaphor—cohesiveness—can also be turned around to create problems for a business,
for this very cohesiveness presupposes the existence of outsiders,
aliens. As Carse has noted: "The world is elaborately marked by
boundaries of contest, its people finely classified as to their
eligibility."[52]

And the inevitable outcome of these classifications, at all times
and in all places, has been war. War is as natural an entailment of
the idea of society as meaning or harmony for the "insiders." We
have explored the war metaphor in business and have found rather
clearly, that the idea of a nation at war has serious shortcomings
as a model. The idea of a society seems to carry with it the idea of
cooperation with fellow employees but, at the same time, the idea
of a contest, a profound lack of cooperation, even hostility to those
outside the firm.

Another feature of society—the generation gap—is also being
noted in modern companies as a reflection of this gap in the larger
society. Companies may try to hold to old ways and old structures—virtually all societies are conservative in that way—but the

new entrants bring not only new ideas of business and technology but also new beliefs about values, hierarchy, and the treatment of people.

And there are other ills. Many societies have been plagued with overpopulation in their histories and have coped with the problem in a variety of ways. The way a company deals with this issue of overstaffing would tend to reflect its idea of the type of society that it holds up to itself. Very few—pathological—societies have employed mass murder as a solution to this problem; even the Nazis and Soviets were led to this extreme by ideological considerations, not by the need to reduce the numbers of its citizens. I would speculate that companies that resort to mass layoffs do not conceive of themselves as societies at all but more likely as machines that need "downsizing" or a herds or flocks that must be trimmed.

More normally, primitive societies resort to the abandonment of the aged, in a manner similar to a company's use of "golden handshakes" to ease the retirement of older employees. Infanticide has also been a common practice in many societies; it is noteworthy that in these societies, infants are not given names until the group has decided that they will live. It is also common, even in companies that eschew layoffs and forced retirement, that new employees must go through a probationary period. During that period, the employee is subject to termination on almost any pretext.

More humane methods of population control have been employed in some societies—birth control, for example, which is analogous to a hiring freeze in a business. Some societies, most notably the seventeenth- and eighteenth-century British and the ancient Greeks, resorted to colonization—the establishment of new settlements for the excess populace. This idea has not been widely employed in many companies as a specific for overstaffing, but some have tried to establish new businesses or new products by spinning off subsidiaries that can provide a home for excess staff. Some aerospace companies, for example, have established "body shop" companies to sell the services of engineers made redundant by the loss of major contracts.

All societies at one time or another have either conquered other nations or have been on the receiving end of a conquest. In business terms, this is the familiar takeover, and anyone who has been involved in one can attest to the aptness of the society metaphor—the truth of the idea of "culture" clashes.

Even firms in the same line of business, which are familiar with one another's technology and general business practices, are puzzled by the different approaches, language, and thought processes of their newly acquired partners. These problems seem to be exacerbated when a small company is acquired by a large one or the companies are headquartered in different parts of the country. A whole way of life seems to have gone by the boards when the new regime is installed. Rimbaud expressed this loss in his description of the rupture of a native idyll by modern invaders:

> Les blancs débarquent. Le canon! Il faut se soumetre au bapteme, s'habiller, travailler.[53]

> [The whites disembark. The cannon! We must be baptized, wear clothes, work.]

The experience of takeovers seems a close parallel to the conquest of alien societies. All the harmony and meaning of the old society (organization) appear to have been lost; the common assumptions and values of the old way are misunderstood or scorned by the new masters. And it is not unusual for the acquiring management to feel that their duty lies in rooting out the old ways and bringing the new people to the "right" approach to business. Yes, they must be baptized, wear clothes, work!

If the newcomers are not too heavy-handed and can appreciate the value of these "alien" ways, the new business combination, like the new society, can benefit greatly. The prime example of a heterogeneous society that has embodied the best of its kaleidoscope of sources is, of course, the United States. The "melting pot" is seen more and more as a poor image; in fact, the strength of American society appears to be in the very diversity of its citizen groups, rather than the homogenization of a melting pot. The clash of ideas, world views, and cultures has given the United States its peculiar dynamic.

However, heterogeneity is not necessarily a blessing. In fact, Japan's success as a society seems to be based on precisely the reverse—the almost total homogeneity of language and race that underlies that society's shared assumptions and values. If there is any criticism of this society, it is the one we might expect from its lack of culture clash—a lower level of creativity than is found in the messier, more disorderly American society.

So a recount of the typical ills of a society seems to be a good parallel to the ills of business and the manner in which business leaders, like societies, approach these problems.

Politics and Power

The entailments of politics and power follow naturally from the metaphor of society. Politics has been defined, crudely but accurately, as the study of who gets what, when, and how.[54] Politics in a business environment has a negative connotation for most of us; it seems to suggest something underhanded and unbusinesslike, a method of operation that is outside the norm of appropriate business behavior. The label "political" is seldom a positive one for a business executive. But we should recall Aristotle's dictum that man is a political animal—political by his very nature. The sense of this is that man must live in a society and that politics is a necessary— in fact, positive—concomitant of life in a society. Aristotle saw politics as a creative force, quite simply the creation of order out of the chaos of the inevitably conflicting interests in any society. Bismarck's definition of politics as the art of the possible says the same things: Only through a political process can the conflicting aims and goals of men be sorted out and resolved.

In his book *Power in Organizations*, Pfeffer has provided a good definition of politics as well as the necessary linkage between politics and power:

> Politics involves those activities . . . to acquire, develop and use power and other resources to obtain one's preferred outcome in situations in which there is uncertainty or dissension about choices.[55]

The key here is that in any organization—or any society, for that matter—the model of rationality seldom holds. As we have seen in the discussion of the machine metaphor, the norm of rationality is still a popular mythology in business. We are expected to behave as though there are right answers, obtainable through the rational collection of facts and the development of alternatives that can be evaluated by objective means.[56] Pfeffer provides a completely different perspective: Business is much more ambiguous than this, and there are no really "right" answers, only conflicting interests that must be resolved by political methods—the building of coalitions, currying of favor, manipulation of key actors, trade-offs and deals, and so forth.

Pfeffer has approached the study of organizations, not from the normal business outlook of rationality but from a sociological standpoint. His premise is that power processes are ubiquitous in organizations but are also beneficial, rather than harmful, to the firm—again, Aristotle's notion of the creative nature of politics. Pfeffer proposes a "Law of Political Entropy": "Given the opportunity, an organization will tend to seek and maintain a political character."[57]

If businesses are, in fact, political in nature, and if the law of political entropy obtains, it is surely helpful to understand this and to consider our actions in terms of this new norm. Pfeffer urges organizational leaders to accept this proposition and to recognize that "leadership is a language game."[58] The leader must recognize the political process at work in his organization and must actively engage in the process through symbolic activity:

> The task of political language and symbolic activity is to rationalize . . . decisions that are largely the result of power and influence in order to make these results acceptable.[59]

It should be noted that decisions are normally legitimized by clothing them in the language of the rational model. Even though results were achieved through a process of bargaining and influence, the organization is normally told that careful, objective study has been made, alternatives have been considered, and the decision "made itself" through an objective process.

The political entailment of the society metaphor has a good deal of merit. The idea encourages us to see all organizational activity as interest-based, and this is not far from the truth.[60] Under this metaphor, we can see the nature of power as a central theme for organizational analysis, just as Pfeffer has done. There is a positive aspect to exploding the myth of corporate rationality. In fact, actions and decisions are seldom based on pure rationality, as the mechanistic theorists would propose. Reg Jones knew this when he spoke of "working with the grain." His actions and decisions were circumscribed by the culture and thinking of the GE people; he could not act arbitrarily, no matter how "rational" the action might appear to be.

But the idea can be quite harmful to an organization. However useful the idea is in *analyzing* corporate behavior, it can be quite damaging in the actual operations of a company if the myth of rationality is replaced by the notion of a political free-for-all where only power and influence decide the major issues. The insight can further politicize an organization—confirming the law of political entropy—and generate cynicism and mistrust among the employees. If the employees truly believe that the business is nothing more than a power game for the management—that all activities are really just a way to jockey for pride of place—the atmosphere will hardly be conducive to success. Who would put out his maximum effort, knowing that the path to success in a career really depends on influence and political maneuvering? Employees who believe that they are in a zero-sum game, that political deals are the true reality, will quickly lose all motivation to make the business succeed.

Shared Entailments

The society metaphor shares a number of entailments with other common business metaphors. For example, organizations can develop a distinct "personality." In fact, as Selznick has shown,[61] this should be the aim of a business leader: to develop distinctive outlooks and habits that will promote both cohesiveness and performance. We are all familiar with the distinct personalities of different national groups, usually in the form of unflattering stereotypes of others and self-congratulatory descriptions of our own national character.

As I noted earlier, though, some organizations do exhibit an apparently dominant type, just as nations and races seem to do. If there is anything at all to the idea of the effect of language and culture on mentality—and I have to believe that there is a great deal to that notion—we would certainly expect that differing cultures would produce different types. Companies with strong "culture"—that is, highly distinctive attitudes and practices—such as IBM or Citicorp, do, in fact, have a large number of people who seem to be possible only as employees of these firms.

Another entailment that "society" shares with most other business metaphors is the key idea of *purpose*. We commonly believe nowadays that societies have some transcendental purpose, but they do not *by necessity* have purposes—they choose to do so. A society without a purpose, but rather with merely the *function* to provide order and security for its members, has the familiar "negative liberty" of Isaiah Berlin. In such societies, the purposes belong to the individuals, not to the society; this is the proper function that Aristotle prescribed for government. The revolutionary government of France espoused "positive liberty" and had a clear purpose— the installation of virtue in the citizens—and resorted to terror, secret police, and mass executions to obtain the result. We in the United States, with our Bill of Rights, operate under the assumption that we enjoy "negative liberty"—the right to have the government leave us alone—but there is a strong countertrend in our society. It is common to ascribe noble, transcendent purposes to the American way; we all tend to be caught up by the vision that we are the last, best hope for humanity. In common thinking, for better or for worse, societies do have a purpose, and the entailment is a good fit for business.

I have already covered, in passing, the ambiguous nature of any society. This is, in fact, the root cause for political activity: the resolution of intractably ambiguous situations. Again, a business shares this characteristic, and Pfeffer's insight is probably correct: Businesses fall into politics to resolve ambiguity as naturally and as necessarily as societies do.

The society metaphor can also speak to the business person about a two-faced coin: the need for cooperation but also the inevitability of competition. A society, like a successful business, must

foster a good deal of harmony and a spirit of close-knit cooperation. However, people, by their nature, seem to be both cooperative
and competitive. Marcus Aurelius spoke of the former attribute:

> We are made for cooperation, like feet, like hands, like eye lids,
> like the rows of the upper and lower teeth. To act against one
> another then is contrary to nature.[62]

But as we have seen, Social Darwinism raised the notion of
man's competitiveness to the level of pseudoscience and placed the
contest between man and man as the essential creative force in
society. We saw examples of this way of thinking in the notions of
Walter Wriston, who believed that Citicorp benefited from the clash
of ideas and personalities. There is certainly a balance between
cooperation and competition in an ideal society or a perfect business environment. The war of all against all is anarchy, but total
cooperation without the leaven of competition would probably not
have got mankind down from the trees or a business beyond its
first year.

The last entailment of the society metaphor, shared with the
journey, game, and war metaphors, is the notion of leadership. By
the nature of this metaphor, it provides to the business leader a
range of very clear and specific leadership models. Let us look at
these now.

The Leader as Shaman

As we have seen, many business writers portray the business executive as the agent to instill values in the firm, using the technique
of myth, ritual, and symbolism. This is precisely the age-old function of the shaman in a traditional hunting society; the shaman is
the one who has the visions and interprets the tribe's experience
through the medium of another world. The shaman's art is based
on an intuitive grasp of the emotional, unconscious elements of
human psychology; he has the ability to plumb these depths in his
own psyche and articulate them for his fellows. Shamans, or medicine men, have been a fixture of human society since the dawn of

time. One of the Paleolithic cave paintings at Les Trois Freres depicts a shaman, outfitted in an owl mask, with an animal tail and a deer-antler headdress.[63] The animal features symbolize the instinctive, prērational elements of the human psyche; the bird reference is a common theme in all shaman lore. Many shaman stories revolve around his ability to transform himself into a bird and fly into the netherworld—the world beyond discursive thought, where the true foundation of reality lies. In modern psychological terms, this is the world of the unconscious.

Joseph Campbell, in his study of mankind's myths, has shown the key role of the shaman:

> The medicine men are simply making both visible and public the systems of symbolic functioning that are present in the psyche of every adult member of their society.[64]

The shaman finds the true reality deep in his own thought and makes it public in a way that resonates with the thought of his less-gifted brothers. The shaman's technique is based on metaphor, myth, and symbol:

> The metaphors by which [shamans] live . . . have been brooded upon, searched and discussed for centuries—they have served whole societies as the mainstays of thought and life. They actually touch and bring into play the vital energies of the whole human psyche. They link the unconscious to the fields of practical action.[65]

Most business leaders would probably find it comical to view themselves in the same light as cave-dwelling shamans or the medicine men of primitive tribes, but their approaches and their effects are remarkably similar. As Bert Snider, president of Bournes, Inc., has said: "My mission is to communicate who we are, what our dream is, and why it is going to work for us."[66] This is a far cry from a self-induced trance, a mythical flight into the underworld, and a return bearing the tribe's vision. Or is it? It has become increasingly common for chief executives to speak of their "vision"; in fact, an executive without a vision is considered a pretty poor sort. Donald Burr of People Express, for example, was proud to "have a vision—a low-cost airline, run with a minimum of bureaucracy and hierarchy. . . . workers manage themselves. . . . [their] enthusiasm would translate into higher quality customer service."[67] And Ian MacGregor, the self-styled gambler, still saw his role in a shamanistic light: "working with people and imbuing them with the same kind of thinking."[68]

The shaman role has been widely applauded and encouraged by business theorists. James Bryan Quinn, a highly respected scholar of strategic planning, stresses the need for "amplifying understanding" and "changing symbols" when the leader is implementing a new strategy. He prescribes the leader role as one of "labeler"— the provider of values and symbols.[69] Selznick, speaking to organizational leaders, says:

> For creative leadership, it is not the communication of a myth that counts; rather, creativity depends on having the will and insight to see the necessity of myth. . . . The institutional leader . . . is primarily an expert in the promotion and protection of values.[70]

Values—values are the cornerstone of an organization—the set of beliefs that makes it worthwhile for the employees to entrust their careers to a particular firm. Peters and Waterman cite "value-driven" as a key characteristic of their "excellent" companies. The leaders, in one way or another, have formulated a set of principles and have been able to articulate them to the employees, much like a shaman, who "sees" the grounding of reality in spiritual and emotional terms and then carries these values back to the tribe in the form of ritual and myth. In the process of establishing values, the shaman or the executive has solved the principle puzzle of anyone's existence: What are we doing here? What is the meaning? The shaman's answer is that we are involved not in a brute struggle for animal existence but in a marvelous pageantry of spirits, demons, and heroes. The executive can convey the sense that this is not just the drudgery of a job; this is participation in a noble cause— this company is doing fine things for humanity. Good managers create meanings as well as making money,[71] just as good tribal leaders bring meaning to individuals as well as looking out for their material welfare.

Peters and Waterman are clear and emphatic about the shaman role for the business executive: "The leader [must be] the creator of symbols, ideologies, language, belief, rituals, myths."[72] Again, this is Selznick's point: The leader cannot merely mouth the conventional wisdom; he must be the active *creator* of values and beliefs. And he must clothe them in the language of ritual and myth in order to tap into the emotional, unconscious side of his employees' thinking—the seat of their own creativity and their commitment to the goals of the firm.

I would expect, as I have said, that many will find the shaman role bizarre or distasteful, at least in terms of direct comparison to outlandish medicine men. But the shoe seems to fit; the self-descriptions of the actors and the prescriptions of business theorists are right in the center of the tribal shaman notion. Even Pfeffer, the advocate of a Machiavellian political stance for the business executive, still can speak to the shaman role:

> The effectiveness of a leader lies in his ability to make activity meaningful for those in his role set. . . . [The capacity] to make sense of things and to put them into language meaningful to large numbers of people gives the person who has it enormous leverage.[73]

Pfeffer circles back to his political and power model, noting that the shamanistic arts can project a person into a position of substantial power. If we require confirmation of this, we need only recall the story of Joseph, who interpreted Pharoah's dreams and parlayed that skill into a place only second to the Pharoah-God in the land of Egypt.

One further point should be made about the shaman syndrome in modern business: the position of the bird motif. As I have noted, shamans commonly identify themselves with birds; and the bird symbol, from the Paleolithic to modern primitive hunters, is a constant accompaniment of the medicine man. I will not pretend to have done a scientific survey, but I have noticed the attraction that bird images have for modern business executives. It is probably unfortunate, but fierce and rapacious birds, especially eagles, seem to have captured the imagination of executives, rather than the wise owl of the Les Trois Freres shaman. Nonetheless, birds we have aplenty in modern business. If an executive has an animal image at all in his office, it is probably a bird. Ross Perot, for example, has fixed on the eagle as EDS's symbol and has decorated the Dallas headquarters with an immense bronze eagle. If asked, these bird fanciers would probably speak of the eagle's presumed virtues: courage, daring, individual strength. (Sadly, the American bald eagle is principally a scavenger.) But how different is the present-day attraction to the bird motif from the unconscious use of the symbol by the shaman of Les Trois Freres, unimaginably long ago?

The Statesman

Many business leaders have found the idea of themselves as a statesman much more congenial than the myth-shaping, emotional role of a shaman. We saw, earlier, Petersen's description of management as the balancing of the conflicts of interests of a variety of constituencies, in an attempt to maximize the benefits for all those involved.[74] Alfred Sloan held this same conception and expressed it in a variety of ways. One of his biographers states that Sloan recognized his responsibility for economic statesmanship. The following was among the tenets of his business philosophy:

> Fairness to all groups in the industrial process—dividends to shareholders, good wages, incentives for managers, value to customers, profits for dealers, wholesome relationships with suppliers, products and policies that the public would respect.[75]

Sloan himself said:

> Customers benefit from lower prices. Labor benefits from higher wages. Investors benefit from fair and steady dividends. Management benefits by the identification of its own interests with the prospects of the Corporation.[76]

And he also said: "Employees, shareholders, dealers, consumers, suppliers and the government have shared in the success of GM."[77]

This conception of a business as having a constitutional form, with rights and privileges for various people, is in the starkest contrast to Iacocca's view of the Ford Motor Company under Henry Ford II. As we have seen, Iacocca saw Ford as an absolute monarch with the arbitrary power of life and death over his subjects.[78]

The idea of a business as a balance of interests has been enshrined in the "stakeholder" view of the firm—a highly popular theory at present. The firm's stakeholders include employees, suppliers, host communities, and government, as well as the shareholders. In fact, the theory postulates that the shareholders' long-term interests are best served by satisfying the legitimate claims of *all* the stakeholders, not just the shareholders themselves. The CEO of one of O'Toole's "vanguard" companies is neither an independent actor nor a slave of the shareholders; he is more a politician, balancing the competing claims of all his constituents.[79]

Ackoff has derived the stakeholder view from the three fundamental responsibilities of corporate management: the responsibilities to the purposes of the system they manage, the purposes of the people involved, and the purposes of the "containing system."[80] The corporation must serve all of these often incompatible purposes and sort out the rights of all of these competing interests.

The theory of the stakeholder view rests on the primacy of the shareholder; the idea is justified, not on the basis of simple equity but on the long-run benefits to the shareholders. This is not entirely ingenuous. A manager who, in fact, operated a public company for any reason other than the prime benefit of the shareholders would do so at his peril. Even with a sympathetic board, the manager would be subject to shareholder suits, for the law is quite clear: A company must be operated for the benefit of the owners, and every expenditure, policy, or action must be justified in that light.

Once having made this necessary obeisance to the shareholder's pride of place, though, the emphasis shifts to the equal rights of all stakeholders: employees, suppliers, customers, and so on, as well as the shareholder. This development in business thought of a constitutional basis parallels the development in political thought, of course. The idea seems strange to us now, but until the very recent past, most societies took it for granted that there were naturally endowed "owners"—clergy or aristocracy—whose privileges were part of the nature of things and whose needs and wants all other segments of society were there to serve.

Perhaps because of our own political experience in free societies, the stakeholder view has a great attraction for us. It is certainly a satisfying role for a chief executive to play; he becomes more a social actor and wise judge of interests than a mere businessman. But are businessmen in fact becoming statesmen—are they capable of it? Not in the view of "real" statesmen.

In Helmut Schmidt's eyes, the differences between political leaders and business people are fundamental—practically unbridgeable. The similarities are really superficial; the differences stem from the exceptionally disparate personal experiences of business people and politicians. Schmidt repeats an old saw: There are very few cases of successful CEOs making their way in politics, or vice versa.[81]

James Callaghan also saw little similarity between politicians and executives and, in general, thought the business leaders he knew were lacking a sufficiently broad view to succeed in government. He noted their incapacity to bring together separate pieces of information about different problems.[82]

Callaghan's and Schmidt's responses could be written off as natural disdain for another profession's abilities, but there has to be more to it than that—for Schmidt is largely correct: There seem to be very few cases of successful business-trained people succeeding in politics, or vice versa. I must conclude that the experiences and training are in some way fundamentally different, which puts the entire concept of "political" leadership and stakeholder balancing in question. It seems natural for us to talk about business statesmen—with the notion of their evenhanded balancing of the interests of shareholders, employees, customers, and so on—but if this were the true role, any experienced governor would be expected to be an instant success at business. Clearly, the skill set is different, which has to mean that the processes of government and business are fundamentally different.

Perhaps an insight of Jay Gould's biographer is the answer. Describing the time when Gould was trying to salvage his position at the Union Pacific Railroad, Klein comments: "It was difficult to play the part of statesman with the barbarians knocking at the gates."[83]

The orderly, rational playing off of disparate interest groups is a fine model and a dignified and noble role, but in business, the truth probably lies elsewhere: The barbarians are always at the gates, and the role of statesman is inappropriate most of the time.

The Hero and the Saint

A common strain in business autobiography is the business leader as hero—the man who has undergone the vicissitudes of fortune, has suffered fools (gladly or not), and has finally won over all. This is the general sense of Iacocca's autobiography, and there are elements of it in Geneen's work and even in Alfred Sloan's. But in the real sense, these were not heroic activities; true heroism, at least in the sense of the hero's contribution to society, lies, rather, in its creative force. As Ortega puts it:

> Such men aim at altering the course of things; they refuse to repeat the gestures that custom, tradition or biological instinct force them to make. These men we call heroes.[84]

It is the entrepreneurs who fulfill this function—who make something from nothing, who "refuse to repeat the gestures" of others but, rather, strike out on their own and contribute to economic growth.

Another social type—the saint—also figures in business life. Hero and saint may seem like radically different roles, but in Church terminology, a saint is one who has led a heroic life in the faith. We tend to think of saints as otherworldly figures, almost antisocial. But not all were people like St. Simeon Stylites, who spent years atop a column. Social activists—Ambrose, Augustine, Francis—abound in the annals of hagiography. These men changed the world and certainly fit Ortega's definition of *hero*.

George Gilder describes the entrepreneur in terms of sainthood, not heroism. Gilder seeks an intellectually and morally sound basis for capitalism; he finds Adam Smith's idea—that the wealth of nations springs from a Faustian pact, a deal through which men gain wealth by yielding to greed—morally bankrupt.[85] Rather, Gilder states:

> Capitalism begins with giving. Not from greed, avarice or even self-love can one expect the rewards of commerce. . . . Giving, risking and creating are the characteristic roles of the capitalist, the key provider of the wealth of nations.[86]

The "gifts" of advanced capitalism are, of course, the investment of the entrepreneur's capital. He relinquishes his resources to others to spur economic growth, with all the social benefits that will entail.

Beyond his charity and inherent optimism or hope, the capitalist must also have faith: "Faith in man, faith in the future, faith in the rising returns of giving are all essential to successful Capitalism."[87] Gilder shows the influence of Max Weber, whose *The Protestant Ethic and the Spirit of Capitalism* described influences on the early capitalists. Weber traces the entrepreneurial impulse to the teachings of Martin Luther, who stressed man's "calling" in the world—the command to action in the business of living.[88]

The modern businessman as a secular saint may sound far-fetched, but some believe that we have one in DEC's Ken Olsen. *Fortune* reports that Olsen is a very religious man, with a strong Puritan strain. Olsen has said that the Puritans were "the toughest men this world has seen." In a recent address to Yale business students, Olsen contended that businessmen should pay attention to the old virtues—humility, gentleness, peace, temperance, long suffering. It seems, however, that the students were looking for heroes, not saints—they booed.[89]

But societies and businesses both need their saints and heroes, and each of us needs that ideal for himself. The psychology of Otto Rank centers on each individual's need to see his own life as a stage for heroic action. And Evan Connell has put this thought into verse:

> Each life is a myth, a song given out
> of darkness, a tale for children, the

legend we create.
Are we not heroes, each of us
in one fashion or another,
wandering through mysterious labyrinths?[90]

Strengths of the Metaphor

The present-day popularity of the society metaphor is not without reason; the idea has a good deal to recommend it. With society as the dominant metaphor, business people can recognize an obvious fact that other metaphors slough off: A business is, in fact, an assemblage of people, and its operations are really a succession of human interactions. Closely related to this concept is the need for cohesiveness in an organization if it is to be successful—a basic attribute of society in its best form. In this chapter's epigraph, I quoted Marx's belief that men's consciousness is determined by their social being. A person's way of thinking is largely determined by his total social experience—not least his inherited language, religion, and culture—as well as his individual upbringing. People bring all this baggage to a workplace, but the work environment itself can color and change beliefs. Knowing this, we have achieved at the very least a handhold for understanding behavior in organizations; and at best, we can use this fact to try to mold an organizational environment in which people's thinking is modified so that their behavior will be useful to the business.

One goal of organizational management that the society metaphor helps greatly is the establishment of a common world view—a set of common ideas that will help achieve effective social control and obviate tiresome and largely ineffective supervision of each and every employee and each and every action.[91] This very social control through a shared outlook benefits not only the company but also the employee, by giving him the comfort and assurance of a place in a larger whole. Durkheim has noted:

> The believer is not deceiving himself when he puts his faith in the existence of a moral potency, on which he is dependent, and to which he owes his better part; this Power exists; it is Society.[92]

The metaphor also serves us well in directing our attention to the central importance of meaning in everyone's life and the role that a business can play in providing this meaning. Beyond the recognition of meaning's importance, the metaphor can provide some guides to action—paralleling the means by which societies help provide meaning for people through language, folklore, ceremonies, and other social practices.[93] This can be exceptionally difficult for an organizational leader, but deft action by a highly sensitive and intuitive leader can create the right formulations and establish the practices that will resonate with the employee's innermost needs.

As I have noted, these actions center on attaching symbolic significance to the mundane activities of a business. A meeting or a retirement ceremony becomes not a routine practice but a Passion play, infused with symbols and rites that strike the right chords in people's psyches. If it is done correctly—and we should not underestimate the difficulty—symbolic behavior can create a unified sense of mission and can add to the harmony of the whole, a feeling of common purpose, and ultimately, a higher level of performance.

Viewing the business as a society, we can also recognize the opportunities and pitfalls of change. The society and machine metaphors are starkly contrasted in this regard. An organizational change for a "machine" business appears simple and obvious; it is merely a rearrangement of parts. In a "society" model, change is recognized as inherently a social process—a process that must revise not abstract or mechanical things, such as reporting relationships or physical arrangements, but attitudes and images in people's minds.[94] Change must always be undertaken with a view toward the people's acceptance of the need for change, the use of clear but also symbolically "right" communications, and the recognition that new folklore and myth will be generated by the change. There is an opportunity to guide the creation of a new and helpful, rather than destructive, mythology.

It should be noted that if a company has achieved a good deal of social cohesiveness—has become a "society" in that sense—organizational change can be fairly trouble-free. If the management has won the trust of the employees, if the workers and the management share the same values, then a change can be viewed as routine—simply a new approach to common problems, rather than a change in values, purposes, and meanings. This raises another point that the society metaphor can elucidate—the problem of change in an organization with the "wrong" culture. I am referring to a company in which each department or group has a great deal of cohesion and shared values but there is no overall integrating influence—a society similar to what Iacocca found at Chrysler, with many small fiefdoms. This is the condition that Montague calls "races, nations, locked in their dream of history." "Culture" exists in each of these small units—harmony, meaning, and so forth—all the things that we would hope to gain by the emphasis on a societal view. But there is a pathology in that there is no company-wide harmony, trust, or shared values. Organizational change under these conditions is perilous; the leader will need every bit of talent, wit, and intuition he can bring to bear on the problem, but viewing it as a social and political problem—recognizing that he must focus on attitudes and images—should be very helpful.

As we have seen, the entailment of politics in a society can be a useful notion for a business leader. If nothing else, it helps explain the seemingly irrational, interest-based activities that are so common in any organization. The appreciation of the essential ambiguity of a business environment can be a real tonic for an executive brought up on scientific management and other mechanical ways of thought. Pfeffer touches on this point:

> If everyone knew what was best and could agree on it, there would not be any use of power in the decision making in the first place. It is because of the fundamentally irreducible nature of the uncertainty about the relationships between actions and their future consequences . . . that power and its use arise.[95]

Recognizing the ambiguity and the essential unknowability of outcomes can be healthy and can guide the leader to the appropriate role of power and politics in his organization and to his own duty to engage in these processes.

I have already discussed takeover situations and how the society metaphor seems to illuminate the hazards of these actions. The leader gains by recognizing that a takeover can be interpreted as a clash of alien cultures and that the participants do not have shared values, language, or modes of thought, even if their businesses seem similar on the surface. The executive will see that his task is to create shared values in these circumstances. But first, he must appreciate the nuances of the other "culture"—its symbols, role models, rites, and myths. He must create a new meaning for these people, basing it on an amalgamation of the original culture and the new one—much as the Spanish friars tried to do in post-conquest Mexico, by incorporating the Indian deities, ceremonies, and sacred places into the Catholic calendar of saints, rites, and pilgrimage sites. If the acquired employees see only the irretrievable loss of their own ways and the destruction of their precious values and folkways, any economic gain that the merger sought will never be realized. The people—the asset that in most cases was the prime reason for the acquisition—will simply leave.

The last strength of this metaphor is the one emphasized so heavily by Peters and Waterman: the focus on values. The leader of an enterprise that is thought of as a society must concern himself with this task—the infusion of values in the organization. The business will achieve high performance when the employees believe that the company stands for something, that their role is not the mere accumulation of stockholder wealth but a contribution to society in the form of excellent products or services. This idea of a transcendent purpose for society, so ingrained in our thinking, can be highly efficacious if it is carried over to our feeling for the company in which we work.

Weaknesses of the Metaphor

In many ways, the society metaphor is the best available to us. It speaks to the employees and the management in language that strikes responsive chords in their psyches: the need for meaning, harmony, and social cohesiveness. It also speaks to the importance of symbolic action and the need to achieve a transcendent purpose for work life. But the metaphor has some serious shortcomings, some fatally wrong features, that must concern us.

One weakness of this metaphor is the innate weakness of all

metaphors—its unwarranted extension in the mind of the actor. In this case, the weakness shows up in the type of society that the business leader envisions for his firm. Look at Walter Wriston's model for Citicorp: a free society, in which the clash of ideas is a creative force. Another attribute of a free society is that it is participative; the social actors participate in the society's decisions, and there is a great deal of social mobility—an ideal meritocracy. This description fits our general concept of a modern society. But this is also the type of society that Tönnies claimed lack *community (Gemeinschaft)*, even if it is a *society (Gesellschaft)*. The point has already been made: Modern societies have a great deal less harmony and provide less meaning to their members than traditional societies. And any exposure to Citicorp would demonstrate that it is an excellent, highly professional, and competitive business, but not a warm, homey environment. Wriston's emphasis on the "free, modern society" seems to have achieved just that, but at the expense of a comfortable "traditional" work climate.

On the other hand, we have those who espouse the traditional, almost tribal, approach in which the emphasis is on values, meaning, and harmony, as in a traditional society—feudal, say, or a primitive tribe. As we have seen, such societies are also characterized by a very rigid social structure, with little or no mobility. This type of environment is often found in family-run businesses. There is little or no chance for nonfamily employees to rise to the top; but in many of these companies, there is a real "family" feeling among the employees, good feeling for the paternalistic management, and a good sense of harmony and purpose. The "society" is free and open, not participative, but there is a sense of harmony, meaning, and purpose among the employees. As I have noted, Peters and Waterman, the prime proponents of the traditional society, have warned that the employees could lose their "freedom" in their search for meaning in such companies—precisely the bargain that traditional society members have made (or that has been made for them).

The prime entailment of the metaphor—culture—has simply been overdone. Benjamin DeMott, who reviewed today's business literature in a recent *New York Times Book Review* article, excoriates the entire "cultural" movement. He sees business theorists

committed to the notion that sensitivity, not performance, should
be the emphasis of entrepreneurs; they should exhibit "flower-power
compassion and playfulness," and they should "make love, not
deals" in organizations that are portrayed as "religious assemblies"
or "theaters."[96] I am not sure that DeMott is being entirely fair,
but there is certainly a risk that the metaphor's outcome can be
little more than plain silliness. Ridicule has destroyed more theories
than any amount of intellectual challenge has done.

Old Henry Ford was a forerunner of the modern critique of the
society metaphor, with its emphasis on feelings, good communication and meaning. He claimed that a business "is a collection of
people who are brought together to do work and not to write
letters to one another."[97] And: "A great business is really too big
to be human."[98] And, summing it all up: "A factory is not a drawing room."[99]

Aside from the distaste that Ford felt for the whole idea, the
metaphor has some serious limitations as a guide for the businessman. There are two strains to the idea of a society and its culture.
First, there is the old concept that we have associated with Burke—
that a society is like an organism, a historical product that has been
produced by the intuitive genius of countless generations. Men
tamper with it, like a machine, at their peril. There is some merit
to this view, but as we saw with the organism metaphor, the idea
can be seriously limiting. The fate of a society or an organization
could appear much too fixed, too determined. Not an organism's
genes but a society's history becomes a limiting factor. Lenin saw
this trap in orthodox Marxism and revolted against it: "History
doesn't make itself; it is made by individuals."[100] And this is what
Henry Ford's famous dictum was all about:

> History is more or less the bunk. We want to live in the present,
> and the only history that is worth a tinker's dam is the history
> we make today.[101]

Ford spoke against the conservative strain of the society metaphor—the notion that we are given a society and a history, that
our fate is so determined, very much like Heraclitus's expression
of the Greek belief that "character is fate,"[102] and, of course, that

character is assumed to be immutable. We saw the limitations of this way of thinking in the People Express response, or nonresponse, to its troubles: "This is our philosophy. We can't change it."[103]

That is the conservative side—a set of beliefs that I feel can be limiting for an organization. The "liberal" side is another matter; it can be highly dangerous. The liberal or interventionist approach to culture is that it is a man-made artifact, as Vico taught, and that it can be changed to suit men's purposes. This self-conscious intervention into culture can be hazardous in the extreme. Regardless of its man-made quality, which is unarguable, culture is a *spontaneous* creation of men's unconscious nature, built over long expanses of time. Let us return to the Jacobins' attempt to make radical changes in French culture—an attempt that utterly failed. Why? After all, on the surface, the Cult of Reason should have been every bit as socially bonding as the Christian faith it sought to replace. The issue is one of authenticity; ritual is not artificially contrived for a practical purpose, not consciously created for social solidarity. The roots of authentic myth and ritual are deeper than any conscious purpose; the roots are in the need to express fundamental—and largely unconscious—human needs.[104]

So culture, myth, and ritual are forms of expression of fundamental human beliefs, not things that can be manipulated for a society's purpose. At best, the attempts to change these modes of behavior are merely silly, like the revolutionary Cult of Reason. At worst, the attempt leads to disaster. Consider the Shah's attempt to change Iranian culture, probably the root cause of his downfall. The same approach in business—culture change, root and branch— as recommended by Peters and Waterman, simply won't work.[105]

The current advocates of cultural change are obsessed with superficial levels of cultural artifacts, such as logos and management style; and this will produce nothing. Basic values must be changed; the management must change its assumptions about work and the workers, the purposes of the corporation, and its responsibilities to the shareholders.[106] This is a critical point—that some managers may be using metaphor verbally and behaviorally in an uncommitted, even dishonest way. True metaphor must spring from one's basic assumptions, one's "paradigm." To change, the paradigm must change.

These are the dangers of the interventionist or liberal view of culture. Burke's insight, however moss-backed it may appear, must be considered. Changing a whole culture—its symbols and meanings that express fundamental ideas—is a very, very difficult, maybe even impossible task. But the limitations and dangers of the society idea aside, there is one further weakness: It just may be dead wrong.

We are all so taken by the idea because it seems to have great descriptive value and seems to match the reality of a business—an assemblage of people, just as a society is. Having made this step, it is easy, then, to apply the lore of anthropology, sociology, and psychology to a business, but this is more than likely an unwarranted extension. Even if the metaphor is a fair description, it can be dangerous to conclude that it is a prescription as well. Managers can begin to see their role as ideological control and manipulation, and the employees will quickly sees themselves in an Orwellian world of thought control.[107] The notion that people's attitudes can be controlled and manipulated is a subtle mechanistic concept—the idea that people are merely complex machines and that management is the job of finding the right buttons to push to get them in the proper frame of mind. Even Peters and Waterman have seen dangers, although they still hold to the view that culture change and thought control are possible. They fear that people will sacrifice their latitude and freedom in order to get the necessary meaning in their lives. "Most worrisome . . . the possibility of abuse—the need for security is fulfilled, but then people yield to authority."[108]

But I believe that the society metaphor is most wrong in its overemphasis on myth and symbolism. To call stories about founders or projects "myth" is a serious misuse of the term, a trivialization of one of mankind's most sacred and enduring possessions. True myth has a much more fundamental basis than anything that could relate to a business:

> Myth is taken with religious seriousness. . . . Its typical theme
> is tragic. . . . [It is] a recognition of natural conflicts, of human

desires frustrated by non-human powers, hostile oppressions or contrary desires; it is a story of the birth, passion and defeat by death which is man's common fate.[109]

Myth, ritual, and symbolism—these are vital commentaries on first and last things, the struggle of humanity to find a deep purpose and meaning in individual life. To use these terms glibly to describe the economic activities of a firm is to trivialize them. It is at best an absurdity, at worst an affront.

Summary

- Two types of societies have occupied us: a traditional society, with its strong social cohesiveness and immutable classes; and a modern society, which is much less cohesive, provides less comfort and meaning, but provides social mobility and many freedoms. Businesses have been modeled on—and expressed as—both types.

- Businesses have been likened to societies since early in the twentieth century, but the popularity of the view peaked in the 1970s and has substantially declined since 1975.

- The current vogue of "corporate culture" betrays a society metaphor, principally referring to a traditional society, in which culture provides meaning and social cohesiveness to its members.

- The work of Peters and Waterman, where it is not based on an organic analogy, is founded on the idea of a business as a society—principally, a traditional society.

- The stakeholder view of the firm is also based on an implicit society metaphor.

- The society metaphor suggests a number of actions for the executive: a stress on "myth, symbol, and ritual" to convey meaning and purpose to the employees; employment and other practices to control "population"; his task of providing a vision and values to the organization; the recognition of politics as a reality in an organization, not necessarily a pernicious reality; and the appropriate behavior and attitudes toward mergers.

- The metaphor also suggests some roles for the leader: the shaman, creator of the society/corporation's vision, values, and rituals; the statesman, concerned with all the corporation's constituents; and the hero/saint, the one who makes a profound creative impact on the world.

- The metaphor's main strengths are in focusing the leader on the need to provide meaning for his employees and in reminding him that organizational change must be considered in social terms.

- The metaphor's weakness is mainly in its overemphasis on culture, particularly on the idea that a corporate culture can be artificially created. If the culture does not spring from deeply held beliefs about the purpose of business and the nature of man, the insincerity of the attempt will be painfully obvious to the employees.

II
Purpose in Business

10
Purposes and Paradigms

Not to describe the motion and matter of a thing, but to see its purpose, is to understand it.

—Susanne Langer[1]

The Shifting Tides

We have now reviewed the principal business metaphors, their origins, and their implications for business people. Let us pause a moment and review what we have learned. We have answered a number of the questions posed in Chapter 1:

- We have determined the most popular metaphors used by business people.

- We have found the source of these metaphors in wider realms of thought: the journey in the world's literature, the game in classical Greece, war in the earliest Greek philosophy, the machine in the thought of the Enlightenment, the organism in the Romantic movement, and the society in political writings from Aristotle to Burke.

- We have seen how the businessman's actions and attitudes will be quite different, depending on the metaphor he chooses.

- We have also seen that the leader's role will take on the cast of his chosen metaphor: the captain of a ship in a storm; the master gamesman or coach; the war leader (strategic or guerrilla); the machine tender or semidivine machine creator; the brains of an organism, its parent/mentor, or its shepherd; and the society's statesman, shaman, or hero/saint.

- In our survey, we have also commented on the aptness of these metaphors to the reality of business management, their efficacy, and their ability to provide useful guides and roles.

As I have noted, the viewpoint in part I was inward—the implications for business activities and the leader's role. And the critique had to do with the efficacy of these metaphors, their ability to describe a business, and their ability to suggest useful actions.

We now move on to other, in Locke's phrase, "ideas in men's minds that constantly govern them"—the *purposes* that leaders attribute to their businesses, the ultimate objectives of their companies and themselves. Here, the level of critique shifts. My concern is less with the impact on the business itself and more with the effects of these purposes on our civilization. The viewpoint becomes outward from the business—away from the internal workings of the corporation and toward the larger society

In part II we will answer our other set of questions:

- What have been the principal purposes of business?

- How are purpose and metaphor related?

- How have these purposes changed over time?

- What are the economic and cultural sources of these purposes?

- What do these purposes imply for our civilization?

Our first task is to determine the linkage of business metaphor and business purpose. To begin, let us review the dynamics of metaphorical usage—the changes in the popularity of these metaphors over time. Look, again, at the historical data in table 3–3 (page 32).

Clearly, there have been major shifts over time in the use of the various metaphors. The journey metaphor offers a particularly interesting case; in the early days, no one thought to use this analogy, but in all other eras, more than half the speakers employ it. The period 1770–1905 includes the Romantic period in art and thought. In that time, the most popular idea of a journey was *le voyage sans but*—the journey without a purpose—as contrasted with the other major entailment of the metaphor—a search for order and meaning in existence. As I have said earlier, the idea of a *voyage sans but* would be particularly unappealing to business-men of that era, who had a clear objective in mind (as we shall see): wealth. I would speculate that the purposeless journey—so popular in literature—would not strike a chord with our speakers, but as the sense of the metaphor in popular usage shifted toward the journey with a goal, business speakers found it more to their taste.

The machine analogy's changing fortunes seem to be directly related to the way business is done and the way it is thought of. In the two early periods, the metaphor was extremely popular, even dominant. In the period 1770–1905, the formative period of the Industrial Revolution, the concept of a business as a machine must have seemed simple and natural to the actors of the time. The mechanical view of the universe—the mechanistic concept of real-ity itself—was a strong current in higher thought well into this period and only began to wane in philosophy with the coming of the Romantic period and its organic cast of mind. However, me-chanical thought retained its popularity in the later period, 1905–1945, well beyond the time when higher thought found this idea very congenial. I would think that the substantial influence of Tay-lor and his scientific management—a direct carryover of mechan-istic philosophy—accounts for this strong strain of machine metaphor in business thought.

Since 1945, the mechanical analogy has fallen into virtual dis-use. Two factors are probably responsible: the loss of general cur-rency for the mechanical view of reality and the setbacks that Taylorism has suffered. Despite the emphasis in business schools on analysis, precision, and calculability of business problems, in-dustrial leaders seem to have rejected an overall mechanical view of the processes of business.

The organism as a description of a business has grown more and more common as time goes by. In the period 1905–45, the organism metaphor was almost as common as the machine anal-ogy, and its popularity has grown since then. As we have seen, there are two strains of this idea of an organism: the notion of a domesticated animal and the notion of a being, like a human, with a transcendent purpose. The domesticated animal analogy is closely related to the machine idea—the belief that the business is a tool to serve the owner's purpose. And in the period 1905–45, the organism metaphor was almost as widely used as the machine metaphor, perhaps for the same reason—the useful, shared entailment of a tool.

The postwar period (1945–75), showed a continuing strength of the organism metaphor, although the use of machine analogies had disappeared. But in this era, the business *qua* society became a dominant figure. The society and organism metaphors share a key entailment: the idea of a business as a being with a transcendent purpose, an entity that has value in and of itself. In the postwar period, America stood alone, the strongest by far of any economy. In such times, without real competition of any type (owning the teams, the ballpark, and the equipment, as Ross Perot said), it would be rather natural to view a business as a type of special person or ordained society, with purposes that were self-contained—to view it, in fact, as an autonomous institution, as I will demonstrate later.

In the most recent period (1975–present), the organism metaphor has remained as popular as ever; in fact, it has been the most commonly used analogy (with journey). This is in contradiction to Russell Ackoff's view. Ackoff thought that the idea of a business as an organism had become passé after World War II.[2] Nothing could be further from the truth.

War has had an up-and-down career as a metaphor for business. Relatively popular in the formative period, it disappeared in the years 1905–45. This is hardly surprising. In that turbulent half-century, with real wars everywhere around them, it could not have been a matter of good taste to speak of business as warfare. Even in the postwar period, war was not especially common as a figure, probably because of the memories of the horror of the actual conflict. Memories fade, however.

As Frederick the Great foresaw:

> Other ambitious rulers will . . . start new wars and cause new disasters, for it is characteristic of humans that no one learns

from experience: the follies of the fathers are lost on their children; each generation has to commit its own.[3]

Frederick was right; the present generation has found the conduct of business and the conduct of war somehow similar, and war has become a remarkably popular metaphor.

The game idea has not been a strong factor in business metaphor, except in the postwar period. Again, recall the condition of that time and Ross Perot's apt description. When everything was so easy and one would have to be an awful fool not to succeed, how natural it would be to view business as a great game.

The society metaphor has had a most interesting career. Never especially popular, it became the dominant mode of business thought in the postwar period, but its use soon fell precipitously. As I have noted, the idea of a business as a society could be quite congenial in the very good times; its popularity in the postwar period does make sense in that regard. In the most recent period, since the oil crisis, American industry has faced a stern test, and this comfortable, ennobling metaphor has virtually disappeared from the speech of business leaders. This has not been so, however, in academic writings. The most influential and widely read business book of the era (if not of all time)—Peters and Waterman's *In Search of Excellence*—has trumpeted the society idea, especially its key entailment of corporate culture. This is all well and good, but nowadays, four times as many business speakers find the organism idea more congenial, and three times as many find war a better fit with their business life.

We should now proceed with the exploration of purposes for business and the correlation of these purposes with metaphor. First, however, it will be useful to summarize the work of Thomas Kuhn, because I believe that this work can both structure our discussion of purposes and illuminate the role of metaphor.

The Work of Thomas Kuhn

Kuhn's work, presented in *The Structure of Scientific Revolutions*, concerns scientific theories—especially the "hard" sciences of physics and chemistry—and how these theories have changed over time.

His work is centered in an important body of thought—the basic idea that Pepper has expressed: "Among the variety of objects we find in the world are hypotheses about the world itself."[4]

This is the idea—clearly metaphorical—that theories, concepts, and processes, are in some way objects that have a structure (see Kuhn's title) and a dynamic and that are subject to analysis. Kuhn shows the influence of Kant, who postulated that the mind contains organizing principles that impose order on experience.[5] We have seen this same strain of thought in Johnson and Lakoff's theory that metaphor structures our thought, and in the work of Pepper himself, who showed how world hypotheses order our experience. Kant, however, thought that the categories of our minds were fixed *a priori*—that is, determined before experience and thus immutable. In Kuhn's view, the theories that determine our thought processes are subject to change, and he describes the manner in which this change takes place.

Kuhn first attacks the popular view of science: the belief that scientific knowledge is a sort of edifice that grows year by year toward some ultimate truth.[6] He claims, rather, that the history of science is better viewed as a series of theories or conceptions of reality and that the series—science—proceeds by discontinuous changes; earlier theories often play no part in the structure of later theories. To describe a new theory as better or worse than its predecessors is beside the point; it is simply new—a new way of viewing things that drives scientific work to the limits of that view of reality. When a theory has gained nearly universal acceptance, it becomes a paradigm—the essential manner in which thought is organized for the particular field. On the point of the theory being "superior," Kuhn remarks:

> To be accepted as a paradigm, a theory must seem better than its competitors, but it need not, and in fact never does, explain all the facts with which it is confronted.[7]

It is in this sense that I am suggesting that the purpose of a business is a paradigm—a way of looking at the world that has gained wide acceptance and that structures the way the leader looks at his business.

The word *paradigm* has the twin meanings of a model and an example; Kuhn exploits this duality. A paradigm is at the same time a model for our view of the world and an example given by some highly significant work. This is Kuhn's key contribution: an explanation of the mechanism by which theories change and the structure of revolutions in thought. Newtonian physics is the best example of a paradigm in the sense of an exemplar. Newton's work gave physics a model for centuries. And the exceptional intellectual accomplishment overawed any competitors, so that the shortcomings of the theory, the areas left unexplained—such as gravitation—remained nonproblems for two hundred years.

In a similar way, exceptional business successes have produced examples for all to follow. Henry Ford revolutionized, if he did not create, the automobile industry, and his emphasis on production influenced an entire period of business history. Alfred Sloan, in the same industry, built General Motors into the largest corporation in the world through his emphasis on shareholder wealth, and many followed this example.

Returning to Kuhn, paradigms, by their structuring of reality, have a key characteristic for scientific work: They produce puzzles.[8] Once a paradigm has gained acceptance, scientific work virtually deserts theory making and becomes a matter of solving a series of puzzles through experimentation and calculation—puzzles that the theory has produced. It is important to understand that these puzzles are not grounded in any ultimate reality; rather, they are a direct result of the theory or paradigm itself. The physicist Heisenberg said: "We have to understand that what we observe is not nature in itself, but nature exposed to our method of questioning."[9]

For example, Ford saw production as the goal of business and grasped the nature of the downward sloping demand curve: Lower price means more demand—that is, more production. He spent his working life in thrall of this view of business and in solving the puzzle thereby created—the continued reduction in the costs of production through mass production techniques.

The paradigm that essentially controls a scientist's thinking gives him a particular picture of what the world is all about. This picture gives him expectations of the type of data that should be available for experimentation, the type of phenomenon that he can expect to find.[10] This will determine for him the types of tools, or apparatus, that he will use—in short, his method of questioning. (You have to know what you are looking for to determine how to go about looking for it.) This can have some curious results, especially the result that certain data are either ignored or never sought. And business problems have been business problems since Wedgwood's time—alienated workers, production setbacks, and so forth. But as one's view of the business's purpose changes—as one adopts a new business paradigm—new problems or puzzles seem to arise; in reality, however, they have always been there. Further, some problems are simply pushed into the background; they are never really seen as problems at all.

Elton Mayo, in his Hawthorne experiments, was either a lucky man or a genius with a new paradigm when he did not discard the key results of his experiments—that is, that workers were motivated merely by being noticed by management. He had sought data on the productivity effect of light level in the workplace, presumably under the old theory that workers were complex machines who would respond to varied input levels.

When paradigms are in conflict, the antagonists cannot seem to argue in rational terms. The disputes do not center on facts or logical deduction, since the basic assumptions are so different. Kuhn says: "What differentiated these [different] schools was not a failure of method . . . but their incommensurable ways of seeing the world."[11]

Earlier, we saw the reaction of corporate management, viewing their business as an institution under siege by raiders who hold a business to be a source of wealth. The debate, if there is one, is meaningless and irreconcilable when such different views are held. What possible facts or economic theories could make one understand the other?

Because of the incommensurable ways of thinking, Kuhn states that a change in paradigms is not a gradual thing, not a process of seeing both sides and then coming down on one. Rather it is a Gestalt shift: One must see it one way or the other; it is impossible to see both ways at the same time.[12] This accounts for the heat of the debates and the failure of reasoned argument in these cases:

When paradigms enter, as they must, into a debate about paradigm choice, their role is necessarily circular. Each group uses its
own paradigm to argue in that paradigm's defense.[13]

How can an institution builder convince a wealth seeker, or
vice versa, about the nature and purpose of a business? Both are
right within their charmed circle of opinion. Surely this is a collection of assets with economic *raison d'être?* No, this is an institution
with values, history, a course to run. To view it both ways is simply
impossible.

There comes a time when paradigms shift or begin to shift.
These periods are characterized by frequent and deep debates over
legitimate methods, problems, and standards—the kinds of debates
that simply don't happen when all share the same view of reality.[14]
As the old paradigm reaches its limits—that is, phenomena are
uncovered that are more difficult to explain—attempts are made
to modify the theory and eliminate the apparent conflict.[15] In as-
tronomy, for example, the Ptolemaic theory of an earth-centered
universe seemed to work well for centuries. (It is still used for a
variety of practical purposes.) But the theory had to be modified
to account for the apparent motions of the planets. The idea of
epicycles was introduced, and the model grew excessively complex,
though still viable from a computational viewpoint. The Coperni-
can sun-centered universe replaced this paradigm and was itself
modified by Kepler and later by Einsteinian physics.

We can see a similar phenomenon in business when the advocates of the stakeholder view, which in reality is antithetical to the
wealth paradigm, still base their theory on the primacy of shareholder wealth. They have held to their view of a business as an
institution only by adding to the theory the "epicycle" of shareholder wealth.

A new paradigm deals harshly with the world of its predeces-
sor. Some old problems or puzzles simply become nonproblems;
they are forgotten, relegated to another science, or declared un-
scientific.[16] For example, pre-Newtonian physics was concerned with
the nature of gravity—a respectable problem that Newton never
attempted and that was virtually forgotten until Einstein. And
chemistry before Lavoisier sought the origin of the qualities of com-

pounds (texture, color, etc.); modern chemistry left that problem behind with its quantitative bent. One could calculate precisely how much potassium permanganate was produced by a combination of elements, but no one cared any more to ask why it was blue. This phenomenon—leaving behind old but real concerns as the paradigm changes—will occupy us later when we look at the applications to business, but the point is important. A particular paradigm can insulate its acolytes from really important problems simply because these problems, or the "facts" they present, cannot be fitted into their mind-set, so they are never even noticed.

Lastly, and important for us, Kuhn shows the linkage between paradigm and metaphor:

> [Paradigms] supply the group with preferred or permissible analogies and metaphors. By doing so, they help to determine what will be accepted as an explanation and as a puzzle solution; conversely, they assist in the roster of unsolved problems.[17]

Kuhn's theory seems to fit our review of business metaphor quite well. As only one example: If you view the purpose of your business as wealth, you are likely to see the entity as a machine or as a domesticated animal. Viewing it as such offers a number of suggestions for action, some mistaken perhaps. But problems and puzzles are seen in that light, and solutions can be framed in the context of the metaphor: The good shepherd can be attentive to his sheep, the machine tender can be sure to provide fuel, and so on.

Let me sum up Kuhn's principal findings as they relate to this work:

- A body of knowledge does not grow in a linear and inexorable fashion toward some ultimate explanation. Rather, our world view is shaped by a model, a paradigm, that changes in a discontinuous fashion.

- The paradigm that holds us in its sway in some sense creates the phenomena we see, suggests the data we collect, and presents particular puzzles that are unique to that paradigm.

- Paradigms become dominant through the influence of exemplars—men or women who have done some extraordinary work.

- When paradigms are changing, the conflict between exponents is marked by irrational debate—the result of incommensurate thinking.

- A paradigm will blind one to certain facts, data, and problems because their acceptance would not be compatible with the paradigm.

- A paradigm suggests metaphors that themselves are helpful in framing problems and ultimately solving them. When paradigms are changing, metaphor changes are noted, signaling a shift to a new way of thinking. Recall that paradigms are fundamental beliefs about the world—how it is organized, how it is structured. Metaphors express and articulate these basic credos, and in that sense, true and useful metaphors must spring from a paradigm—a sincere belief about reality.

Purposes

As we have seen earlier, the use of the various metaphors has ebbed and flowed—influenced, no doubt, by the patterns of general speech, which themselves were surely influenced by the currents of thought in art and philosophy. The choices of metaphor also must have been influenced by the prevailing business conditions of the time. Peters and Waterman have suggested that there has been a paradigm shift, particularly a shift away from Taylor's mechanistic view of business. There has certainly been a shift in metaphor, but a paradigm shift in Kuhn's sense is another matter. As we just saw, Kuhn has postulated that metaphor changes are a *result* of paradigm shifts; metaphors are not themselves paradigms. Metaphors are a description of a process, an event, or a thing. Paradigms are more profound; they relate to the actor's fundamental notions of what the world is all about. Metaphors, which of course color our thinking in a substantial way, are chosen, or chosen for us, by our world view—in short, by our paradigm.

The business leaders' basic view of their business must be ultimately traceable to their basic view of the world, their notion of their own place in the world, and their conception of the place that the business holds in that world. Very closely tied to this, in my view, is the fundamental *purpose* that they see for the business. I believe that the purpose the leaders see for their business is inextricably bound with the paradigm that lies at the basis of their thought. Now, it may seem that all business people have a single purpose in mind for starting a business or for devoting their lives to operating one. Probably, the common view is that people are in it for the money—Marx's economic explanation for virtually all human activity has become the pervasive view of our time. But this is not really the case if we turn to the speech of our business actors. In fact, business people voice three quite distinct purposes for their activities.

First is the commonsense view: The purpose of a business is to produce wealth for the shareholders—the owners. This is a popular view in business and in economic theory: the notion that the purpose of business is the maximization of shareholder wealth. All transactions, investments, and decisions are assumed to stem from this basic tenet. As we have seen, this notion is enshrined in the law governing public companies; directors are charged with the responsibility to safeguard the shareholders' economic interests. A variant of this purpose is, of course, the individual's desire for personal wealth, whether as employee or stockholder. Lee Iacocca was quite candid in this regard, stating that he entered business to become a millionaire.[18]

But there is a second basic purpose for business: the very simple notion that a business exists to produce goods and services for the benefit of society, not just to enrich the owners. This purpose forms the background for a good deal of classical economic theory; increased production is the key to the continued improvement in living standards and the general well-being of society. That the owners are enriched can be seen as some sort of epiphenomenon—a necessary and perhaps desirable outcome, but not the real objective. The basic task of business is to *produce* .

The third major purpose for business activity is entirely non-economic in nature; it is the purpose of building or perpetuating an institution, establishing or directing an organization of indefinite duration. Wealth, whether corporate or individual, and the needs of society are quite secondary concerns. The real concern is the organization itself—its well-being and its indefinitely continued existence. Surprisingly, when we consider the contrary weight of legal and economic theory, this purpose for business is not at all rare.

These three purposes—the personalities who exemplify them, the metaphors they call forth, the clash of ideas they engender—will occupy us in later sections. For now let us turn to some data on the purposes of actual business leaders. Table 10–1 shows the purposes that can be attributed to business leaders from 1770 up to the present, based on their own words. Table 10–2 presents these data by historical period.

The data are rather dramatic. Until 1900, apparently no one conceived of a business as having any other purpose than the generation of wealth for the owners. Then, in a rather short time, the tide turned, and production became the conventional wisdom. But in the postwar period, again influenced no doubt by the American position in the world, the idea of an institution became dominant. That lasted hardly any time at all; under the shock of the oil crisis and rising foreign competition, the idea of building or perpetuating an institution lost favor. I think that these changes can be illustrated by reference to Kuhn's theories, and I will show that a bit later. Now, following Kuhn, let us look at the correlation of these purposes with the metaphors that the actors have chosen.

First, let us look at some more data. Table 10–3 shows the frequency of use of the various metaphors by the actors voicing different purposes. The chart can be read as the percentage of actors with a particular purpose who use a particular metaphor. The sample size is fairly small—thirty-four actors (thirteen for production, eleven for wealth, and ten for institution) employing metaphor sixty-four times. (Most speakers use more than one metaphor.) However, I think that the data suggest a number of conclusions.

The information can be expressed less quantitatively as follows:

- The production paradigm: The journey is the most frequently used metaphor. Other metaphors are important—especially

Table 10–1
Actors and Purposes

Actor	Year	Wealth	Production	Institution
			Purpose	
Wedgwood	1770	X		
Owen	1813	X		
Towne	1866	X		
Gould	1870	X		
Carnegie	1870	X		
Gantt	1901		X	
Taylor	1903		X	
Ford	1908		X	
Gilbreth	1923		X	
Sheldon	1923		X	
Sloan	1923	X		
Draper-Dayton	1932		X	
Chester	1936		X	
Nichol	1941	X		
Ford II	1946		X	
Robertson	1946		X	
Petersen	1955			X
Ackerman	1958	X		
Jones	1970			X
Wriston	1970			X
MacGregor	1970			X
Haley	1970			X
Watson	1970			X
Geneen	1984	X		
Cook	1984			X
Sanford	1984		X	
Sperlich	1984			X
Anderson	1984	X		
Frisbee	1984		X	
Azzato	1985		X	
Ferguson	1985			X
Stone	1985		X	
Burr	1986		X	
Iacocca	1986	X		
Perot	1986	X		
Roderick	1986	X		
Hanson	1986		X	
Olsen	1986		X	
Kissinger	1986			X
Borman	1986			X

Table 10–2

Actors' Attribution of Purpose

(percentage of actors citing the purpose)

	Purpose		
Period	*Wealth*	*Production*	*Institution*
1770–1905	100	0	0
1905–45	22	78	0
1945–75	11	22	67
1975–present	29	41	29

Table 10–3

Metaphor and Purpose

(percentage of actors using the metaphor)

	Metaphor					
Purpose	*Journey*	*Game*	*War*	*Machine*	*Organism*	*Society*
Production	46	23	15	23	23	8
Wealth	36	46	36	27	45	18
Institution	60	50	30	10	40	50

Note: Totals exceed 100 percent because most actors use more than one metaphor.

game, machine, and organism—but none achieve substantial use, since the "votes" are split among them.

- The wealth paradigm: The game and organism metaphors are the most frequently used.

- The institutional paradigm: The journey, the game, and the society are the most popular metaphors.

In the next several chapters, we shall look further at the three basic purposes of business, and I shall discuss the role that metaphors play in articulating these purposes for business leaders. The metaphors will be seen to have entailments that help define the leader's role and help condition his actions along the lines of his basic purpose.

Summary

- The viewpoint in this part of the book has changed from metaphors and their effect on business practices to the purposes of business and their impact on society.

- The popularity of metaphors has changed greatly over the years.

- The use of metaphor is rather well correlated with the business purpose of the speaker. Wealth seekers speak of games and organisms; the production-minded talk of journeys but also allude to games, machines, and organisms; the institution builders favor journeys, games and societies.

- Kuhn's model of changes in scientific theory provides clues to the analysis of business purpose: the notion of exemplars; the discontinuity of change; the puzzles created by the new paradigms; the incommensurability of different paradigms; and, critically, the idea that metaphor springs from a paradigm—that a useful metaphor is a natural expression of a deeply held belief.

Now let us move on to an exploration of the three fundamental purposes, or paradigms, of business: production, wealth, and institution building.

11
The New Messiah

The Paradigm of Production

On the importance of production, there is no difference between Republicans and Democrats, right and left, white and colored, Catholic or Protestant.

—John Kenneth Galbraith[1]

Background

Production—the supply of goods and services to better mankind's lot—has been a rallying cry for generations of businessmen, and with good reason. The improvement in living standards that industry brings can justify our industrial civilization as well as the business participants. We may have struck many bargains with nature and suffered loss of identity and social cohesiveness, but no one can deny that we have all benefited from improved housing, nutrition, health care, and leisure.

Many have championed this altruistic purpose for a business; Gilbreth epitomizes this view, stating flatly that "production is the universal need of all times."[2] And this is difficult to deny; in any human society, some sector must provide the necessary services and artifacts that the group needs to subsist and to prosper. Modern industrial civilization has simply rationalized and extended the productive sector, which has always met the "universal need of all times." But as we have seen, the consensus on this purpose for business has ebbed and flowed. And there is a certain discomfort among many business thinkers when the consensus seems to stray from this fundamental role of business. The 1954 film *Executive*

Suite portrayed these conflicts in stylized form: Surrounded by his money-grubbing (and physically unattractive) peers, the handsome young lion (Bill Holden) captures the allegiance of the board, as well as the audience, when he proclaims:

> We're going to give people what they want—at prices they can afford, and as fresh needs come up we'll satisfy them, too.[3]

The film seemed really to explain business for a lot of people— the general population as well as businessmen. Business was not a gold rush; it was a humanitarian enterprise. Business people were not in it for the money; they served a key purpose for society. Altruism triumphed over greed, noble purpose over petty self-interest. The paradigm of production had entered the popular consciousness.

Production and Economics

The primacy of production has its roots deep in economic theory. Adam Smith took production more or less for granted and focused his considerable intellect on the distribution of goods. He sought, and largely found, the mechanism that holds an economic society together: the market system that provides the goods that society wants, in the quantities desired, and at the prices it is prepared to pay.[4] The great contribution of Smith's analysis has been in this understanding of the rational operations of a free market economy; he brought order out of a scene in which everyone else had seen random, individual profit seeking. But again, his focus was on the distribution of goods as the primary problem to be explained; producing the goods was a given. His market mechanism theory gave to distribution the trappings of natural law.

Smith wrote in 1776, really before the advent of large-scale industrialization. John Stuart Mill published *Principles of Political Economy* in 1848, when England was well into the Industrial Revolution. Countering Smith, Mill saw the true province of economic law in production, not distribution. In his view, distribution does not follow natural law; on the contrary, patterns of distribution are established by society in arbitrary ways. Distribution obeys no laws but human ones.[5]

This insight was seized on by socialists of all persuasions, not least Freidrich Engels. Engels, paradoxically, was an industrialist as well as a social revolutionary and communist theorist. His business background led him to see production as primary, but further, he saw that the production and exchange of products was the basis of every social order. Engels taught that in every society, not only the distribution of goods but also the establishment of social classes is determined by the type of goods produced, the method of production, and the way in which products are distributed.[6]

Another radical thinker, Thorstein Veblen, writing around 1900, provided a sharp critique of business leaders but maintained the prime role of production as the force that improves society. Veblen's critique of businessmen centers on his theory that in all times and all places, leisure classes have emerged that enjoy their ease at the expense of the productive sectors of society. Through force or cunning, not sweat or skill, these people gain the material benefits of society's productive output.[7] Veblen also proposed the novel thesis that businessmen actually hamper production. They are not merely a necessary evil; they actively get in the way of the essential role of production.

In his time, around the turn of the century, he had grounds for this view. This was the age of Morgan, Frick, Rockefeller, and Gould—men "far more interested in the exciting manipulation of huge masses of intangible wealth than the humdrum business of turning out goods."[8] In Veblen's view, these financial manipulations did nothing but distract industry from its key role: production. Veblen thought that business leaders actively sought to slow down the engines of production through breakdowns, so that scarcities would result, prices rise, and profits soar.[9] For our purposes, it is enough to note that Veblen, along with other nineteenth-century economists, saw production as the rock that society stood on; his quarrel was with the leisure class, which impeded the smooth operations of industrial production.

It was left to John Maynard Keynes, writing in the first third of this century, to show the essential coupling of production and the demand for goods. An expanding economy results because supply (production) creates its own demand. Keynes showed the mechanism: To produce goods, a firm must pay workers, suppliers, and, of course, the government. These payments are recycled to the production sector because when people or institutions have money, they spend it. The payments back to the production units not only permit them to continue producing; the surplus payments (profit) may be used to invest in increased production capacity.[10] Keynes had radical ideas—the naturalness of depression, the need for pump priming—but he believed implicitly that production was paramount.

In more recent times, Galbraith has pursued the debate on production, essentially by posing a new question: production of what? I will postpone discussion of his critique until later in this chapter, but his writings on production show its primacy in contemporary thought. The epigraph for this chapter presents his view on the worldwide consensus on production. Galbraith has also written:

> The importance of production transcends our boundaries. We are regularly told [it] is the justification of our civilization.[11]

Galbraith writes mainly tongue-in-cheek, but his statements can be taken as an accurate picture of the conventional wisdom: production is the *ne plus ultra* of our civilization.

Even George Gilder, that champion of the entrepreneur and apologist for his wealth, justifies the riches of the entrepreneur in terms of the primacy of production:

> Capitalists need capital to fulfill their role in launching and financing enterprises. . . . [They] must be allowed to retain their wealth for the practical reasons that only they, collectively, can possibly know where it should go, to whom it should be given.[12]

So from Adam Smith through the great names of classical and Marxist economics, and even into modern times, Galbraith's commentary is correct: There is no dispute on the importance of production.

The Actors

Josiah Wedgwood can be counted as a precursor of later figures who embraced production as the root purpose of business. Wedgwood flirted with this idea, but in the company of the other early actors, he came down on the side of wealth. Writing in 1769, Wedgwood showed his discomfort with the wealth paradigm, specifically on the question of sharing his designs with other pottery makers:

> The foundation of my argument is money getting. If instead you substitute Fame and the good of Manufacturers at large for our principles of action, then we would do the contrary of what I have been recommending. . . . I wish to be released from these degrading, selfish chains, these mean selfish fears of other people copying my works.[13]

But his partner, Bentley, talked him out of it, remarking that "posterity is great, but not at the cost of lost profits."[14]

Wedgwood clearly had to struggle with what his business was all about, what purpose it served. In many ways, though, he indicated that his purpose was money-making: He drove his workers to the wall on wages, held his designs in closest secrecy, and worked against the emigration of potters at the same time as he worked for the emigration of pots—that is, free trade. Wedgwood, though, first raised the question—honestly—of what the essential purpose of a business is. To his credit, he believed that wealth alone was "degrading," although he eventually opted for it. He made another essential contribution—the discovery of the downward-sloping demand curve and its implications. Faced with a high overhead in equipment and wages, and spurred by his workers' demand for even higher wages, Wedgwood had his inspiration. If more could be produced with the same overhead, the unit cost would go down, so prices could go down. Lower price would attract more buyers and yet more could be produced—and so on, around the closed loop of decreasing cost and increasing production. He grasped, as he said, "the vast consequences in most manufacturers of making the greatest quantity in a given time."[15] The consequence for Wedgwood—the goal he sought—was riches beyond counting. But we owe to him this fundamental idea, an idea that Henry Ford rediscovered generations later and put to the purpose of production.

I have been focusing this discussion on one aspect of the paradigm I have called production—the aspect of producing goods or services. The paradigm is actually broader; it includes the larger realm of serving society. Many business people see this as their essential role—to serve society's needs for food, shelter, health care, and other essential services through the output of their productive capacities.

This theme was first articulated in the early twentieth century. Henry Gantt stated it concisely: "The first aim of business should be to render service."[16]

And many others have taken up this theme—especially Frederick Taylor. Taylor has been treated harshly by later generations, (even in these pages), but his goal was a clear and noble one; it is his technique that is questionable. Taylor believed fundamentally in production as the goal of business, the clear imperative for any business enterprise:

> There is hardly any worse crime to my mind than that of deliberately restricting output; of failing to bring the only things into the world that are of real use to the world, the products of men and soils.[17]

Taylor's view coincides with Veblen's outrage at the business leaders of their era, who restricted output for the sake of personal gain. And Henry Ford, the exemplar for this whole body of thought, in turn railed against the "money" people, who contributed nothing: "It is the function of a business to produce for consumption and not for money or speculation."[18]

Ford professed a belief in service—that industry's function was quite simply to make the world a better place in which to live.[19] Writing in later life, he looked back at the time of his founding of Ford Motor Company (1903):

> The most surprising feature of business . . . then was the large attention to finance and the small attention to service. That seemed . . . to be reversing the natural process.[20]

As we have seen from our earlier review, Ford was right in his assessment. Before 1900, virtually everyone conceived of business as a means to generate wealth. Ford's enormous success revolutionized this thinking. It became much more common, more acceptable, to talk about business in terms of its service to society. For example, George Draper-Dayton, a founder of Dayton-Hudson, wrote in 1932:

> Shall we agree to start with the assumption that success is making ourselves useful in the world, valuable to society? The business of business is serving society, not just money making.[21]

Even Alfred Sloan, the exemplar of the wealth paradigm, could catch the spirit of production. One of his biographers saw as Sloan's constant theme: "Provide more things for more people in more places."[22]

The theme of service and production has continued into our own time. Foster Wheeler's CEO, Louis Azzato, wrote in 1985: "We're not producing to satisfy a sales quota, we're producing to satisfy the customer."[23]

And Donald Burr, of the late People Express, typified the production paradigm in the airline business. Burr's vision (as described earlier) was a low-cost airline that could provide air transportation for the masses and, through some new style management, provide high-quality service at the low price.[24]

The sense we get from those who hold to the production paradigm is that they are doing something important, even ennobling. These are people with a strong sense of mission. Listen to Robert Hanson, CEO of Deere: "We are proud because we are engaged in a necessary kind of business. . . . We're in the business of feeding the world."[25]

Hanson puts himself in the company of Frederick Taylor, Henry Ford, and George Draper-Dayton—men who saw their responsibilities almost in terms of the Christian corporal works of mercy: feed the hungry, clothe the naked, shelter the homeless, and so on. Theirs was an altruistic vision, not always confirmed by their deeds, but fine sentiments nevertheless. It may be more difficult to see this imperative in the computer business, but Ken Olsen of Digital Equipment really follows the same paradigm. Olsen has devoted his energies to a compatible range of computers, a family that gives users what he thinks they want. He has stated his determination to build products so appealing and useful that an aggressive sales force would be unnecessary.[26]

Olsen's obsession with the product and his deemphasis of selling (the product should "sell itself") is a radical break with the pioneer in the computer business—Thomas Watson. Watson's concern was IBM itself—IBM as an enduring institution. Within IBM, he developed the primacy of selling, the excellence of the sales force and customer service as means to establish account control and thus assure the indefinite existence of the IBM institution. In contrast, Olsen follows the production paradigm: Build a superior, useful product and all else will follow.

Ford the Exemplar

Let us explore this paradigm of production in terms of the structure that we have learned from Thomas Kuhn. And let us start with the key figure of the "exemplar," the person whose work sets an example and determines the thinking of other workers in the field— in our case, other business leaders. This exemplar is, of course, Henry Ford the elder.

Ford was an odd, complex man, an unlikely candidate for the role he finally assumed—industrial giant and folk hero. But his gifts were exceptional; he combined mechanical genius and an eye for talent with single-minded devotion to one idea: mass production. He was pathetically ignorant of the history he dismissed as "bunk"; under questioning at a libel trial, he volunteered that the American Revolution took place in 1812. But he also revealed the bent of his personality when, criticized for this gap in his knowledge, he said: "I could find a man in five minutes who could tell me all about it."[27]

Beneath all his grasping, ignorance, and deviousness, though, Ford held firmly to the essence of the production paradigm. As he expressed it: "The foundations of society are the men and the means to make things, to grow things and to carry things."[28]

And to secure these foundations for society, Ford—and he was the first (save Wedgwood)—saw that mass production and mass consumption must go hand in hand. His life-long passion became mass production as an end in itself.[29] He was hardly the first to make an automobile; the German G. Daimler invented and demonstrated the first car in 1886, when Ford was a twenty-three-year-old farm worker and tinkerer. Ford was not even the first American to produce a car; Charles Duryea had done that in 1892, when Ford was a mechanical engineer with the Detroit Illuminating Company. But Duryea inspired him, and Ford, still employed at Edison, set out to build his own car. In 1899, he found some investors and formed the Detroit Automobile Company, serving as chief engineer. But the Model T and Ford's later inspiration on mass production lay in the future; his interest then was in high-priced racing cars. He designed and produced one but failed, and the company folded. Undaunted, he found new investors in 1901, formed the Ford Automobile Company, and tried another racer. Again, he failed within a year. Ford then became a famous racing driver, competing in cars he designed and built himself. The publicity he received attracted new investors and he was ready in 1903, at the age of forty, to try again.[30]

We often suppose that Ford created the entire automobile industry from absolutely nothing; but he, like all great men, found the conditions ripe for his success. The United States at the turn of the century had all the factors needed for a mass automobile business (except an extensive highway system). America had endless coal and iron and a thriving steel business; oil production had begun; and there was an enormous potential internal market for motor cars.

Also, a great deal of the necessary technology and skills were already available, ready to be tapped. The railroad industry, the bicycle and carriage industries, even the sewing machine business had created an infrastructure of machine shops and had sparked the development of machine tools. It was all ready—the market, the technology, the material resources—ready for the hand of the genius to assemble into a vast new industry.[31]

In a similar way, we often suppose that Albert Einstein, like Ford in his field, created post-Newtonian physics out of thin air. But again—and, curiously, at the same time that Ford emerged— the conditions in the world of theoretical physics were set for a major breakthrough. The experiments had been performed, yielding results that Newtonian physics could not explain. The mathematics had been developed—the mathematics of non-Euclidean geometry. Everything awaited the master stroke of a genius. And such a genius was alive and active in the mainstream of theoretical physics and mathematics; in fact, he had largely created the necessary mathematics himself. This genius was not Albert Einstein; it was Henri Poincaré—the acknowledged mathematical giant of his age—a Sorbonne professor and member of the Academie Française. Poincaré had all the threads in his hands—the experimental results and the mathematical tools—but he never pulled the threads together. Fortune chose Einstein, and an obscure twenty-six-year-old patent clerk in Berne—not the mature, widely honored Sorbonne savant—overturned the centuries-old edifice of Newtonian physics. Einstein is known to every child in every educated society; Poincaré is usually confused, even by the well educated, with his first cousin, the statesman Raymond. And Charles Duryea, from the same time and place as Ford and with the same technical skills (he made a car years before Ford), has sunk into obscurity.

Ford, like Einstein, succeeded because the conditions were favorable but also because he had an idea that had simply never occurred to anyone before. In 1903, the automobile was a luxury item. All the manufacturers, without exception, catered to the rich or to the coterie of racing enthusiasts. Most manufacturers were making money at this trade, and no one saw any reason to change.[32] Enter Ford, with new capital, for another run at the automobile business. In 1903, he produced a practical, well-made vehicle—a nonracer. Priced at $850, the car met a seller's market and was reasonably successful; 1700 cars were sold in fifteen months.[33] Following the conventional wisdom, he then produced a luxury car—a $1,000 model. This failed badly. Then, finally, Ford had the inspiration of a lifetime—perhaps of Western man's lifetime. He lowered the price of the car, and the "effect was magical."[34] In 1907, a "panic" (i.e., recession) year, Ford made his largest profit to date.

Ford's inspiration was nothing more than a grasp of the downward-sloping demand cure, exactly the discovery that Wedgwood had made nearly 150 years before. But Ford saw the full implications of the idea. He would produce a simple, standardized, and inexpensive car—nothing else. He saw that in order to produce a low-cost car, standardization and high volumes were critical. And the tinkerer and race car driver saw more than this; he had the vision of a tool for the people of his roots, the small-time farmers. He would provide a machine to get them to market, pump water, run farm machinery, and do all the endless, back-breaking farm tasks that ingenuity could invent from the simple principle of a power-takeoff point on a low-cost, reliable automobile.[35]

The result, as all the world knows, was the Model T, priced at $850 in 1908. In that year, Ford sold 11,000 cars; he had the trade's bestseller. His efforts for the next twenty years can be read as an obsession with driving down the cost of that car. And the method had to be volume production. In 1908, he said that his heart's desire was to produce a car per minute. He got that wish on February 7, 1920; and by October 31, 1925, he was producing a car every ten seconds.[36] The price continued to drop, and by 1921 he had sold one million cars.[37]

Eventually, 15 million Model Ts were sold—a total value of $7 billion. In its last ten years, the Model T accounted for half of all U.S. automobile production.[38] The principle was simplicity itself—the essential coupling of mass production and mass consumption, the downward-sloping demand curve: Lower the price, sell more, produce more; unit costs will decline, and price can be lowered yet again. The car that had sold for $850 in 1908 went for $290 in 1926, its last year.[39]

Ford's enormous success revolutionized America's—indeed, the world's—industry, but not just in the scale of its operations. His example—his very successful example—was not lost on industrialists in all fields. Mass production, with the essential concomitant of lowered prices to fuel mass consumption, became the new conventional wisdom. The paradigm of production had found its exemplar. As Ford himself said: "Machinery is the new Messiah."[40]

Some Puzzles

Kuhn has shown us that paradigms create puzzles; that is, they create a series of problems that come to light when the paradigm is accepted and that then serve as the plan of work for all practitioners in the field. And so it is in business, and so it is with the production paradigm.

It will be instructive to trace the development of the production paradigm through the career of Henry Ford to illustrate some of the puzzles that arose and his solutions to those puzzles. As we have seen the paradigm of production is a simple mind-set; it is the belief that the production of goods and services is essential to the well-being of mankind. Put so baldly, it is almost a tautology——of course men need goods and services. The essential puzzle, though, is how to provide these goods on such a scale that they will be useful to the bulk of humanity. And I don't speak only of the physical problems in large-scale production; the first problem is an economic one: How can the goods be produced so that they are within the reach of most people? Ford got right to the heart of this problem, stating: "It is better to sell a large number of articles at a small profit than to sell a few at a large profit—more can buy."[41]

Ford's answer to the essential puzzle that mass production presents was, of course, mass consumption. This, in turn, raises another puzzle: How can mass consumption be fueled? That is answered by the demand curve, which Ford intuitively understood—low price. But low price, in its turn, raises its own conundrum. The solution to that is perhaps obvious as well—low cost. And here, at the innermost of the "Chinese boxes" of puzzles, is where Ford made his contribution—solutions to the puzzle of low cost.

His answers were several. First, as Wedgwood had learned, high volume in itself would lower unit costs as the high volumes absorbed the fixed costs of equipment and some of the overhead labor. But Ford found other ways: standardized parts, a very narrow product line (one product—the Model T), and the newly coined techniques of Taylor's scientific management. Ford even took Wedgwood one better in his understanding of high volume; he actually priced his car *below* cost, dropping the price from $575 to $440 in 1920, on the conviction that he could drive the costs low enough to earn a profit.[42]

Although he never articulated it, his actions showed that Ford understood what is now called the *experience curve*. This phenomenon was first noted in the aerospace industry after World War II. Industrial engineers found that there was a relationship between the volume of an article produced and the *variable* costs (not just the unit costs, which would decline automatically as fixed costs are covered by higher volume). The rule of thumb became that a doubling of the total number of articles produced since the first run would reduce variable costs by 20 or 25 percent. The explanation was "experience"—hence the phenomenon's name. As a company produced more and more of an article, more experience with the process was gained, the process equipment was perfected, the workers increased their skills, better raw materials were found, and so on.

In the electronics industry of the 1970s, the experience curve became an article of faith, and some companies—Texas Instrument was the most prominent—launched new products, with very low volumes, at prices that related to production levels they expected to reach at some time in the future. The theory was that the low price—well below cost—would create the demand that would generate the low cost levels. It was a self-fulfilling prophecy. Ford did much the same thing: lowering the price below cost, gaining the volume, and then forcing his organization to become more and more efficient. He drove his people unmercifully. He told his top men that their jobs depended on increasing production every day and reducing costs to catch up with his reduced prices.[43]

But, lowering the price, increasing demand, and hectoring his men were not enough; Ford needed better methods. Demand was very high in 1908, but Ford was using the same techniques and the same plant that he had started with in 1903. The techniques were the same that he had found in all of the mechanical industry of the day: A skilled mechanic, a real jack-of-all-trades, moved around the shop from machine center to machine center with his parts and assemblies. The entire manufacturing industry, from its low-volume heritage, had found it efficient to group similar machine tools in these machine centers. The strain of Ford's volumes drove this system to its breaking point.

In 1910, Ford, with his sure eye for talent, hired a production expert, Walter Flanders, who was a disciple of Frederick Taylor.

With Flanders's scientific management principles in mind, Ford built a new plant at Highland Park. Using Taylor's methods, Flanders eliminated the machine centers and introduced the line concept—bringing the work to the mechanic and his tools, rather than the mechanic bringing the work to the tools.

Even with standardized parts, in 1913 it still took twelve hours and twenty-eight minutes to assemble a Model T.[44] In that year, the first assembly line was introduced—the chassis dragged along by rope and windlass. This reduced assembly time by 50 percent. When a continuous belt was installed (in early 1914), assembly time was down to ninety-three minutes—less than one-tenth of the time it had taken eight months earlier.

The assembly line solution created puzzles in its turn. It was found that the machine tools—those hangovers from the machine center era—were too generalized for the highly specific job of Model T production.[45] New tools were designed and installed along the assembly line. Ford's (and Flanders's) innovative work on machine tools and the assembly line made all the difference. Their innovation was in *process* technology. That is the essential story of the Model T. Very little about the product itself was innovative; the new fact was the manner in which it was built and the cost and productivity results of how it was built. Ford solved the puzzles of mass consumption by production technique, not by a new and better product design.

The highly successful installation of the new process technology created another puzzle, one that Ford and his contemporaries never really solved adequately: the problem of people. Ford thought that he had solved the problem—or more accurately, he did not see a problem at all: "The average worker . . . wants a job in which he does not have to think."[46] And this belief dovetailed with the new job requirements. Skilled men were no longer required in production; the day of the skilled mechanic, the jack-of-all-trades, had passed.[47] The new processes inexorably reduced the necessity for thought on the part of the worker.[48] Scientific management had produced the mindless industrial worker.

Ford, as he said, seemed to think that this was a desirable state for the average worker, but the facts proved contrary. The new methods caused catastrophic employee turnover—380 percent in 1913.[49] (To fix that number for you, that means that Ford had to hire 983 people to increase staff by a net 100—and he was expanding rapidly.) The situation was clearly out of control. Ford would never compromise on his techniques of production and the resultant robotlike jobs. He still believed that men wanted mindless jobs; to him, the problem was compensation. Yet again, Ford found the right solution to this latest puzzle. He introduced the $5 per day wage, double the prevailing standard, and an eight-hour day, down from nine. It worked magic. Turnover dropped by 90 percent, but more than that, Ford got the best men. Ford's men produced more efficiently than anyone, and unit labor costs actually declined.[50]

I have spoken of Ford as an exemplar in the context of Kuhn's structure of scientific theory revolution. Ford's incandescent success certainly was an example, and many followed, but his influence was more direct than mere emulation. Alfred Sloan was a subcontractor to Ford at this time, and he felt the full weight of Ford's dedication to the production paradigm—his mania for mass production and incessant cost reduction.[51] Ford's suppliers had only two choices: adopt his methods or perish. He drove his suppliers to the wall on cost and volume of delivery. He had solved the puzzle, and his suppliers had damn well better do the same. As a result of his own efforts, Ford raised the productivity of the entire industry and forced everyone, by economic necessity, to follow his example. He had solved the puzzles of the production paradigm, transforming an industry in the process.

The Problems Left Behind

As we have seen from Kuhn's work, when we are in the grip of a paradigm, we see the world only in that light. We see a series of puzzles, but, very importantly, we do not at all see other issues, other puzzles, other problems. It comes down to the questions that we ask of the world, the questions that the paradigm seems to pose. As Susanne Langer has said:

> The intellectual treatment of any datum, any experience, any subject, is determined by the nature of our questions, and only carried out in the answers.[52]

We have followed Henry Ford's pursuit of the production paradigm and the puzzles, or questions, he uncovered, and we have seen his solutions. But Ford left a lot behind; he relegated to the status of nonproblems some serious issues that had concerned his predecessors and still concern us today. In particular, he blinded himself to the problems of people and the problems of distribution.

First, regarding people, Ford thought this a nonproblem; or more accurately, he believed that his paradigm and his methods were a good fit to human aspirations. He really focused on only one aspect of people's lives: their consumer needs. And all his efforts were bent to satisfy these very legitimate needs through the vehicle of production. But people are workers as well as consumers, and here Ford parted company with the work of millennia: society's goal of ensuring meaning in men's lives—through ritual and custom, but also through meaningful tasks. Ford's noble concern for the material needs of his fellows was matched by his contempt for their abilities; we have seen his remark that workers really want a job that requires no thought. He actually believed that the majority of people were incapable of making a living without the aid of someone like himself.[53]

That men *had* made a living, time out of mind, as hunters, farmers, artisans, and merchants seemed to escape the sage of Dearborn. Medieval society, like all societies until the Industrial Age, had provided meaning—both spiritual consolation and the meaning that work can bring. Despite appalling privations, the medieval serf still had the satisfaction of tilling his fields, reaping the harvest. The guilds honored the skills of craftsmen, men who produced an article shaped by their own hands and sensibilities. The industry that Ford found at the turn of the century was hardly a medieval idyll, but the men were artisans, craftsmen. Ford's reading of the paradigm of production swept it all away; men became no more than complex cogs in the production process. The low volume of output in the pre-Ford days allowed production workers to exercise skill and craftsmanship; Ford's imperative for high volume could not use such men.

As we have seen, Ford was a tough taskmaster, driving his men to higher and higher output. But in the early days, it worked. He had talented people; the atmosphere was electric. It was very hard work, but the rewards were in the success of Ford Motor Company, and there was a fine spirit of camaraderie.[54] As the volume demands grew, though, the atmosphere changed. Men were uprooted from customary tasks as Ford experimented with the process. No skilled men were needed and the workers lost the satisfaction of artisan work. The jobs became routinized, dull. The robot workers had to work faster and faster in cramped surroundings and in set positions for hours at a time.[55]

By 1921, there was no longer much that could be done to improve the process with the current technology. Ford's solution was simple: work faster and harder. Even his vaunted high wage philosophy and professed concerns for his workers disappeared under the whip of the production imperative. By 1926, he was squeezing out the older and slower workers and had cut the labor force and the wages.[56]

The dream of the highly productive worker, satisfied only with his high wage, began to unravel. Ford promoted Harry Bennett to chief of the Ford Service Department, and Bennett used this collection of spies and private police as an agent of repression and regulation. Workers were intimidated; Bennett's men would push and shove a worker into the boss's office. There were reports of beatings and other mistreatment. Bennett established an iron-clad rule against talking at work; one man was even fired for smiling.[57] Ford had said, "A factory is not a drawing room." Clearly, his was not. The man who championed the cause of humanity, the cause of man the consumer, had lost all interest in man the worker.

Ford's other blind spot, which ultimately led to near-disaster for his company, was in the area of distribution. He held firmly to his demand curve thesis: Distribution would take care of itself so long as the prices were low enough. As time went on, this strategy began to fail, as competitors—particularly General Motors—offered consumers better styling. Ford found himself forcing cars on his dealers; in 1921, he made his dealers accept 93,000. Those who refused lost their franchises.[58] Ford simply could not see distribution as a problem. In a meeting with a group of dealers in 1922, he listened to their complaints, then said: "The only problem with the Ford car is that we can't make them fast enough."[59] He held on to the paradigm of production to the end.

But the market was signaling, despite Ford's adamant stand, that there was more to distribution than a low price. Low price even began to work against Ford. In 1926, a Model T cost $290 FOB Detroit. This very low price for a basic car created a new competitor—the used car, which sold for $10 or $15.[60] Worse followed: The Model T, the "Tin Lizzy," became the butt of jokes. Ford resisted as long as he could; not until the final Model T years did he even see the need for national advertising.[61] He finally had to accept the public's mania for the annual model change, and the Model T was discontinued in 1927, after a precipitous drop in sales.[62] Ford nearly destroyed his company by his obstinacy. It was necessary to shut down the plant for a year to retool; 60,000 workers were laid off, while Ford replaced 15,000 machine tools and rebuilt 25,000 more.[63]

Even the admission of the Model T's failure, though, did not change Ford's basic principle. The new Model A was launched, but Ford froze all engineering change, any model improvements, for five years. Chevy gained, Plymouth gained, and the Model A was discontinued in 1932. By the end of 1933, General Motors had outsold Ford three years running, and in 1933, Plymouth outsold Ford. In 1931–32, the Ford Motor company lost $115 million. In fact, General Motors outearned Ford every year from 1924 until the year ending December 31, 1986, when Ford finally bested GM. Ford's obsession with production had made him and his company immensely successful, but his blind spot on distribution—the need to cater to consumer tastes—had nearly brought the firm to ruin and had allowed his competitors to pass him by.

The firm did survive, but in a weakened condition. When old Henry passed away in 1947, the leadership passed to his grandson, Henry II, who directed the company for nearly 40 years. Henry II recruited a group of brilliant scientific managers from the service after World War II, including a future U.S. secretary of defense, Robert McNamara. McNamara appeared to many to be a human computer; all of his decisions were based on rigorous cost analysis and statistical projections. He even looked the part: squarish, balding head and thick, rimless glasses. But McNamara had more than the soul of a cost accountant; in fact, he shared the old dream of Henry Ford, Sr. As his erstwhile colleague Lee Iacocca described it, McNamara believed strongly in the idea of a utilitarian car—a car whose purpose was simply to meet people's basic needs. He believed that luxury cars were simply frivolous.[64] The paradigm of production had found a new champion at Ford Motor Company. But McNamara soon went to Washington; and when Iacocca took over, he killed McNamara's small, cheap, fuel-efficient compact. Iacocca believed that he had learned the lessons of the Model T and the Model A, remarking: "The truth is, we can only sell what people are willing to buy."[65]

In recent times, another proponent of production, Donald Burr of People Express, took another try at solving the production paradigm's puzzles. Burr was highly sensitive to one of the problems that Ford had overlooked: people. He conceived an airline with no hierarchy, where people managed themselves and performed a variety of tasks.[66] He believed that these new-style workers would approach their tasks with enthusiasm and deliver high-quality service at a low cost. Burr got the low cost, but the anarchic management style simply could not deliver the service, and he faced the same problem as Ford: People would not buy, even though the cost was low.

Incommensurate Thinking

Kuhn has described the nature of the debate between proponents of opposing paradigms: It is no debate at all; it is mere "talking through each other"—what the French call *les dialogues des sourdes,* conversations of the deaf. We have already seen Henry Ford's comments on the world of business as he found it around the turn of the century: the enormous attention given to finance and the disinterest in service and production.[67] Ford's response to this was characteristic: "Business as a mere money-making game was not worth giving much thought to."[68]

Thorstein Veblen, writing at the time of Ford's entry into business, saw very much the same thing: Business leaders—Gould, Rockefeller, and the like—seemed interested only in financial manipulations and had no concept of business as a service to humanity. This was anathema to Ford: "Manufacturing is not buying low and selling high."[69]

This conflict between the paradigm of production and the paradigm of wealth is deep-seated and unbridgeable, regardless of attempts to paper over the differences. They are radically opposed views of the nature of business. One aspect of this difference is shown by the attitude toward dividends. Ford believed that profits belong to the business for continued expansion; they do not belong to the shareholders.[70] This was a radical break with the past and seemed like heresy or madness to the financially oriented business people of Ford's day. It is an interesting irony that latter-day proponents of the wealth paradigm share Ford's view, but for a different reason. Modern financial theory states that profits are more appropriately reinvested in the business, because the business should be able to gain a higher return on the funds than the individual shareholders would. The concept of maximizing shareholder wealth—highly popular now—leads to the idea that the shareholder is better served, through future stock price appreciation, by profit reinvestment than by dividend payout. And the tax laws had cooperated: Dividends were taxable at ordinary income rates; sale of appreciated stock was taxed at the lower capital gains rate.

But this was not the issue in Ford's day—it was simply the issue of production versus wealth, the issue of the purpose of the business. If the business existed to enrich the shareholders, the appropriate policy in those times would be to pay out cash dividends. If the purpose was the ever-growing production of goods, clearly the firm must reinvest its profits in more and more productive capacity.

Ford saw the bankers as his opponents at that time, although virtually all business people had the same viewpoint as the bankers: "They think of a factory as making money, not goods."[71] And the debate still goes on. David Roderick, a contemporary chairman of U.S. Steel, has said, flatly: "The duty of management is to make money. Our primary objective is not to make steel."[72]

Roderick has a defensible position, of course, but the position of Ford is equally defensible and ultimately incommensurate with Roderick's succinct statement of the wealth paradigm. No amount of debate, economic theory, or scholarly proofs can bridge this fundamental gap. We have here two internally coherent views of the purpose of a business—two views whose widely separate basic premises can only lead to accusations of folly, bad faith, or immorality. We have *les dialogues des sourdes,* to be sure.

The Metaphors of Production

The Actors

As we saw in Chapter 10, the production-minded favor the metaphor of a journey but also make significant use of the game, machine, and organism analogies. Let us look at the speech of a few of these actors. Ford, as we have seen, spoke of life (and his business *was* his life) as a journey, not a location. And although he denied that a business was a machine, his actions, and some of his words, belied that statement. In his obsession with production, he created Ford Motor Company as a gigantic goods-producing machine, and his treatment of workers relegated them to the status of interchangeable parts in that great machine.

C.M. Chester, president of the National Association of Manufacturers in 1936, sought "more jobs, greater comfort, more leisure, more security"[73] and wrapped his October 19, 1936, speech in the metaphor of the "Great Highway"—American industry journeying, always forward, along a Great Highway that always improves.

We heard Azzato, speaking in 1985, sound the clarion call of production: "We're not producing to satisfy a sales quota, we're producing to satisfy the customer." Then he evoked the images of a sea voyage: "impending difficulties over the horizon," but he would "remain at the helm."[74]

Stone, a clothing manufacturer, spoke in 1984 of the "adventure"; the business had "traveled a path"; "throughout the journey there was a saga of human effort." And he believed that "our mission is to produce a quality garment that people could afford,"[75] just as Ford saw his mission as a quality motorcar for the masses.

We find Robertson, in a 1946 speech, standing four-square for production—"give the people something they want"—and elaborating on the likeness of business to the great Sequoias: "If the climate becomes adverse, they would die"; and "business must breathe and eat every day of the year."[76]

Others of the production school have added their mite. Sanford said that his purpose was "contributions to the progress of mankind," and he saw his business as a "fragile craft launched upon a stormy sea."[77] We have seen DEC's Olsen comparing of business management to solving a jigsaw puzzle. And the great scientific management theoretician, Gilbreth, stated both the production paradigm and the machine metaphor in the simplest possible terms: "Production is the universal need of all times" and "The best results come when everything is standardized down to the smallest and most insignificant detail."[78]

But Frederick Taylor, the great champion of the paradigm of production and the machine approach to business, expressed it best. We have seen earlier his emotional commitment to the paradigm: "There is hardly any worse crime . . . than failing to bring . . . into the world the products of men and soils."[79]

Taylor taught that management's duty includes the "scientific" selection and development of workers, remarking: "It may seem preposterous, but they are studied just like machines."[80] Taylor also saw some aspects of business as analogous to a game, but to the highly regimented, unspontaneous game of football—"a pretty good piece of scientific management."[81]

The Entailments

We see, then, our production-minded leaders employing the rather disparate metaphors of journey, game, machine, and organism. These quite different figures share a few entailments, particularly the notion of an objective, a mission, the production of something of value: the commercial cargo voyage, the game that ends in benefit to the player, the goods-producing machine, the fruits of the labor of domesticated animals. The metaphors also have quite distinct entailments—entailments that provide different guides to the thoughts and actions of the production-minded.

The journey metaphor, in particular, can powerfully evoke the production paradigm's sense of mission and purpose. The paradigm speaks to the noble purpose of serving mankind; a voyage figure neatly captures this sense of high purpose. The other side of the journey metaphor is, of course, *le voyage sans but*—the journey for the sake of the journey. We can see in Ford's career his shift to this form, away from his early concern for the farmer and ordinary people toward a concern only for production for its own sake— the endlessly accelerating out-put of motorcars.

The journey metaphor also suggests the difficulty of the mission, the peril the business faces, the possibilities of catastrophe, shipwreck. This entire complex of ideas—an overarching purpose, fraught with danger and potential failure—is all contained in the simple journey metaphor. The metaphor can provide a compelling mind-set for the leader of a production-oriented enterprise.

The game metaphor provides another case, at first glance an odd choice for the leader who is concerned with the serious business of production. But the figure captures the intricacies and complexities of a business, especially with references to such complex games as chess, football, even jigsaw puzzles. As only one example, consider the task of scheduling a machine shop, routing any number of different parts and jobs through any number of machine centers. The possible number of routings is immense; it can make chess—or anything the Glassbead players imagined—child's play in comparison. Faced with this constant challenge, a game provides a good analogy for the business leader who must struggle with these critical tasks. But by the same token, other entailments of the game metaphor—fun, pastime, nonserious purpose—can cause the "player" to lose sight of the ultimate objective. These "games" can be quite compelling; the intellectual challenge of solving complex production problems can lead the mind away from the purpose that lies behind the problems—the purpose of producing goods and services for society. The Glassbead game can be a real temptation.

The machine is an especially apt metaphor for a business managed for production. The idea fits neatly and naturally: The entire enterprise—facilities, equipment, people—is readily viewed as one complex engine to pour out goods. The idea carries with it the entailment of predictability—a comforting thought for the manager of such an engine. This entailment has some positive benefits, particularly as a spur to the detailed planning that any business demands. As we have seen, the analogy works well for the routine segments of a business or for a business that is stable and, in fact, predictable. The troubles begin when planning is taken for reality; the inevitable gap between plans and brute facts is highly disturbing to a mind set in the ways of a machine metaphor. But the real difficulty with the metaphor is the guide it provides for management of people. People are seen as interchangeable parts of the great machine; and the abuses of Taylorism follow inexorably from this view of business. Even when management is more benign, machine metaphors help create bureaucracy through the inevitable pressure for rationalization, as Weber pointed out many years ago. The "machine mind" seeks order and predictability and attempts to rationalize—and bureaucratize—every process and every facet of the business.

The organism metaphor avoids some of the injurious attitudes of the machine figure. The business is viewed as a much more complex entity; a degree of ambiguity is recognized. The business has needs; this is seen much more clearly with the organism metaphor than with the machine metaphor. Capital, materials, and people are all viewed as necessities to keep the business in operation; it must be "fed." The manager also recognizes that the "organism" is an entity that has evolved, has adapted to changing circumstances, and cannot be rudely changed. This can lead to good decisions—better in most cases than a machine metaphor would yield—but it can also stymie action by a resignation to the limitations of the business, to a feeling of determinism. Change must be slow and within the limits of the organism's inherent nature. This can be a wise caution, but it also can rule out necessary actions in a crisis.

The organism metaphor is applied by production-oriented managers in terms of a domesticated animal. The business is like a workhorse or a flock of sheep. The organism is cared for, but it is fundamentally exploited for the purpose of production.

So the quite disparate metaphors—voyage, game, machine, and organism—have entailments that can be useful guides for the production-minded but can also limit the leader's actions or steer him in the wrong directions.

Production: Pro and Con

We have learned from Kuhn that it is pointless to analyze or criticize a paradigm in terms of another paradigm; to offer a critique of the paradigm of production from the standpoint of the paradigms of wealth or institution would be bootless. But it is certainly fair to examine this paradigm in terms of its own professed aims: the betterment of mankind's lot.

To deny the production paradigm's successes would be folly. The accomplishments of industrial civilization are self-evident: longer, healthier lives; the freeing of men from drudgery; and the virtual elimination of material deprivations in many societies. Ford and his allies can take great pride in this accomplishment. They have truly performed the corporal works of mercy: feeding the hungry, sheltering the homeless, clothing the naked. No one can say that the production of useful goods has not been an enormous benefit to mankind. The production "machine" has largely delivered the goods.

But there is a fallacy at the heart of the production paradigm— its obsession with production pure and simple, irrespective of the content of that production. Earlier, I quoted Robert Hanson, CEO of Deere and Company, and recorded his evident pride in his work and his company: "We're in the business of feeding the world." But Hanson goes on and illustrates the paradox of the production paradigm: "I wouldn't get that feeling if I were marketing bubble gum or soda pop."[82]

But people *are* marketing bubble gum and soda pop and a myriad of goods and services that would be difficult to classify as essential or even beneficial, difficult to place under the rubric of the corporal works of mercy. The measure of success for all economies throughout the world has become gross national product, and this statistic—the banner for all industrial societies—makes no distinction among tractors, automobiles, health services, and bubble gum and soda pop (or worse). This is the salient of our industrial society that Galbraith has attacked in *The Affluent Society:*

> We are curiously unreasonable in the distinctions we make between different kinds of goods and services. We view production of some of the most frivolous goods with pride.[83]

This issue has crept up on us. The basic economic theories of Adam Smith, John Stuart Mill, and even John Maynard Keynes were developed at a time when production meant, largely, production of utilitarian goods—more food for the hungry, more houses for the homeless, more clothing for the cold. Today, according to Galbraith:

> Increased output satisfies the craving for more elegant autos, more erotic clothing, more elaborate entertainment—indeed for the entire modern range of sensuous, edifying and lethal desires.[84]

There are dangers in this obsession with production, especially with the production of ultimately frivolous things. Production of basic, utilitarian goods has been enormously liberating for mankind, and freedom from want has been achieved in most industrialized societies. But as our needs are satisfied, as we attain that basic freedom, we run the risk of enslavement to consumerism.

Galbraith bores in on this aspect of consumer society—the fact that wants are no longer plain physical imperatives but rather are created by the producers of goods. If the wants are contrived by the process of production that satisfies them, then:

> The whole case for the urgency of production based on the urgency of wants, falls to the ground. One cannot defend production as satisfying wants if that production creates the wants.[85]

This brings into question the whole logic of the paradigm of production. The paradigm purports to serve a noble purpose: providing for the needs of mankind. But if the needs are not true needs—if, in fact (which appears to be the case), the needs are actually created by the agents of production through advertising and promotion—the whole enterprise becomes suspect. What is really the point of this production?

Galbraith illustrates this in a passage that shows the keenness of his analysis as well as his literary gift:

> Were it so that a man in arising each morning was assailed by demons which instilled in him a passion sometimes for silk shirts

. . . sometimes for chamber pots . . . there would be every reason to applaud the efforts to find the goods, however odd, that
quenched the flame. But should it be that his passion was the
result of his having cultivated the demons, and . . . his effort to
allay it stirred the demons to ever greater and greater efforts,
there would be a question as to how rational was his solution.
. . . He might wonder if the solution lay with more goods or
fewer demons.[86]

There is much yet to be done through the paradigm of production. Millions of our fellow creatures lack the necessities of life that
production can bring, and the elevation of living standards remains
a noble—and unattained—goal in most parts of the world. But
Galbraith's critique must be considered. Our passion for silk shirts
and chamber pots is an artificial passion, one we generate for ourselves by the production sector's advertising, which fuels these spurious needs. Galbraith's solution—higher taxation, which will allow
government to decide the appropriate content of production—will
not appeal to many in contemporary society. But if his solution is
questionable, his critique is valid. There is something ignoble, even
obscene, about the spectacle of people in want while others revel
in surfeit of frivolous consumer goods. Viewed in its own terms—
the production paradigm's goal of benefiting mankind—it is ar-
guable that the paradigm has gone astray in modern industrial
civilization.

There is another result of the paradigm that further calls its
own objective into question: the problem of environmental damage. If the goal is to better mankind, wholesale destruction of the
environment, even if short-term benefits are realized, is a bad bargain. Unfortunately, this process seems to be well under way. The
Worldwatch Institute recently published a report, "State of the
World 1987".[87] The outlook is bleak. The pressures of population
growth and economic expansion are starting to exceed the ability
of the earth's natural systems to sustain economic activity.

The Worldwatch Institute is concerned that we are approaching
thresholds of use of air, water, land, and forests that will cause
permanent damage. Already, food and fuel production is declining
in many parts of the world because of contamination of the atmosphere, climatic change, and the extinction of plant and animal

species. We are beginning to face a cruel paradox: Efforts to increase economic growth and thereby raise living standards are, in some cases, actually lowering standards through pollution and the extinction of needed species.

Again, in terms of its own purposes—the improvement of man's lot—the paradigm of production can be questioned. The headlong pursuit of economic growth is beginning to strike the outer limits of the planet's ability to sustain that growth. This is an exceptionally difficult problem. Societies that see their children die young, their young people without work, their very society's fabric rent by poverty and want are unlikely to heed the call for environmental limits. But the consequences, in the not too long run, are probably catastrophic; the paradigm of production may prove our undoing. When we consider what we may be doing to satisfy consumer appetites, we should recall Byron's comment on Buonaparte:

"To think that God's fair world hath been
the footstool of a thing so mean."[88]

The problems with the paradigm can be highlighted by reviewing the leader roles that some of the paradigm's metaphors suggest. For the voyage we have, of course, the captain of the ship. And a ship's captain, since the dawn of time, has had complete, unquestioned authority over the crew. In no other sphere can we picture one human being having so much control over the lives and fortunes of his fellows. Ford, the paradigm's exemplar, acted in every way in this manner. He was the complete autocrat—firing people for petty offenses, or no offense at all; bullying his senior people; and making all the important decisions with total arbitrariness. And as I have noted, the later Ford represents, as well, the leader of a *voyage sans but;* after his initial successes, he seemed to lose sight entirely of societal benefit in his absorption with production—more and more production.

Ford also became the quintessential machine designer, the creator of his business/machine who was omniscient in his sphere. It seems clear that Ford believed, in time, that he had created not just Ford Motor Company but the entire automobile industry. (In fairness, he largely had.) He set the standards for suppliers as well as competitors. His hubris became apparent, however, when he acted as though he had created the automobile *buyer* as well. His own role was to produce; the consumers' role was to buy. As we have seen, when his distributors rebelled against his forcing cars on them, he remarked that the only problem he could (still) see was that Ford Motor could not produce enough.

Summary

- The paradigm of production had no adherents in the period 1770–1905 but became the majority view in the period 1905–45, largely thorough Henry Ford's influence and example. Production lost favor in the postwar period but is now the most popular, although not a majority, view (41 percent).

- Production as a goal for business is deeply rooted in economic theory. Economists from Smith and Mill, through Marx and Veblen, on up to Galbraith in our day agree on the primacy of production: Business exists to produce goods and services for mankind.

- Henry Ford is the exemplar of the paradigm—the man whose work inspired business people to focus their attention on production, particularly mass production.

- As Kuhn predicted, a new paradigm produces puzzles. The main puzzle that Ford found, and solved, was the creation of mass consumption to fuel mass production. Price was the answer there, which led to further puzzles on costs. Ford's overall answer involved the discovery of the downward-sloping demand curve (more buy at lower prices) and the experience curve (as more is produced, costs are lowered).

- Kuhn also predicted that a new paradigm leaves some old problems behind—that is, ignores them. For Ford, these were the problems of the worker and his aspirations and the problem of distribution—the need to keep people buying a standard, low-price car. His failure to even recognize these as problems nearly finished Ford Motor Company.

- The paradigm is best articulated in the forms of journey, game, machine, and organism metaphors. Apt entailments include a goal, complexity, intellectual challenge, predictability, and exploitation.

- The paradigm of production has brought us all the blessings of material civilization. But there are serious problems with this paradigm: There is no distinction between useful and frivolous goods; and environmental damage from excess production is a possibility, even a reality.

- The leader roles suggested by the metaphors contribute to the paradigm's problems—an autocratic ship's captain on a *voyage sans but,* or an omniscient machine designer who tries to bend the world to his own purpose: more and more production.

12
Treasures upon Earth

The Paradigm of Wealth

Lay not up for yourselves treasures upon earth, where moth doth corrupt, and where thieves break through and steal; for where your treasure is, there will your heart be also.

—Matthew[1]

Background

That a business exists to produce wealth is a commonplace, a statement that would appear to brook no contradiction. The pronouncement "We are in business to make money" has ended many debates. The purpose seems so obviously true, such a direct appeal to common sense, that it was virtually the conventional wisdom in the past; it still remains so for many today. (The term *cash cow* finds few detractors.) But as we have seen in the preceding chapter, there is a serious body of theoretical and practical opinion that speaks against this paradigm. It has not always been so; in the early days of industrialization, no one ever held a contrary opinion: The purpose of business *was* to produce wealth. It was taken as a matter of immutable law, akin to a revelation of science or theology. There have been, and still are, quibbles about the distribution of the wealth, of course. Some hold to the view that the purpose is personal wealth; others believe that the value of the firm is the ultimate objective; and some theoreticians see the final goal as the increase in the wealth of a society or nation. But wealth it is that all seem to seek, and in the fine tradition of Kuhn's "incommensurate thinking," the devotees of wealth scorn any who hold to another opinion about the purpose for a business.

Alfred Sloan, whom I will present as the exemplar of this paradigm, stated it very succinctly: "It is the strategic aim of a business to earn a return on capital."[2] Nothing ambivalent about that. All of Sloan's considerable talent and energy were aimed at that single objective. As a practical man of business, this basic goal served as the lodestone for Sloan's years of effort at General Motors; his example inspired many others in business. But let us look now at the theoretical foundations of this paradigm.

We speak, of course, of the profit motive—the very foundation of capitalism. The idea is fundamental to Western industrial civilization and appears to have great explanatory powers for human behavior. Just as the Freudians have taught modern man to look for basic motivation in our sexuality, Marxists have pointed us elsewhere—to the personal or class economic motives that underlie behavior. It is curious that Marx's work, generally considered a tissue of lies by capitalist thinkers, has nonetheless had its root concept embedded in modern man's thinking: Economic motives are dominant.

We are so inured to this way of thinking that we can forget that the profit motive, as an all-pervasive motivator, is really a modern invention, like printing or electricity. Even today, a large portion of the world's population finds the idea curious, even distasteful. Even in the West, social sanction for the idea of profit came quite late in our history. In the Middle Ages, the Church could still teach that no Christian should be a merchant; the ideas of living a worthy life and striving for wealth were simply incompatible. Early capitalists were hardly the pillars of society; more accurately, they were outcasts. This chapter's epigraph was taken quite literally in the medieval world.[3] And Thomas Aquinas said:

> [Commerce] is justly condemned, for it encourages the passion for money. . . . Therefore, commerce, considered in itself, has something shameful about it.[4]

But just as religion provided sanctions against profit-making in the time before industrialization, as the world turned, religious thought became a secure foundation for these same practices. Max Weber has traced the transmutation of the Protestant sects' genuine religious feeling into the drive for worldly success. As we have seen, Weber bases early capitalistic behavior on the concept of a man's duty. The intense piety and devotion of the Calvinists were combined with an extraordinary capitalistic business sense; a fanatical devotion to business was accepted as the proper channel for fulfilling one's duty in this world.[5]

But to link the modern spirit of capitalism to the religious feeling of the Protestant Reformation is really to misread Weber. In his analysis, the true spirit of capitalism arose only when the religious feeling had waned, leaving behind only the strong compulsion toward a duty or calling in life. Weber puts forward the figure of Benjamin Franklin as the exemplar of this new spirit; in Franklin, he sees personified:

> The peculiarity of this philosophy of avarice . . . and above all the idea of a duty of the individual toward the increase of his capital, which is assumed as an end in itself.[6]

Here, we no longer have the Calvinist's joyless pursuit of worldly success as confirmation of his predestination; simply the increase of a man's capital was his sole purpose for being.

Adam Smith provided a social purpose for the capitalist's accumulation of wealth. In Smith's well-known analysis, the aggregation of the individually selfish activities of Franklin and his type produced a great benefit to society—nothing less than the "wealth of nations." Smith's market system is a beautifully intricate game in which society benefits when each individual strives to do what is to his best financial advantage.[7] A great, automatic balance is achieved as each pursues his own interests in a freely competitive environment. The goods that society wants, in the quantities desired, and at the prices society is prepared to pay are provided by this wonderful market mechanism, based at bottom on individual self-interest. Smith's famous aphorism gets to the root of the matter:

> It is not from the benevolence of the butcher, the brewer or the baker that we expect our dinner, but from their regard to their own interest.[8]

Here we have individual profit as the mainspring that drives an entire society toward a better material existence. Smith extended his analysis from this basic assumption of self-interest. There are three factors of production: land, labor, and capital. Each factor must receive its financial reward for the factors to be employed in production, so we have rent, wages, and profit. Smith highlights the role of profit as the compensation to the capitalist for his strategic role in combining the factors of production.[9] The role of profit, then, is seen as the critical underpinning of our entire industrial civilization. Without the capitalist's willingness to risk his capital and his energy, land lies fallow, men are without work, and production simply does not take place. Alfred Sloan's comment that a return on capital is the strategic aim of any business is right in the mainstream of Smith's view of industrial society.

Seventy-five years after Smith, and after the substantial industrialization of England and the attendant social disruption, Marx and Engels launched their critique of Smith and capitalism. They saw the need for self-interest in an industrial society but believed in a future where it would be unnecessary. To Marx and Engels, the technical base, as well as the utility, of capitalism was industrial production—production that logically should be highly organized and disciplined. Over this base, capitalism had reared an incompatible superstructure—the institution of private property. Private property, by its nature, is highly individualistic, disorganized if you will, in comparison to the highly organized nature, real or desired, of industrial production.[10] The Marxist critique claimed that the incompatibility of capitalism's base and its superstructure would ultimately prove fatal. Smith saw an intricate system, the Brownian movement of individual self-interests somehow organizing themselves into a complex machine—industrial production. The Marxists saw the fate of capitalism written in an irrational marriage of private greed and public purpose. History has proved neither side really right. Unchecked competition and unfettered avarice led to such social evils that even conservative governments saw the need for regulation of total self-interest. By the same token, Marxist societies have nowhere solved the puzzle of beneficial production nearly as well as the capitalists—even capitalism in the modern, governmentally controlled form. If the modern capitalists, the heirs of Smith, have bested the heirs of Marx, it must be said that the profit motive, even constrained by society's overall concerns, has been the prime mover.

But the debate on the purposes of business goes on into the present day, as we saw from the proponents of the production paradigm. Those proponents, at bottom, have questioned the social utility of business, the contribution of business to society. Smith had ready a basic answer: Self-interested capitalists supply our dinner. But others continue to raise the issue—the fundamental question of a business' social role. The Nobel Prize–winning economist Milton Friedman has given his answer in his own turn: "The only social responsibility of business is to increase its profits."[11]

Milton Friedman is a highly conservative, free-market econo mist—a lineal heir of Adam Smith. Curiously, John Kenneth Galbraith, a man of the Left, agrees with Friedman. Galbraith, though, comes to his conclusion from a different view of business purpose. As we have seen, he proposes not unalloyed production—the production of any goods no matter how useless—but rather the production of necessities. Rather than force business to produce these, Galbraith believes in working the demand side. High personal taxation will take funds from consumers so they can buy only real necessities. High taxes on business—which is why Galbraith sees their role as increasing profits—will permit society as a whole (in the rather dubious form of the federal government) to invest in socially useful things: infrastructure, foreign aid, support for the arts, and so forth. Galbraith believes, then, that business is the wrong actor to fund these "socially useful" expenditures and that business should, as Friedman says, concentrate on its only socially useful role—to increase profits so that they can be the cash cow for society's needs.

Galbraith's view of capitalism—a capitalism constrained by regulations and heavily taxed for social purposes—is a long way from Adam Smith's, or even Milton Friedman's, ideas. But they share the fundamental paradigm of wealth: Business exists only to generate profit, wealth. And this view is enshrined in modern financial theory. The entire, very considerable theory of corporate finance is based on the notion of maximizing shareholder wealth. This is the root purpose of a business that underlies the dazzling intellectual edifice of modern financial thinking. The theories of Modigliani and Miller on the arcana of dividend policy and debt structure, the net present value approach to capital budgeting—all are based on the paradigm of wealth: Maximize the owners' (share-holders') wealth. Modern business, at least in its financial aspects, is lashed tightly to the mast of the wealth paradigm.

Smith's invisible hand and modern financial theory are mar-velous creations of the mind, and their intellectual elegance and practical utility are compelling. But a certain uneasiness persists. Is self-interest a worthy, even a secure basis for our civilization? Were the medieval churchmen so far wrong in condemning this para-digm? Put any character you wish on it, we are fundamentally talking about avarice—one of the seven deadly sins. Although there may be a utilitarian reason to accept this—and there must be, as we look at the triumphs of capitalism all around us—is there a moral sanction for capitalism?

George Gilder has entered the lists on this issue, as we saw earlier. He rejects the notion that capitalism is morally vacant—that it is based on the crudest forms of greed and atomic self-interest. Rather, Gilder finds the moral center of capitalism in the Christian virtue of giving—charity.[12] The capitalist *gives* his capital to society, risks his wealth for the benefit of all. Gilder cannot accept the utilitarian justification for capitalism:

> Smith and his followers believe that the wealth of nations springs from a kind of Faustian pact, a deal with the devil through which humans gain wealth by giving in to greed and avarice.[13]

It is a matter of psychological analysis, a parlous exercise, to accept either Smith's view or Gilder's. Are the butcher, the brewer, and the baker moved by self-interest or by an altruistic spirit, the spirit of giving? In any event, we must still count Gilder among the proponents of the wealth paradigm: The only way the capitalist can continue to give, if that is his function, is to make a return on his capital, precisely as Sloan has said. Gilder enters into the non-economic realm of human motivation, just as Weber had done in postulating the call of duty as the mainspring for the capitalist. But economic theory, from Adam Smith to the present—regardless of the actors' motivations—seems to be based largely on the necessity for the profit motive. Profit is the engine that drives the economic machine; a business must earn a profit to continue to produce, continue to exist, and continue to invest in further productive capacity. That seems unarguable. If we confine ourselves to the economic realm, the paradigm of wealth must be seriously considered.

The Actors

As we have seen, all actors in the early days took wealth as the principal purpose of their business. We have followed Josiah Wedgwood as he struggled with this ultimately ignoble (in his view) purpose for his efforts. But Wedgwood finally came down on the side of wealth; his letters to his partner, Bentley, show his ultimate conviction that he meant to make money—a great deal of money—from his pottery business.[14] Once he had overcome his doubts, Wedgwood seemed very comfortable with the image of his business as a farm from which he expected to get "ample recompense."[15]

Another early figure, Robert Owen, demonstrated by his later philanthropy that he was a good friend to the laboring class. But in his working life, Owen subscribed to the prevalent view that business was really wealth production; he stated flatly that the objective was "to produce the greatest pecuniary gain to the proprietors."[16]

There seemed to be little doubt about purposes in the minds or actions of the later nineteenth-century businessman. Andrew Carnegie's greed was legendary, and it would be easy to attribute his later generosity to justifiable guilt feelings. But while he was in business, "the end was money and yet more money,"[17] and Carnegie piled up a hoard of staggering dimensions. The speculator Jay Gould, in his turn, amassed a very large fortune. I have shown earlier that Gould was a master gamesman and that his compulsion went beyond mere greed to fascination with the great game of business and finance. But the counters in Gould's game were dollar bills; his objective in any enterprise or any deal was an increase in his personal fortune. He was not the type to play for matchsticks. Further, the idea of benefiting society by producing goods or by building an institution that would survive his life would have been a strange notion, indeed, to Jay Gould. The name of the game was money.

Frederick Taylor, as I have noted, was fundamentally interested in production and took that paradigm as almost a sacred trust. But another of the early theorists of scientific management, Henry Towne, saw the application of these techniques as aimed more correctly at the wealth of the firm. In an article entitled, "The Engineer as Economist" (1866), Towne stated:

> The organization of productive labor must be directed and controlled by those with economics in mind. . . . Dollars and cents are the keys.[18]

It is interesting to compare Towne and Taylor. Both espoused scientific management, and both employed the mechanical metaphor for a business. It can be seen that both the technique and the metaphor were just tools in their hands, tools that could be applied to fundamentally diverse purposes. The machine, constructed and tuned by scientific management, could be Taylor's engine for progress through production or a money machine, as Towne believed.

As we move into the twentieth century, we can see the impact of Henry Ford, as more and more business leaders bought into Ford's production techniques and even into his fundamental paradigm of production. Even those who held to the wealth paradigm often made the obligatory obeisance to the key role of production. In 1941, Major Nichol, general manager of IBM, showed his allegiance to the wealth paradigm but recognized the necessity for production, at least the necessity for production as a means to attain wealth: "The only way we can create wealth is by keeping people buying—by production and thus selling that production."[19] I believe that Nichol shows the influence of Alfred Sloan, as I will detail later, but it is instructive to note that the status of production, here, has been relegated from Ford's ultimate end to that of a means. Ford had convinced most observers that production was essential, but perhaps not as an end in itself, as he believed.

Contemporary business leaders have also subscribed to the wealth paradigm, if not in the crude, grasping form of Gould or

Carnegie. In his autobiography, Harold Geneen of ITT has provided a subtle and illuminating picture of business management. We have seen some of his metaphorical expressions—cooking on a wood stove and business as a "fluid, ever changing, living thing."[20] Geneen also wrote:

> To my mind, the process of conducting business is fascinating, demanding and creative—worthy of being classed with the high arts.[21]

This is a far cry from a crude mechanical view of the business money machine or the predations of Andrew Carnegie. But at the end of the day, Geneen remained convinced that however great an art it was, the practice of business was aimed at a simple end—the bottom line: "It was the end to which all my efforts at ITT would be directed."[22]

Lee Iacocca is the best-known modern proponent of the wealth paradigm. For Iacocca, the purpose seemed to be not even corporate wealth, but simply his personal fortune. We find none of the subtlety or artistry of Geneen, but rather a throwback to the days of Gould and Carnegie. Iaccoca is candid about his motives. In his youth, his "philosophy" was, "I want to be a millionaire."[23] Even as a mature man, the head of car and truck marketing for Ford Motor Company, Iaccoca recalls, "It wasn't prestige or power I wanted, it was money."[24] Or look at this statement and compare it to old Henry Ford and his belief in machinery as the new Messiah—a boon to mankind: "I began to develop my own ideas about doing a car that would be popular and make us a ton of money."[25]

Iacocca at least has the virtue of clarity of thinking. His purpose—wealth—could not escape anyone. Other moderns have struggled, though, as Nichol did, with the power of the production paradigm and its hold on business consciousness. In a recent speech, Richard Ferris, former chairman of Allegis (United Airlines), tried to merge the paradigms, seeking to show that the problem is to balance the need for profit and the need to serve society: "I believe that business' first priority is producing a product that people need, doing it ethically and making a profit."[26]

That he had proposed three quite distinct and possibly incompatible goals as "first priority" probably escaped Mr. Ferris. He is right, of course, about the difficulty in striking a balance, but being steadfastly in favor of service and profit at the same time and with the same primacy is not a matter of balance; it is an attempt to square the circle. Perhaps Ferris is an example of F. Scott Fitzgerald's idea of a first-class intellect—one who can hold two mutually exclusive ideas in his mind at the same time.

The last actor to get our attention is David Roderick, chairman of U.S. Steel. For Roderick, there is no flirting with social utility or any other purpose of a business. We have seen his statement: "The duty of management is to make money. Our primary objective is not to make steel."[27] This is a flat rejection of the paradigm of production. There are no echoes, here, of service to mankind or any other purpose. Roderick is on the side of Milton Friedman: His job is to make money. His phrasing, however, is curious. The statement that the "primary objective is not to make steel" could be awkward English, or it could betray his intentions—that is, to stop making steel. In any event, we have a candid admission that the days (if they ever existed) of steel making as a fundamental service to humanity lie far behind us. The corporation called U.S. Steel is in the business of making money.

Roderick's four-square devotion to the wealth paradigm has been tested in recent times—by the corporate raiders. Roderick joined other CEOs in recent congressional testimony, condemning the raiders for their attempts to gain control of his and other businesses.[28] Curious. If U.S. Steel is nothing more than some real assets that exist to make money, it is fair game. Anyone who thinks he can make more money than Roderick with those assets should surely have the opportunity to bid up the shares in the equity market and gain control of the assets. But if U.S. Steel's role is to make steel—if that is the fundamental purpose—society had better take a hard look before those *steel*-producing assets are traded about by speculators.

Sloan the Exemplar

Alfred Sloan was Henry Ford's greatest student and also his greatest critic. He learned the critical importance of mass production from Ford, absorbed his techniques, but turned Ford's example on its head: Production was not an end in itself but a means toward the increase of shareholder wealth. Born in New Haven in 1875, Sloan was a Connecticut Yankee, an MIT engineer, and one of America's truly great industrialists.

After a few engineering jobs, Sloan helped form the Hyatt Roller Bearing Company and found himself a supplier to the young automobile industry. The pressures of that business—the demand for high precision, interchangeable parts, and huge volumes—made a lasting impression on Sloan. This, of course, was the business that Henry Ford had transformed into the epitome of mass production. Sloan learned that the success of a supplier hinged on high quality, ever-decreasing price, and ever-increasing volume. The Hyatt Company eventually sold out to United Motors, and Sloan became a major stockholder and the company's president. When United merged with General Motors, Sloan again held a major block of stock; his initial role was vice-president and director, and he moved into the presidency of General Motors in 1923. Sloan's status of shareholder, as well as manager, was critical to his thinking. He always viewed his activities and his interests from the shareholder viewpoint; it is not surprising that he believed that a business's aim must be a return on capital.[29] (The title of one of his books, *Adventures of a White Collar Man*, is disingenuous; Sloan was no more the hired man than Andrew Carnegie or Jay Gould).

Sloan's constant theme was return on capital, and he attempted to apply this principle in every aspect of the business. He made a system out of the motto, "Every dollar must make a showing for itself."[30] The system had two important features: rigorous cost accounting and decentralization. The idea of decentralization, one of Sloan's lasting contributions, stemmed from his basic principle— return on capital: Put more managers in profit-and-loss jobs, and the overall earnings of the corporation will be maximized.

As I have noted, Sloan adopted almost all of Henry Ford's techniques and ideas—precision manufacturing to ensure interchangeability of parts, high-volume output to drive down unit costs, the increased market that lower price would bring—all the means that Ford had employed to transform the automobile industry.

Sloan's quarrel with Ford, though was on the purpose for all this. In a 1927 speech, he was explicitly critical of Ford's intent:

> The sole idea was to make as many cars as the factory could possibly turn out and then the sales department would force the dealers to take and pay for the cars, irrespective of economic justification. . . . That certainly was wrong.[31]

It was not that Sloan was not a true believer in mass production. His credo, constantly repeated, could have been Henry Ford's: "More goods for more people in more places."[32] But again, recall that Sloan viewed all of this from the shareholder's perspective; more goods for more people meant more revenue and earnings, and that was the ultimate objective—the return on capital.

With Sloan at the helm, General Motors was consistently successful, passing Ford in both revenues and earnings. This obsession with profitability was tested in the Great Depression, when General Motors' sales dropped precipitously: 1929—$1.5 billion; 1930—$983 million; 1931—$809 million; 1932—$437 million.[33] It seems impossible, but even with revenue falling off by 75 percent in four years, General Motors made a profit every year. The human costs were, of course, severe. A great number of people were furloughed, and those remaining suffered salary reductions of 20 and 30 percent. But GM made a profit.

Sloan became a cheerleader for American industry during the Depression—preaching progress, competition, and, of course, more goods for more people. But those were the words, the words that Ford had sunk deeply into the American consciousness—the paradigm of production, the new Messiah. Sloan's deeds were more where his heart was; production dropped by 75 percent, people lost their livelihoods or worked for less, but GM made a profit. Sloan had promised no less—in words that anticipated David Roderick: "The primary objective of the corporation . . . was to make money, not just to make motor cars."[34]

Sloan's success was a beacon for American and, eventually, world business leaders. His approach was in many ways a refinement of scientific management; his contribution was the application of rigorous techniques to the general management function.

Taylor and his disciples had focused mainly on the jobs of mid-management—those struggling with recalcitrant workers or complex machine processes. Sloan brought an order and a rigor to top management—those who must deal with finance, marketing, and profitability, as well as operational questions. As he put it:

> An essential aspect of our management philosophy is a factual approach to business judgement. The final act of business judgement is intuitive, but the big work is finding and acknowledging the facts.[35]

His criticism of Ford lay precisely in this realm; Sloan thought that Ford had injected his genius as a subjective factor into the company without the discipline of management by method and objective fact.[36] Sloan's way won out, both in the relative success of General Motors and Ford Motor Company and in the example to others. Sloan's approach became (for a time) the distinctively American way of doing business. For example, Harold Geneen's autobiography shows him to be Sloan's heir; irrefutable facts were Geneen's constant demand. (And, of course, Geneen followed Sloan as an advocate of the wealth paradigm.)

For a variety of reasons, not least its untouched institutions and productive capacity, American industry stood astride the industrial world after World War II. In that period, the management techniques of Sloan also were widely embraced in the United States, and those techniques were given a great deal of credit for U.S. success. The French thinker Servan-Schreiber published *The American Challenge,* warning Europeans either to copy American management practices or face U.S. takeover of their markets. The practices that Servan-Schreiber praised—rational management, management by analysis and "facts"—were those that Sloan had introduced at General Motors.

It is nostalgic to remember that American management practices were once the envy of others; we are so accustomed now to criticism of American management and adulation for the Japanese. But we did, in fact, ride high in the 1950s and 1960s, in part because of our favored geopolitical position, but certainly in part because of our methods—Sloan's methods.

Kuhn and Sloan

We have seen Sloan as the exemplar of the wealth paradigm. Taking the side of the shareholders—the people who had invested their funds—he stressed return on capital as the strategic aim of a corporation. His success was almost beyond belief; he bested Henry Ford at the game Ford had invented and made General Motors the largest industrial corporation in the world. An exemplar, indeed.

Let us look, using Kuhn's terms, at the puzzles that confronted Sloan as he worked through the paradigm of wealth, and at the problems that he left behind. First, the main puzzle was how to compete with Ford, how to find a strategy that could be successful against such a formidable force in the automobile industry. Sloan recognized the strength of Ford's position and first determined that Ford could not be touched by anyone who tried to compete on that ground.

But Sloan had other ideas, and he picked up on the problem Ford had left behind—distribution, sales. Sloan could have been reading Michael Porter, the Harvard strategist, sixty years before Porter wrote. The strategy of Sloan can be seen as brilliant exploitation of Porter's basic principles—the idea that all corporate strategies can be reduced to three fundamental approaches: low cost, differentiation, or focus.[37] (There is more than one way to skin this cat, but no more than three.)

A cost leadership position in an industry can be attained by a variety of means, including high market share, favorable access to raw materials, or state-of-the-art manufacturing. In fact, Henry Ford used all three: market share (through low cost and price, the strategy doubling back on and reenforcing itself); the River Rouge plant, which gave Ford his coke and steel; and Ford's obsession with process technology.

The differentiation strategy is entirely different; a company creates something that is perceived by the market to be unique and valuable and thus worthy of a premium price. There are many ways this can be accomplished, such as high-quality image, technology, features, customer service, and the like. The third generic strategy, focus, is the establishment of a niche market—a relatively small group of buyers or a restricted product line. Within that niche, which becomes a market unto itself, the firm then can, and must, apply either a low-cost or a differentiation strategy.

Sloan seemed to grasp these fundamentals instinctively. It was clear that Ford had seized the high ground in the industry with his cost leadership approach. Sloan's basic problem in achieving a profitable business was, simply, Ford: "No one had figured out how to compete with [him]."[38] Sloan's solution was a highly sophisticated application of Porter's ideas—before Porter was born. Sloan formulated an approach that consisted of a *series* of niche markets—a grouping of buyer preferences that ran from the low end (the Ford market) to the high end (the luxury cars). In each sector, or niche, Sloan adopted the strategy that could win. Against Ford, the cost and price leader, he chose the differentiation strategy at the low end, distinguishing his somewhat higher priced cars by styling. At the high end, General Motors could leverage its *total* volume (all lines), by using a number of common parts, and could compete as a cost leader in the luxury car market. Further, by keeping a family resemblance in the styling, General Motors could build long-term customer loyalty by showing buyers an upwardly mobile path from car purchase to car purchase, but all within the General Motors line—from Chevrolet for the young family of modest means to the Cadillac as the ultimate symbol of worldly success. Sloan had found a way—superior styling—to compete with Ford at the low end and had used Ford's own technique—high volume and common parts—to go one better and compete successfully at the higher ends. Brilliant.

The key to Sloan's differentiation strategy was, in his word, quality, but it really amounted to styling. This was essentially the approach Iacocca took years later at Ford Motor Company when he conceived the Mustang, a program he based on a car with great styling at a reasonable price.[39] (Incidentally, this was the car that Iacocca thought would make "a ton of money." It did.) Iacocca paid his homage to Sloan, calling him the greatest genius that the automobile industry had ever produced, tacitly conceding that his own company's founder was not in Sloan's class.[40] The lesson that Iacocca learned was Sloan's lesson. The American buying public wanted more from a car than transportation, old Henry's belief to the contrary. The public wanted an *experience*, a car whose styling had emotional appeal. The early Mustang ads included a jingle: "Only Mustang makes you happy." The goal of human existence— yours for under $4,000!

Going back to Sloan and his strategy—so far, so good. He had a broad product line, a series of niche markets, that could compete in one sector on quality (styling) and in another on price. But Sloan again learned from Ford's failures: Distribution was a continuing problem. How could people be induced to buy, especially when the used car market offered such an inexpensive alternative? As Sloan saw it, GM's "survival depended on winning the favor of buyers of new cars each year."[41] Sloan's solution, inspired by the success of his styling innovations, was a masterstroke: the annual model change. The way to make a car owner dissatisfied with his perfectly functional car was simply to introduce a new model, with new features and new styling—something (apparently) better. In a short time, General Motors had made a national habit of the desire for annual model changes.[42]

Sloan's strategy worked, worked marvelously. By 1930, Ford had lost the industry leadership with his concept of a low-priced, static product. Sloan had transformed the industry from Ford's "mass" market to a "mass/class" market—an ingenious combination of Ford's way and the original luxury-car, low-volume automobile business.[43] By adopting Ford's mass production techniques, he had found the way to produce "luxury" cars at mass production costs. He had differentiated General Motors through styling and had established the company in a series of profitable niches. Sloan solved the problem that Ford left behind—distribution—and he carried all before him.

But in solving the puzzle, Sloan, in his turn, left some problems behind. His formula for success contained the seeds of General Motor's subsequent difficulties. At bottom, the General Motors strategy was based on styling as the differentiator and as the means to drive the annual model change. As time went by, the styling became more and more forced—after all, there is *some* limit to what a motorcar can look like. Styling became the mainspring of the business, and the world marveled as General Motors (and its competitors, in time) twisted the cars' form into such absurdities as the tail fins.

The question of the car's basic utility seemed to have been forgotten; quality—in terms of the vehicle's maintainability and functionality—became a low priority, and gas mileage was neglected as R&D expenditures concentrated on styling issues.

The bubble burst in the 1960s with the invasion of the Volkswagen—ugly, almost *anti*-styled, but functional, a good bargain for the price, highly reliable, serviceable, and economical to run. The Japanese quickly learned the lesson and produced cars of high quality and low gas mileage. They followed up their successes with cars of clean, attractive styling, and General Motors began to lose the war.

In short, Sloan's solution to the puzzle—his brilliant differentiation and niche strategy—at last had deteriorated in the hands of his successors. (He retired in 1956.) The empty husk of that strategy—the mania for trivial and bizarre styling changes to drive the annual model change—eventually failed General Motors. The company became one of Galbraith's bad examples—an example of industrial production of frivolous goods, fueled by the demons of advertising.

The Metaphors of Wealth

The Actors

The most widely used metaphors for the wealth-seekers are the game and the organism. Andrew Carnegie, whose end was "money and yet more money,"[44] said it all: "Business is the greatest game in the world."[45] And Jay Gould echoed this feeling, regarding the Erie Railroad as his "plaything."[46]

We have seen Lee Iacocca, the man whose objective was to "make a ton of money," employing numerous sport analogies: football (the Lombardi admirer), baseball, track, boxing. The more cerebral Harold Geneen, whose energies were focused on the corporate bottom line, in his turn resorted to game analogies: ITT was "a team" that "huddled"and needed "new players" and a "game plan."

Both Iacocca and Geneen favored the organism idea as well.

Geneen thought of his business as a "fluid, ever changing, living thing."[47] Iacocca's imagery was more pathological. He spoke of "Chrysler's brush with death";[48] its "bleeding, hemorrhaging"[49] and its "cancer";[50] and the need for "survival, radical surgery, triage."[51] He wrote to the *Wall Street Journal*, complaining that their editorials proposed that "the patient, not yet restored to full health, should be put to death."[52] And Iacocca used perhaps the perfect organic metaphor for a wealth seeker: "In the 60's and 70's, the car industry was like a golden goose."[53]

We have already noted other wealth-seekers and their attachment to the organic metaphor: Wedgwood—the business as his mistress;[54] Anderson—his company "an entity deeper and broader than any of its constituent parts."[55] And our exemplar for the paradigm, the man who defined the objective of a corporation as return on capital—Alfred Sloan—referred to "the evolution of the enterprise";[56] "survival, respond or die";[57] and "growth, essential to the good health of the enterprise."[58]

The Entailments

The game and organism metaphors share a number of entailments that are important to the wealth paradigm: a goal or purpose; profit production (Iacocca's "golden goose," Carnegie's "greatest game"); a gamble, an unpredictable entity; and competition (game opponents and Darwinian competitors).

The game is, all in all, an excellent metaphor for a wealth-producing business. It captures the notion of risk and uncertainty as well as the idea of financial reward (the games cited are mainly professional sports). The idea of a nonserious purpose—fun, in short—is also contained within the game metaphor. The idea of business as a pastime is clearly pernicious but not inappropriate for a wealth-seeker. The game also implies the ideas of winning and losing—ideas that are foremost in the minds of a wealth-seeker, however inappropriate they may be to the real processes of business.

The organism metaphor's entailments for the wealth paradigm are closely matched with those for production: ambiguity, evolution, needs, limitations. But the notion of a domesticated animal captures the spirit of the wealth paradigm best. Animals are domesticated for clearly economic reasons. Men brought animals under their control to produce wealth; animals were the "capital equipment" for mankind from the Neolithic era to the coming of the steam engine. We relied on animals for power and for transportation, and we still rely on them for food and clothing. The "cash cow"—the business operated to throw off cash—is a fixture of the business lexicon, and the image sharply portrays the notion of business as a wealth-producing activity.

The Eye of the Needle

Let us look further at this paradigm of wealth, this great game, this cash cow. The appeal—the "correctness"—of the paradigm lies fundamentally in the economic realm. Adam Smith and his heirs over the past 200 years have made the point very well: Profit is the engine that drives industrial production and, thus, the increase in material well-being.

Capital formation is the mainspring of material progress—that seems unarguable. Even the Chinese, staunch Marxist-Leninists, understand the necessity for profit and operate a socialist economy according to these principles. O'Toole has written about a recent tour of state-owned factories in the PRC, reporting that the factory managers are measured on the profitability of their operations.[59] The managers, who are very comfortable with this approach, informed the visitors that profit is a necessity: Profits are needed for investment, to maintain employment, to support the community and retirees, and—significantly—to maintain production. And Ota Sik, a Czech socialist later associated with the University of Basel, has said: "The optimum development of capital . . . the most effective use of capital [is] the foundation of every social development."[60]

So in any advanced society, socialist or capitalist, there seems to be a consensus on the key role of profit and capital formation. Of course, the socialists are turning the wealth paradigm on its head, as Sloan did with Ford's production paradigm: Profit, wealth, is a means to an end, the fuel that will provide the real objective—production.

In a way, this was Adam Smith's point: Individual self-interest—greed, if you like—will drive improvements in material well-being. Smith put it this way:

> Though their sole aim can be the gratification of their own vain and insatiable desires, they are led, as though by an invisible hand, to serve the interests of society.[61]

This, of course, is the Smithian idea that George Gilder finds so objectionable—the pact with the devil that will transform evil (greed) into good (material progress). As we have seen, Gilder searched for another impulse on the part of the capitalist—an altruistic purpose, turning good deeds into good results. Is this realistic?

Perhaps it is. Weber provides some support for Gilder's position:

> Unlimited greed for gain is not in the least identical with capitalism, and is still less its spirit. Capitalism may even be identical with the restraint, or at least a rational tempering, of this irrational impulse.[62]

And Michael Novack, a scholar with the conservative American Enterprise Institute, has weighed in with a similar critique of Adam Smith.[63] Novack sees the political economy of the West deeply rooted in Judeo-Christian values—particularly those cultural values that inspire people to believe in the future and in their ability to shape that future toward a better world. He suggests that the biblical injunctions against riches stemmed from the economic conditions of that time—static, unremitting scarcity. Economic life was then a zero-sum game; if someone was rich, he was rich at someone else's expense. Novack contrasts this with the modern world, the world of capitalism, in which economic growth is possible through profit and investment and man now has the means to satisfy material needs—an unthinkable possibility in biblical times. So the strictures against wealth in Judeo-Christian thought could be outdated; economic growth can provide enough for all.

Novack also downplays the unseemly avarice of Smith's "invisible hand" players. These types are not essential, as Weber has said; rather, they are a product of a historical accident. Capitalism just "happened," in Novack's view, to arise in eighteenth- and nineteenth-century England, with its tradition of individualism and utilitarianism. Then, in the nineteenth century, Social Darwinism became England's credo, and this reinforced the coupling of capitalism with the greed impulse. Novack believes that this "did immeasurable damage to the theory of capitalism."[64]

Novack has some strong arguments: the fact that the biblical injunctions against wealth were made in a time of stagnant economies and the taint that Social Darwinism and English individualism have given to capitalism. But the biblical injunctions remain and are incorporated in the values and ideas of our Western culture. And there is nothing ambiguous about the scriptures; Novack to the contrary, Matthew's rendering of Christ's words is very clear: "Lay not up for yourselves treasures on earth." And Matthew also wrote:

> It is easier for a camel to go through the eye of a needle, than for
> a rich man to enter into the Kingdom of Heaven.[65]

Matthew's Christ had no ambivalence on the subject of wealth: "Blessed are the poor in spirit"—one of the Beatitudes. And there was a clear injunction: "If thou wilt be perfect, go and sell that thou hast, and give to the poor."[66] This was the command that St. Francis of Assisi took so literally in the thirteenth century—a time when the economy of Europe was improving and merchants, and the Church, were growing increasingly rich. Francis, a rich man's son, gave away everything, lived on alms, and helped reform the Church.

Much later, in Elizabethan England, Shakespeare also lived in a healthy, growing economy but expressed his adherence to the old values:

> If thou art rich, thou'rt poor;
> For like an ass whose back with ingots bows,
> Thou bear'st thy heavy riches but a journey,
> And death unloads thee.[67]

Shakespeare was hardly Francis of Assisi; he did well enough for himself. But he certainly expressed a strong streak in Western consciousness—the idea that there was something unseemly, and ultimately futile, about riches. Ancient Palestine, medieval Umbria, Elizabethan England, the modern West—in all times and all places, avarice was and is one of the deadly sins.

And we see all around us today a certain revulsion against this impulse. The Wall Street scandals, the corporate raiders and their "greenmail"—it seems little has changed since Veblen wrote, almost a hundred years ago. Even one of the age's most admired businessmen, Lee Iacocca, comes through in his autobiography as less interested in the survival of Chrysler and its productive capacity than in his own personal wealth.

Veblen railed against the capitalists, not so much for their greed as for their superfluity. He believed that they were worse than useless—they actually got in the way of production. And that is the basic question: From an economic viewpoint, from within the paradigms of production or wealth, do we need such people? Was Adam Smith right—must we have rapacious men in order to benefit mankind? Is the success of Western civilization dependent on tolerating—or even encouraging—men like Ivan Boesky and Dennis Levine?

Perhaps it is so; nowhere are we told that good can only come from good. The world of nature teaches us that growth and flowering follow from corruption and death—good, if you will, from evil. The concern we must have, though, with the acceptance, even reward, of avarice is a moral one and a cultural one. What does the sanctioning of these impulses do to the fabric of our society? We have already seen Engels's critique, and it was a moral concern, not a social or political one. His words are worth repeating:

> The middle classes have a truly extraordinary conception of society. They really believe that all human beings (themselves included) and indeed all living things and inanimate objects have a real existence only if they make money or help to make it.[68]

That was Engels's impression of English society, circa 1845. And there is an eerie echo of his critique in modern life: Is that all there is? Should people be concerned only with money and view *all* of nature as means to that end? What types of characters are we building? Weber spoke to this last question; he saw Franklin as archetypical, a man whose moral attitude was colored by utilitarianism: Honesty is useful because it assures credit, and so on. For Franklin, the mere appearance of virtue was always sufficient to ensure that his dealings would produce more and more money.[69]

Here we have the serious weakness of the wealth paradigm: first of all, its ultimate futility as an end in itself—Shakespeare's ass that carries ingots, only to the grave; and second, its impact, in its extreme form, on the fabric of society—the enshrinement of avarice as an acceptable posture. Forty years ago, Karl Polanyi showed the dangers of the system we have created. He reflected on Adam Smith's, and later economists', abstraction of the factors of production: land, labor, and capital—treated as commodities. Treating these as objects produced for sale, a metaphorical trick, is extremely helpful in the advance of economic theory, but we pay the normal price for the use of metaphor: We forget what these things actually are. "Labor," for example is neither an object nor a factor in an equation; "labor" is individual human beings—you and I, if you like. As Polanyi writes:

> The alleged commodity, "labor power" cannot be shoved about, used indiscriminately, or even left unused, without affecting the human individual who happened to be the bearer of this peculiar commodity.[70]

In a similar way, "land"—the economists' shorthand for the yield of soils and mines—is in no way a commodity either; it is God's green, limited planet Earth, not an inexhaustible cornucopia for man's ever-increasing needs. Polanyi anticipates the World-watch Institute report mentioned in the last chapter:

> Nature would be reduced to its elements, neighborhoods and landscapes defiled, rivers polluted . . . the power to produce food and raw materials destroyed.[71]

Polanyi's dark picture converges with that of Engels a hundred years earlier—nature and mankind reduced to one role: profit-making.

It all goes back to Smith and his "invisible hand"—the need for greed so that it can be channeled for a society's purpose. But we must remember that Smith wrote at a time when production was almost exclusively meeting real material necessities; his example of a "product"—his own dinner—to describe the benefits of self-interest was well chosen. But we live in a time (at least in the fortunate countries) when our necessities are satisfied. Why, then, should we accept the corrosive effects of institutionalized greed so that we can produce frivolous goods?

Peter Drucker has suggested an answer, an answer that Richard Ferris seemed to be struggling toward. Drucker says, simply: "The first job of a business manager is to convert social needs into profitable opportunities."[72] *That* seems right—but it is essentially a synthesis of the wealth and production paradigm, a synthesis that Kuhn tells us is impossible. (We will return to Drucker in chapter 15.) The key, though, must be meeting social needs. The businessman is the businessman; he cannot be expected to throw his money away—nor should he. Society needs capital accumulation. But he should find real social needs—and they are everywhere—and apply his energy and capital to them. The medieval world of the "just" price and the "just" wage lies far behind us, and for good reason. Modern capitalism and industrialization, with all their true benefits, would be impossible under the medieval formula. We need market-clearing prices for efficient allocation of goods and capital; that is unarguable. We need profit and capital formation. But we also need new, innovative ways to steer business toward the production of socially useful goods and services. The market system has served us well; there is a great deal of merit to the idea that the decentralized nature of investment decisions is the key to material progress. Nowhere have governments—bureaucrats—shown that they can make better decisions than the aggregrate of individual entrepreneurs pursuing their own ends. But we have also seen the down side of those individual decisions—environmental destruction and the coarsening of society's values. Somehow, we must develop in the spirit of capitalism a merger of the entrepreneurial instinct with a greater social responsibility. The wealth paradigm eschews this responsibility, and its favorite metaphors—game and organism—reveal that disdain.

The leader role that the game metaphor suggests to the wealth-seeker is, of course, the gambler, the speculator, the man responsible only to himself. The metaphor reinforces the worst feature of the paradigm: the exclusive focus on money. And the game notion also entails winning and losing that money, an idea that distorts the true processes of business. Everyone who has conducted business has been caught up in complex negotiations and hectic-paced deals, and the excitement is real—it *does* seem like a great game. But the wealth-seeker's preoccupation with the monetary result—seeing the conduct of business as a gambling game—can only lead to a neglect of the leader's responsibilities to employees and to society at large.

The organism metaphor projects another leader role that is equally pernicious. I refer, of course, to the "bad shepherd"—the shepherd who, again, is responsible only to himself. The bad shepherd exploits his sheep, exploits them purely for economic reasons. He has no emotional link to the dumb beasts, no bond, no caring. They are economic units. He slaughters them when their feed costs exceed their cash output. He tends and feeds them at a minimal level, without other concern for their well-being. And businesses *are* run that way; the wealth paradigm can degenerate into that degree of exploitation.

The gambler, the bad shepherd—these leader roles that the paradigm calls forth—argue strongly against wealth as a suitable purpose for business. Wealth alone cannot be our guide. The Kingdom of Heaven is real, if only in our own hearts, and the old wisdom is still valid: It is easier for a camel to pass through the eye of a needle than for a rich man to enter that Kingdom.

Summary

- In the period 1770–1905, *all* business speakers embraced the paradigm of wealth. However, this purpose has had only minority representation in subsequent periods.

- The paradigm of wealth is closely linked with the profit motive. This motive is a unique feature of Western industrial society and is the foundation for classical economics. Adam Smith saw the capitalist's gain as the mainspring for better material existence. In brief, the capitalist's self-interest supplies our dinner.

- Alfred Sloan is the exemplar of this paradigm. In the same time and the same industry as Henry Ford, he held to a fundamentally different view of business. His statement, "The primary objective of the corporation was to make money, not just to make motor cars," signaled his disagreement with Ford and his adherence to the wealth paradigm.

- The Kuhnian puzzle that Sloan faced was how to make money in competition with Ford. He solved the puzzle through a mixture of differentiation and cost leadership, in the process moving auto styling to the fore as a differentiator and creating the annual model change.

- The problem that Sloan left behind was one of quality and utility of the automobile.

- The wealth paradigm is difficult to refute in pure economic terms. The uneasiness with the paradigm stems from its cultural impact—the embodiment of greed as a necessity for our material civilization.

- The wealth paradigm engenders the metaphors of a game or an organism. The key entailments are a goal, profit production (Iacocca's "golden goose" and Carnegie's "greatest game"), a gamble, and competition.

- Our uneasiness with the paradigm is accentuated by the leader roles that the metaphors call forth.

- The metaphors project two leader roles—the gambler and the bad shepherd—neither of which is helpful to responsible business management.

13
Stonecutters Fighting Time

The Paradigm of the Institution

Stonecutters fighting time with marble
                    you foredefeated
challengers of oblivion
. . .
For man will be blotted out, the blithe
                    earth die, the
Brave sun
Die blind and blacken to the heart;
Yet stones have stood for a thousand
                    years.

—Robinson Jeffers[1]

Institutions

We have now reviewed two fundamental purposes for business: production and wealth. These purposes are largely based on economic motives, and their analysis can be conducted in economic terms—although, as we have seen, their ramifications go well beyond economics and enter the realm of cultural values. The third paradigm, or purpose, is the idea of business as an institution; in short, the purpose of business is to stay in business, to endure. This is an entirely introspective purpose; economics, the pressures of the larger society, even the fate of individuals are means to an end— the paramount purpose is the existence of the enterprise through time. Walter Wriston has expressed this point of view rather clearly. Speaking of Citicorp, he said: "This is a continuing outfit. It's been here since 1812 and my monument will be that we didn't total it."[2]

We have here a radically different concept of an organization. For Ford and Sloan, the organization was a means—either Ford's tool for production or Sloan's cash cow. For Wriston and his type, the organization was *pour-soi*—an end in itself. It is this paradigm that will occupy us in this chapter.

Any institution—a university, a government, a corporation— is a peculiar entity, that is part idea, part process, part physical. To a large extent, an institution exists only in the minds of the people who make it up or deal with it. Should everyone decide tomorrow that Harvard University no longer exists, it surely would not, despite its buildings, capital equipment, and billion dollar endowment. But as Marcuse has noted, over time, things and people have been organized, integrated, and administered; and this process produces an entity that is far more than the sum of its component parts.[3] Harvard is not the physical plant, the students, the faculty, the administration, and the alumni, but all of these—integrated, ongoing. It is a place in the mind as much as any, or all, of its parts.

Institutions also have a very distinctive characteristic: They embody values. An institution stands for something; it is this characteristic that makes it a place in people's minds, that keeps everyone from deciding one morning that there is no such thing. As Selznick writes:

> The formation of an institution is marked by the making of value commitments . . . as to the nature of the enterprise—its distinctive aims, methods and role in the community.[4]

But Selznick makes this sound too precise, too self-conscious and deliberate. Most institutions, I believe, originate in irrational impulses and simply grow. However, if they are to endure, Selznick is right: An institution must, consciously or not, develop a set of values, a unique stance on its merit and purposes.

The most successful extant institution in terms of longevity is the Roman Catholic Church. Tradition tells us that Simon Peter established the papacy in 42 A.D.; Korol Wojtyla, Pope John Paul II, reigns today, more than 1,900 years later. In that time, there have been vast changes in the Church—in its doctrine, its wealth, its position in the world. But the institution has endured, and even its organizational form—pastors who are responsible to a bishop, who in turn is responsible to the pope—is unchanged. St. Augustine was bishop of Hippo at his death in 430 A.D. The world of late antiquity is unimaginably different from our day and different again from the medieval and Renaissance worlds. But Augustine was a bishop of the Roman Church, responsible to his pope, Celestine I, and with duties toward his flock—in no way fundamentally different from a bishop today in the space age or bishops 500 or 1,000 years after his time. The institution has endured.

John Paul II is recognized as the 263d pope; 263 men have reigned over the Roman Church as it has moved through time. But clearly, the Church is much more than its leader; few names could be recalled from this long march of the popes. Some are remembered for their works, some for their crimes, some for their patronage of immortal artists. But in the main, they are anonymous; they were stewards of an institution who served their time and passed the duty on to a successor. The institution, not the men, is the story of the Church. And the institution itself, not the men who serve it, is generally the important thing; the indefinite prolongation of the organization's life is the true story.

Origins

The world is filled with institutions of every description; an alien anthropologist would probably describe man as an institution builder. What is behind this inclination, this drive to build and maintain these peculiar forms that endure beyond individual lifetimes? We can see some inkling of this impulse in art, even from the earliest articles that have come down to us. From the great Paleolithic cave art and "Venus" sculptures of middle Europe up to the present-day articles of paint, canvas, wood, and steel—all represent a simple motivation: to translate the world of the individual spirit into imperishable matter, to transcend the finite life of the individual by creating something lasting—Robinson Jeffers's stonecutters, fighting time.

Earlier, we touched on Ernest Becker's work, especially man's need for meaning in his life. Becker based his work on the essential fact about the human condition: man's creatureliness, his finitude. To Becker, the most important fact about man is his consciousness that he is a creature, an assemblage of matter that knows it will die. Becker's title, *The Denial of Death*, signals the basic motivation for human behavior:

> Man erected symbols which do not age or decay to quiet his fears of his ultimate end—and of more immediate concern, to provide the promise of indefinite duration.[5]

We owe to Kierkegaard the illumination of modern man's dread, anxiety, *angst*. It stems from nothing less than the human paradox—the fact that man is an animal who is conscious of his animal limitation. And John Montague has put these ideas into poetry of considerable power in his poem "Process". The first verse reads:

> The structure of process,
> time's gullet devouring
> parents whose children
> are swallowed in turn.
> Families, houses, towns
> Built or battered down,
> only the earth and sky
> Unchanging in change,
> everything else fragile
> as a wild bird's wing:
> Bulldozer and butterfly
> dogrose and snowflake
> climb the unending stair
> into God's golden eye.[6]

The whole world of matter—bulldozers and butterflies, families, houses, towns, and we as well, we human individuals—will climb that unending stair. But the difference is that we *know* we will climb that stair. Becker says, "It is a terrifying dilemma to be in and to have to live with."[7]

It is this terror that gripped Blaise Pascal when he meditated on his lot—a small, time-bound creature, lost in the eternities of space and time, unaccountably placed in his particular locale and age. His comment anticipates Becker: *"Le silence eternal de des espaces infinis m'effraie"*[8] (the eternal silence of those infinite spaces frightens me).

Pascal saw most human activity—the pursuit of pleasure, the absorption in work—just as Becker did, as a denial of death, a way not to think about the ultimate end. Pascal's ultimate answer to the human dilemma was salvation within the Roman Church. But Pascal was a great mind and a great spirit; his was not an unthinking and abject surrender to the arms of Holy Mother Church. Pascal showed that man can transcend his creatureliness, the brute fact of his animal finitude, through his mind and the works of his mind.

The products of men's minds, far nobler than the world of matter, will endure; Pascal's words will live so long as men reflect on their fate—so long as there are men.

Poets and writers, painters and sculptors, artists of all descriptions—surely there we see the denial of death, and in a noble form: not an escape, but an expression of strength of spirit, a statement that they have transcended their creatureliness.

The impulse is also seen in leaders who raise enormous material monuments to themselves—the Pyramids of Egypt, to cite only the most famous example. That this is ultimately futile, as Jeffers says in this chapter's epigraph, is undeniable. But stones *do* last a thousand years; that *is* something. Shelley caught the futility in his "Ozymandias"; the poet describes the ruin of a great portrait statue, then says:

And on the pedestal these words appear:
"My name is Ozymandias, king of kings:
Look on my works ye Mighty and despair!"
Nothing beside remains. Round the decay
of that colossal wreck, boundless and bare
the lone and level sands stretch far away.[9]

Shelley could have been describing Yucatan in the 1840s—strewn with the remains of colossal palaces and pyramids, but a thick forest, not a desert. Yet, more ironic than Shelley's poem, the area was not uninhabited; in fact, it was thickly populated. More-over, it was populated by the descendants of the men—the Ozy-mandiases—who built these monuments. The irony lies in the discovery of the first modern explorer, John Lloyd Stephens: The inhabitants knew nothing of these ruins, had no idea who built them, and had absolutely no tradition that the builders were their own ancestors. In less than 300 years, the memory of these men—the men who sought immortality in these structures—had been lost to their own descendants.

But the experiences of the Maya and Ozymandias only tell us that nothing is guaranteed. The impulse to deny death, to build monuments in words or in stone, to extend ourselves in time be-yond our material existence is a powerful drive and hardly foolish or ignoble. In fact, the most noble works of man can be ascribed to the impulse. And men do not build only in stone or words; they build institutions—organizations that endure, move forward in time well beyond individual lives and careers.

Carse's concept of "infinite play" can be interpreted as insti-tution building—the players not playing for themselves but to con-tinue the play in others.[10] The man who builds an institution or carries it on feels this strongly: His duty lies in strengthening the institution so that his successors can continue the indefinite life of the enterprise. Carse uses the term *evil* in the same way as Becker. For Becker, evil (one of his titles is *Escape from Evil*) is simply death. For Carse, evil is the termination of infinite play—the end of the institution.[11]

In all of these thinkers, then, we see a profound consensus, an agreement on the human condition. Man is a paradox: an infinite spirit and a material body. A man cannot accept that he is no better than a bulldozer or butterfly and will be annihilated without a trace. A man is more than that; he is an infinite spirit, and he must strive to fix his immortality somehow in the world of matter—through words, through monuments, through works of art, or through institutions that he can create, serve, and perpetuate. That the task is futile, that even the "brave sun die blind and blacken to the heart"—that is not the point. The impulse is too strong in our nature; we must attempt immortality in our works; we must deny our creatureliness and our death, if not in art or thought, then in business institutions.

The Actors

As we saw in chapter 9, the institutional paradigm has had an interesting career. Let me review the data again. In the period 1770–1905, no one expressed this view. Similarly, in the period 1905–45, there were no proponents. But in the postwar period 1945–75, fully 67 percent of the actors surveyed held this view. Since 1975, the number has dropped to 29 percent.

The extreme popularity of the paradigm in the postwar period may be due to its very nature: The viewpoint is basically noneconomic. The organization is not seen as a tool for production or wealth, but rather as a thing in itself, a monument—a piece of immortality, if you will. This is not inappropriate, and it was also quite feasible when America had little competition. When the tide turned against us after 1975, it became more difficult to sustain these views. Economics became grim necessity; transcendence and immortality had to be sought elsewhere.

In Clifford and Cavanagh's review of successful midsize companies, they find precisely the viewpoint we have been discussing: "[Their] mission is to create an institution, leave a legacy, make a difference."[12] Clifford and Cavanagh though, seem to think that this is today's paradigm (they wrote in 1985). My data suggest that the dominance of this view has passed. Since the impulse toward institution building is so fundamental to human nature, it is likely that the view has always existed in some form in business. In fact, Clifford and Cavanagh quote Joseph Schumpeter, who wrote in the 1940s that entrepreneurs have "the dream and the will to found a private kingdom, and also a dynasty."[13]

Donaldson and Lorsch studied twelve CEOs of large companies—in the *Fortune* 500. Their work, which was published in 1983, reflects the thinking of the latter part of the postwar period. One of the CEOs expressed the paradigm this way:

> "The highest priority to me is perpetuation of the enterprise. I'd like to leave this place in better shape than when someone passed me the baton. I don't sweat the shareholders too much."[14]

Donaldson and Lorsch demonstrate how far these CEOs have come from the paradigms of wealth and production. They see their companies as much more than financial entities; rather, they see the organization as a conflation of people, ideas, and products—all worth perpetuating—but the institution itself is especially worth perpetuating.[15] To accomplish this, they seek independence—ironically, independence from just those constituencies that the stakeholder view of the firm holds so dear: customers, suppliers, shareholders. ("I don't sweat the shareholders too much.") The task is to be self-sufficient, to free oneself from the strictures of the equity market (the shareholders), the capital markets (the banks and bond holders), dependencies on large customers or suppliers, demands of the government, and so forth. They seem to believe that to perpetuate the institution, the stakeholders must be placated but not in any way allowed to control the business. Control is for the steward; the institution must endure. To see this, let us look at the man who epitomized the steward.

Reginald Jones became CEO of General Electric in 1972. He was a man of deep religious conviction, an inveterate churchgoer. From his Christianity, he took the concept of stewardship and grafted it onto his approach to the leadership of GE: "I spoke of stewardship from Day One . . . [stewardship for] the distinctive spirit of General Electric."[16] Asked about his role by a company historian who wanted to write about the "Jones era," he was concerned that the GE story would appear to be the Jones story, and he remarked: "This is an institution, and I'm steward here. I have it for a while, and then I move on."[17]

Ian MacGregor was quite a different man from Reg Jones. Hardly the corporate type at all, he was more the gambler and plunger than the corporate manager. His skills were in making deals, and his deals built Amax into a major corporation after he took over in 1967. Interviewed in retirement, he expressed satisfaction in building a large company, in taking a "minor-league player" and transforming it into the world's largest mining company.[18] Of his own legacy, he said: "I am a kind of cynic about the individual in an organization. He leaves no enduring mark."[19]

Monsanto's John Hanley, another CEO of this era, also thought in terms of succession, continuity, the indefinite existence of the corporation: "When I lay down the hod, one of the greatest satisfactions I'm going to get is watching those younger people . . . succeed."[20]

This penchant for succession, for the heirs to the institution, has been clearly expressed by the chairman of Weyerhauser: "The philosophy is: 'We do things not for ourselves, or for our children, but our grandchildren.' "[21] This is a paraphrase of Carse: infinite players playing to continue the game in others. And it is noteworthy that the game metaphor figures prominently in the speech of institution-minded leaders.

I quoted earlier the words of Walter Kissinger, chairman of the Allen Group, raging against the corporate raiders. Kissinger excoriates the raiders and arbitrageurs:

> It is no interest or concern to these individuals . . . that they destroy the careers of dedicated individuals who have devoted their lives to building a company. . . . It is ludicrous that the speculator [arbitrageur] who may be in the stock for a few hours should have the same moral claim and rights as an investor who has dedicated his whole life to the building of a company.[22]

Here we have incommensurate thinking in its pure form. On one side we have Kissinger, defending the institution—the idea of an entity with a history and a value set, moving indefinitely forward into time. On the other side, we have those of the wealth paradigm, seeing only financial assets and financial gain. Another *dialogue des sourdes.*

Jones the Exemplar

In Reginald Jones, we do not have a towering figure like Henry Ford or Alfred Sloan—men who placed their personal stamp on enormous enterprises, even entire industries. Rather, we have the quintessential steward—a man who spent his working life as an employee of a large firm, rose to its leadership, strengthened the institution in many ways, and passed on the duty to others. His success at General Electric and his public visibility, however, popularized and legitimized the idea of business as an institution. In this sense, he was the exemplar for the paradigm.

Jones was in some ways an unlikely choice for the top spot at GE—a business school graduate and financial man in a company whose predominant skill was engineering. Since its foundation in 1878 as the Edison Electric Company, the company had prided itself on technical leadership.[23] Most of the managers were midwesterners; Jones had been born in England and raised in Trenton, New Jersey. But as a young man at General Electric, he had spent eight years as an internal auditor, traveling the country, learning more than anyone else about the diverse GE empire. He rose steadily through the ranks, from management trainee to financial vice-president and head of strategic planning. When he was chosen in 1972 over several more senior colleagues to lead the corporation, he was fifty-five years old.

In 1972, General Electric was a major industrial corporation with many strengths. Sales were over $10 billion, return on stockholder equity was 17.5 percent, and the company enjoyed a record $10 billion backlog.[24] Over its nearly 100-year history, General Electric had developed a particular, sharply defined ethos. Jones's career from management trainee to senior manager was hardly atypical. In his day, the senior managers averaged twenty-five years with the company. This facilitated shared knowledge and tradition, common values, and a clear self-image: moral integrity, hallmark quality, and technical leadership.[25]

The atmosphere was highly conducive to teamwork: a network of friendships, an air of collegial fellowship and informality. Jones himself—somewhat reserved, hardly a backslapper—was universally called Reg (rhymes with Peg) throughout GE. The informality, fellowship, and teamwork muted the political element in GE management; internal competition was reserved and gentlemanly.

Jones was fond of talking about "working with the grain" at GE. The "grain," of course, was this complex of GE traditions and "culture." Jones's job was to harness this energy, this cohesive team, and strengthen GE's business for the indefinite future. His success with General Electric was indisputable, although hardly the incandescent success of Ford or Sloan. He left a record of twenty-six quarters of improved earnings through a period that included two recessions. In his time, annual revenues grew by 163 percent, and GE's return on capital was consistently 50 percent higher than that of its major competitors.[26]

Over this period, Jones had developed into a public figure as well. He was a participant in President Ford's 1974 economic summit, then served on Ford's and President Carter's Labor–Management Group. He became a frequent visitor to Washington—and not simply as a lobbyist for GE. Jones had his own staff develop position papers on a wide range of public issues: individual tax policies, welfare reform, debt policy. He used his position as co-chairman of the Business Round Table (a group of major company CEOs) to help formulate ideas as well as to lead business community opinion on matters of public policy.

Jones won the respect of the business community at large. In fact, a 1979 survey of more than 1,400 business leaders rated Jones as America's most influential businessman.[27] That influence was felt in a number of ways. The GE management style—objectivity coupled with caring—became well known through Jones himself and through the public awareness of GE's success as a business. But Jones's image of himself as the steward, and his image of GE as an institution, also became well known. The example of a highly successful and highly visible figure espousing the idea of stewardship was not lost on the business community. Nor was his frequent use of the society metaphor, a metaphor closely aligned with the institutional purpose. Jones's emphasis on the culture entailment of the metaphor undoubtedly aided its popularity.

The Puzzles

Selznick defines one of the key tasks of leadership as "the defense of institutional integrity."[28] And this is the central Kuhnian puzzle that confronts anyone who sees his business as an institution: survival. How does one ensure the indefinite continuation of the enterprise? The stakeholder view of the firm helps frame this puzzle. Even if the constituents of a firm are not considered stakeholders in the sense that they have rights, those constituents (management, shareholders, employees, customers, suppliers, society) are the forces that bear on the firm, that can in fact determine whether the institution will survive. As we saw earlier, many CEOs really see the issue more in terms of independence from these constituents rather than an obligation to serve them. Their idea is to lessen the influence that these constituents will have on the firm so that the institution can achieve its own ends—particularly indefinite duration. This is not the political balancing of diverse interests and rights so much as it is the lessening of dependence on all or any of the actors that can help or harm the business.

When Jones took over GE, he faced challenges from a number of his constituencies. He solved the institutional puzzle by meeting these challenges in ways that were unique to GE and to GE's position at that time in history. For the puzzle of institutional survival is a continuing one; there is no generic solution—each time and each company is different. The job of the manager or steward of an institution is to recognize the puzzle and to continue to solve it—that is, to maintain institutional independence.

The first key constituency is the shareholders or, more generally, the capital markets. It has become increasingly popular nowadays to "go private"—to take the ownership of a firm out of the public's hands so that the management is no longer subject to the demands and the scrutiny of the public markets. This is one solution to the puzzle, but all but the most fortunate companies cannot thrive and expand with only internally generated cash; they must deal with the banks and bond markets, if not the equity market, for capital. When Jones took over, GE faced a cash crisis and had just borrowed $300 million for working capital. Jones instituted rigorous cost controls and preached financial fundamentals: balance sheet analysis, return on investment criteria. He also saw a threat in GE's high stock price to earnings ratio; a decline in that ratio would limit GE's ability to raise capital in the equity market. Jones spent a good deal of time selling the financial community on the current ratio, convincing them that GE's future profits would justify the high level.[29]

Another key constituency that must be placated and satisfied is the employees—in GE's case, particularly the unions. Contract negotiations were scheduled for 1973, and these had never been easy for the company; in 1969–70 GE had experienced a three-month strike. Prior to Jones's day, GE had taken a tough stand with the unions, which represented half of the employees. Jones modified this stance and orchestrated negotiations that were conducted in a genuine give-and-take manner. General Electric emerged with a new thirty-seven month contract and a satisfied work force.[30]

The next key constituency that occupied Jones was the larger society—the general public as well as the U.S. government. He was not a natural public figure—he was reserved, a poor public speaker, and initially unsure of his abilities to deal with political leaders. But Jones knew that GE could survive only with the sufferance of the public, that he must work to change the political and social climate.[31] The public must be educated on the necessity for reasonable profit; the government must be lobbied for reasonable tax and investment policies. This was Jones's motivation in entering the public milieu: another task, another puzzle to keep GE in business. He became a voice in the councils of government and had an impact on public policy. He also became a public spokesman for American business and tried to educate the general public on key issues that related to business. But as Jones's time drew to a close, he withdrew from public view. He had no aspirations for public office and even turned down the chair of the Business Round Table as he neared retirement. There is no hint in any of his public work that he sought self-aggrandizement. His work was GE's work.

Jones's tenure at GE was marked by these struggles to strengthen the institution, to keep at bay the forces that could lessen its independence. A stonecutter fighting time. And his work and his solutions were fruitful. He placated the financial community by good, fundamental business results. He satisfied the unions with a fair contract. He spent his personal energy in shaping government policy. He worked hard on maintaining the GE atmosphere, the sense of caring for people: phone calls, birthday cards, endless sessions of hand-shaking, and inspirational speeches. But he built no cult of personality; he knew that his time was limited and that the institution needed new leaders. His last years were spent on highly organized succession planning, for he recognized that the institution belonged to its members and that his role was that of a caretaker, a standard-bearer for his turn at the guard.[32]

The Metaphors of the Institution

The Actors

Institution builders favor the journey, game, and society metaphors—metaphors sharing some entailments that well match the

institutional mentality: goal, unpredictability/ambiguity, cooperation, and leadership. Walter Wriston often spoke of Citicorp's
founding in the early nineteenth century and his transient role. And
Wriston also spoke in the language of the institutional metaphors:
"[I] sailed into waters [I] didn't know much about"; "A participative society at Citicorp"; "What counts is winning the game in
the marketplace".[33]

Monsanto's John Hanley employed his metaphors to articulate his personal concerns with leadership and cooperation:
He "wore the company hat";[34] his style was "cheerleading";[35]
and he exhorted the employees to "get in the boat and row
together."[36]

We have seen Ian MacGregor's comparison of business management to playing gin rummy,[37] a metaphor that captures the goal
of business but also the unpredictability. No matter how skilled
the player, he must play the cards that are dealt. But MacGregor
affirmed: "Somebody has to bet."[38] MacGregor also spoke in "society" terms—much like Wriston—in terms of an open society:
"The basic principle is the consent of the governed."[39]

And earlier, we saw Petersen, CEO of Standard Oil in 1955,
make an explicit comparison of a business to the U.S. form of
government—a system of checks and balances.[40]

Our exemplar—Reg Jones, the self-styled steward—used the
society and journey metaphors to express the meaning GE could
bring to its people and his own sense of mission: "This is a family,
we enjoy each other."[41] And his business principles were his "personal roadmap".[42]

The Entailments

We have seen the shared entailments: goal, unpredictability, cooperation, leadership. The journey metaphor is quite apt for all of
these ideas, which are important to the institution builder—the
risky journey of high purpose, requiring the highest degrees of cooperation and leadership. And the journey metaphor also captures
a critical component of institutional thinking—the idea of a transcendent adventure, an undertaking that all can throw themselves
into, something larger and more meaningful than their own small

lives. As we have seen, this notion can become dangerous when the actors lose sight of any overarching purpose; the agency costs mount when the journey becomes a *voyage sans but*.

The game metaphor carries with it some of the same ideas, especially the risk of the enterprise, the uncertainty and potential for failure. The needs for teamwork, cooperation, and leadership are also accentuated; Hanley's rather trite "company hat" is nonetheless a cogent figure for the cohesiveness of a team. To the extent that the speakers have a Carsian infinite game in mind, the metaphor is a fine one for an institution builder. Playing a game to perpetuate the game itself is a very close match to the aspirations of an institutional leader.

Game analogies also project another key idea: the notion that the enterprise should be a source of pleasure—it should be fun. This idea is generally missing from companies that are run for wealth or production (though perhaps not missing for the leaders themselves). For the employee of such a company, the sense he gets from management is that the work is aimed at very serious purposes—profit or goods production; he should get his fun elsewhere. Since an institution is operated, at bottom, for the sake of the employees, the goal is to satisfy all of their human needs, including pleasure.

The society figure incorporates a number of the journey and game ideas, especially the needs for leadership and cooperation. But as we have seen earlier, the idea of business *qua* society is particularly apt for an institution in suggesting the central positions of meaning and values. Institutions, I have argued, are created to enshrine values; they exist to give meaning to individual lives. Every institution has something like the myths, rituals, and symbols we find in traditional societies; they are natural and necessary features of the institutional landscape. The work life in an institution is peculiarly colored by a sense of belonging, a sense of the company as an essential part of life—in all ways comparable to the mentality of a traditional society member.

The society metaphor also calls up the idea of politics—a particular problem for an institution. When the goals are noneconomic, when the objectives are not as clear as this month's quota or next week's factory run, politics naturally flourishes.

Institution: Pro and Con

We have discussed the paradigm of the institution in noneconomic terms, focusing our attention on the essentially irrational impulse toward denial of death—individual death or institutional death. Those who build or serve these institutions are following an impulse as old as man: to be part of something greater than themselves and their time-bound limitations, to leave a legacy, to become a small part of the future. But there are clearly economic implications of this paradigm. For one, in the simplest terms, a business institution simply would not survive if it did not meet at least minimum economic performance standards. If the constituents are to be held at bay, the business must perform in economic terms; the capital markets, employees, and suppliers must be satisfied with some level of profits and financial distribution.

The business scholar North sees a closely related economic role for the institution: the mediator in the economic structure that assures the working of the system:

> Institutions are in effect the filter between individuals and the capital stock and between the capital stock and the output of goods and services and the distribution of income.[43]

Now, this could be said about any corporation, not just those led as institutions. But institutions play a much stronger role. Quaker Oats's Mason elaborates on this:

> I don't think there has ever been an institution to equal the modern corporation in providing society with superb financial, physical, technological and human assets. . . . [Assets are] brains, character, personal integrity and the desire to do some good in the world.[44]

This is not the colorless description of an institution that we just heard from North—not a "filter" between such abstractions as "the capital stock" and the output of goods and services. Mason describes an institution very like Reg Jones's General Electric—a conflation of technology, capital, and unique human skills. It is the combination and the management of these assets that has such economic power. This idea can be lost if the business is viewed solely in terms of wealth-generation or production.

The economic role and impact of institutions are heightened by its central tendency: stability. Classical economics, with its severe abstraction of the real processes of production and exchange, misses this point entirely. For the classical theory to work, it hardly matters whether producers (businesses) are transient or long-lived; one is as good as another. But in the modern world, to create economic benefits, the producers must be capable of managing technology, capital, and human assets over a long stretch of time. The very stability of organizations that are managed as institutions helps this along immensely. General Electric could hardly be a manufacturer of aircraft engines if it had gone into business yesterday. And that business is typical of most high-technology, modern industry: a business that requires a long tradition in design, manufacturing, and marketing, a tradition built up over many years and stored in the minds and life experiences of thousands of people. This point is lost on those who view corporations merely as sets of real and financial assets, lifeless abstractions.

Earlier, we discussed the motivation behind the institutional paradigm: the individual's need to overcome his creatureliness and project his life and spirit into the indefinite future. Our business leaders may or may not be comfortable with the thoughts of Pascal and Kierkegaard—we certainly hear nothing about dread, *angst*, or terror in their remarks. But those are the thoughts of highly sensitive artistic spirits, mankind's eyes into the depths of the human condition. They do, though, reflect universal thoughts that are muted and repressed in ordinary lives and ordinary consciousness. And it is significant that the business leaders who have espoused this paradigm stress their satisfaction with their role. Reading the words of Wriston, Jones, and Hanley, we catch their sense of accomplishment, their firm belief that they have fought the good fight, done their part in an ongoing saga, and left behind successors who can and will continue the struggle. You will find nothing like this in Jay Gould or Andrew Carnegie—men who devoted their lives to piling up wealth. Nor do you find it in Henry Ford, justifiably proud as he was of his accomplishments. These other men, these stewards, or stonecutters, seem to have found the way to be truly human, to engage in a process and a life work far larger than themselves, to fulfill themselves in the continuation of an institution. They are the ships' captains—sailing into the future, voyaging after immortality. They are the infinite players—inspiring the team, gaining its cooperation, playing to perpetuate the game itself.

I speak of the leaders, of course, but organizations operated as institutions can provide much the same benefits to the employees. We saw in our discussion of the society metaphor how a company can provide meaning in people's lives, point them beyond their creature limitations, even give them Montague's "swaying rope ladders across fuming oblivion." Institutions can do this, do it much better than firms that are operated for wealth or production.

It is not surprising that the society metaphor and the institutional paradigm are closely linked in the minds of business leaders. The metaphor follows logically from the paradigm, as Kuhn would have us understand. An institution becomes a society unto itself, with mores, values, behavior patterns, and a sense of a purpose that endure beyond the transient careers of the people who make it up. The institution leader can choose from the variety of roles that the society metaphor suggests: the steward/statesman, the shaman, the politician. All care; all aid the institution.

We have seen Reg Jones, the archetypal steward, managing the affairs of General Electric for its indefinite duration. The statesman role closely fits the institutional leader; his is the task of balancing the claims of the institutional stakeholders, managing the contending forces so that the institution can endure. The shaman role likewise suits the institutional leader. Institutions imply the creation of values and meaning for the members—the timed-honored role of shamans in traditional societies. And institutions need creative politicians—those who recognize Aristotle's insight that politics creates order out of chaos. The institutional politician recognizes the inherent ambiguity of business, the limitations of the rational model, and uses the arts of persuasion, coalition building, "log-rolling," to move the institution along. The statesman, shaman, and creative politician provide the leadership that maintains the institution as a positive force in society.

All that having been said, we must recognize that there are

serious faults with this paradigm. Very simply, we have the issue of agency costs. It is very easy for the principals in an institution to forget that the organization has important economic and social responsibilties; it is easy to interpret the institution's purpose as merely the well-being of those involved. I am sure that I am not alone in a sense of uneasiness about CEOs' drive for independence from their constituencies. It is natural and rational of them to seek such independence, but we all sense that society must have some role in controlling critical institutions—institutions that have such potential for good or ill in the larger society. Similarly, the capital markets are a means to discipline firms so that they do not stray too far from necessary economic performance. The drive toward "privatization" is unsettling, as we see large firms unshackled from that degree of public accountability.

And what will the organizations do with their freedom if they are truly free of constraints from constituents? Pfeffer has already provided us one answer: They will become increasingly political. His law of political entropy states that *"given the opportunity,* an organization will tend to seek and maintain a political character"[45]— and not Aristotle's creative politics but just self-serving politics. Freedom from the constraints of the government and the capital markets would provide precisely that opportunity. An institution without a purpose other than self-perpetuation and without external checks would insensibly sink into politics; would diminish its concerns for suppliers, customers, and shareholders; and would operate to satisfy the transient management and employees. As we have seen, the leader can be a creative politician, but he can also easily fall into the "pol" role—the politician who plays the game for his own interests. And the paradigm's metaphors suggest other negative roles: the leader of a *voyage sans but,*—the captain of a ship of fools, bound on a journey without goal or purpose, *qui partent pour partir.* Even the society's statesman role can be perverted, particularly if the emphasis is on the shaman aspect, the idea that the statesman must have charisma. Peter Drucker has recently commented on this aspect of business leadership.[46] He speaks against the business leader's need for charisma, citing examples not from business but from the political and military realms. Eisenhower, Marshall, and Truman "were singularly effective lead-

ers, yet none had any more charisma than a dead mackerel,"
whereas their contemporaries—Stalin, Hitler, and Mao—had the
gift of charisma but wrought nothing but evil. Drucker's charismatic leaders are concerned only with self-glorification—poor sorts
compared to the statesman/businessman who is focused on performance and the mundane workings of an institution.

So the paradigm's metaphors can set leader roles that reinforce
the tendency of the paradigm toward self-aggrandizement. That is
a dark, perhaps overdrawn picture, but the organization conceived
of as an institution carries within it those seeds—essentially, the
primacy of the needs of the people in the organization. Russell
Ackoff has written of this rather approvingly. He says that profit
is not the reason for a business; it is a means to an end. That
statement fits well within the paradigm of the institution. But he
goes on to say that the need for profit is not necessarily for growth
of the enterprise; growth, in turn, is a means to an end. What is
the end? For Ackoff's managers, it is neither profit not growth, but
rather, "to provide themselves with the quality of work life and
standard of living they deserve."[47]

Ackoff is not apologetic about management's purpose, provided that the quality of working life of all employees is maximized. Growth and profit are a means to this end, since profit is
needed to sustain the life style and attract investors and growth is
needed to absorb employees displaced by improved productivity.

He could be right. But clearly, he is describing the perversion
of the institutional paradigm: the agents—that is, management—
operating the institution solely for their own purposes. Ackoff's
way out of the dilemma is to assume that those agents are smart
enough to realize that their own interests will be best served if the
institution maximizes profits and growth. Perhaps. But it sounds
suspiciously like a new "invisible hand"—private, selfish interest
unconsciously producing public welfare.

Whether Ackoff's analysis is correct or not—that is, whether
or not the agents' behavior will help the institution—he has certainly uncovered a primary weakness of the institutional paradigm.
In any institution that is not operated by the owners (and there are
almost none), those owners are threatened by agency costs—the
actions of the managers that suit their own purposes, not those of

the owners. And literature provides us with a signal example of agency costs, centered in our oldest institution, the Roman Church. I refer to Dostoyevsky's tale of the Grand Inquisitor in *The Brothers Karamazov*.[48]

The story has Christ returning to earth, 1,500 years after his death, and appearing at Seville in the most terrible time of the Inquisition. Christ is immediately recognized and draws throngs; he heals a blind man and raises a young girl from the dead. But the ancient cardinal, the Grand Inquisitor, has Him seized and imprisoned. The cardinal attempts to interrogate the silent Christ, and the remainder of the tale is a self-justifying monologue:

> Why art Thou come to hinder us? We have corrected Thy work. Tomorrow I shall condemn Thee and burn Thee as the worst of heretics.

The cardinal, of course, represents the Church, the agents of Christ—his vicars on earth, in Church terminology. The "correction" of Christ's work followed from the Church's belief that Christ had misread human nature: he had offered men freedom; that was the last thing they wanted: "In the end they will lay their freedom at our feet and say to us: 'make us slaves but feed us.' "

The Church leaders had accepted the crown of Caesar, rejected by Christ in his temptation by the Devil; they had accepted the crown to make men happy.

Again, the cardinal accuses Christ of error: Men do not want freedom; they want authority. They are happy only in slavery.

If you haven't read it, I will not spoil the ending. The point is made. Over the course of 1,500 years, the message of Christ was totally perverted, and deliberately so. His vicars—agents—had made their own judgment about human nature and the purpose of the Church itself and had reversed Christ's teachings, especially "and ye shall know the truth, and the truth shall make you free."[49] When the "owner" (if I can use the analogy without blaspheming) appeared, the agents knew what they had done, regretted it not, and threatened him with death. Agency costs, indeed.

The tale also speaks to the enormous power of an institution— the inertia that has built up over the years. The weight of tradition—the opinions and behavior patterns that are passed along to the young—can produce massive inertia. In Dostoyevsky's tale, the Church, after 1,500 years, had conditioned itself and the populace to its infallibility. Incredibly, no one raised a hand when Christ himself—and they knew who he was—was seized. I have spoken of the benefits from the stability and tradition of institutions, but that very stability can be fatal when the wrong course is chosen. How can an institution be diverted, changed? The poet Evan Connell provides one answer—perhaps the only answer:

> The power of an organization
> like that of an individual,
> shall be tested when some man or
> principle is found which stands
> irrevocably in opposition.
> *Heir stehe ich, ich kann nicht anders.*[50]

The last line is Martin Luther's response to his conviction for heresy at the Diet of Worms in 1521: "Here I stand, I cannot do anything else." Luther was hardly the first to see the problems of the Roman Church, the corruption and godlessness of its princes. In fact, a generation earlier, Erasmus of Rotterdam had recognized the need for reform but had confined his critique to private communications. It took Luther, a man "irrevocably in opposition," to test the power of the Church and, in fact, to win. He died in his own bed, the founder of a new Christian faith outside the Church of Rome. A true Ortegan hero—he changed the world.

We have had a recent example of one man in opposition to a giant organization: Ross Perot versus General Motors. When General Motors acquired Perot's EDS in 1984 for $2.5 billion, Perot became the automaker's largest shareholder. From his position on the board, Perot became GM's greatest critic, publicly excoriating the management on a range of issues: compensation, investment practices, employee relations, and so on. On December 1, 1986, GM's chairman, Roger Smith, had had enough. Perot resigned as a GM director and as the head of EDS, accepting a buy-out of his stock position for $750 million. In this particular challenge to the power of an organization, the organization won, although Perot must be a famous loser, taking away $750 million.[51] The books on this whole affair are still to be written, so it is not certain whether Perot had an opportunity to stay with General Motors and continue the fight but just settled for the cash. He may well have been the Erasmus in this drama—the man who knew he was right but could not bring himself to make the final challenge. General Motors may still need its Martin Luther—the man irrevocably in opposition.

Summary

- Unlike production and wealth, the source of the institution paradigm lies outside economics. The principal basis for the paradigm is a matter of human psychology—what Becker calls the denial of death. Men recognize their physical mortality and seek an indefinite imprint of themselves on timeless institutions.

- Reginald Jones is the exemplar of this paradigm. His leadership of General Electric centered on the maintenance and improvement of an institution; his own description of his role was "steward."

- The principal Kuhnian puzzle of an institution is its indefinite maintenance. To ensure this, institutional leaders seek an accommodation, even independence, from their "stakeholders"— employees (unions), shareholders, government, customers, suppliers.

- The institution serves society in economic ways, mainly because of its central tendency: stability. Economic benefits are derived from the long-run, stable management of technology, assets, and people.

- The institution serves its members (employees) well through its stability as well as through its tendency to instill a sense of purpose, a meaning, in people's lives.

- The principal metaphors of the institution are journey, game, and society. These share entailments that closely fit an institution: goal, unpredictability/ambiguity, cooperation, leadership, meaning, adventure.

- The principal fault of the paradigm lies with agency costs. The managers of institutions do not necessarily have the same interests as their owners or, for that matter, other stakeholders. The risk is that the company will be operated for the sole benefit of the management or, at best, the employees. The paradigm's metaphors reinforce this in the choice of leader roles: the captain of a ship of fools, the team leader playing for the sake of play, the politician grinding his own ax, the charismatic shaman/leader bent on self-glorification.

14
Fin De Siècle

To be modern is to live a life of paradox and contradiction.
—Marshall Berman[1]

A Taste for the Apocalypse

We have now seen the evolution of business thought and business expression—the metaphors and their changes over time, driven by currents of thought and the shifting purposes that men have attributed to business organizations. And we have answered most of the questions posed in chapter 1: the natures of business metaphors and business purposes, their interrelationships, their changes over time, and their sources in wider spheres of thought. Now it is time to look at the present day—the changes that we are in the midst of.

The present age is one of unrest and uncertainty in Western culture, and this has carried over into the subculture of business. We stand on the brink of the twenty-first century, the *fin de siècle*—indeed, more momentously, the *fin de millénaire*, the end of the second millenium.

As the philosopher William Barrett said, the fear of the apocalypse, and even the taste for it, is revelatory of our time.[2] We have, of course, the constant nuclear threat, the fears of resource exhaustion, the turbulence generated by population explosion and widespread poverty. In the United States, new economic times have burst upon us—times of sharp extremes: a record high stock market index, then a record decline; record budget and trade deficits; the dollar at new lows; and the United States in a net deficit to foreign capital.

We have also seen the evolution of three basic business paradigms and their ultimate failures as useful guides to action. These failures, I believe, are related to deeper currents in Western culture. We can sense at this juncture, this *fin de siècle,* a hint of Pascal's fear as he faced the infinities of time and space. Twentieth-century thinkers have sharpened Pascal's insight: Heidegger writes of man's "throwness," an awkward but profound statement of man's lot— thrown into the world and made to make the best of it. Ortega sees modern man as shipwrecked, grasping for salvation in culture.[3]

And we have seen Montague express the same thought—culture as one of the "swaying rope ladders across fuming oblivion." We should recall that in this era, business is a key factor in our culture and still has the capacity to provide those rope ladders, to aid that shipwrecked man. Let us look at the cultural trends we are experiencing at the edge of the twenty-first century and the economic trends that are entwined with culture. Let us also review the failures of past business paradigms and speculate on what the future could hold.

Economic Trends

Apocalyptic talk grows more common in U.S. business circles; it is difficult to pick up a business publication and not read of mortal threats and dire predictions. A good deal of this disquiet centers on the growing U.S. dependence on foreign economies—the loss of America's favored status as an independent economic entity.

The facts bear out this concern. Foreign-owned assets in the United States have grown dramatically: In 1985, Western Europeans increased their U.S. ownership by 21.9 percent over 1984; the Japanese increased their ownership by 50.6 percent.

Perhaps even more alarming, the U.S. economy has become dependent on foreign capital, much of it not for investment in productive capacity but to fund U.S. government deficits. In 1986, foreign purchases of U.S. Treasury securities accounted for 22 percent of the total, up from only 4 percent as recently as 1983. The U.S. economy, with its enormous domestic market, once operated almost as an autarchy; foreign trade and capital were epiphenomena. But in 1985, over 20 percent of the U.S. gross national product was related to the export and import trade; that figure was 10 percent in 1965. The result of these changes in capital movements, investment, and trade has made the United States a debtor nation; we achieved that status in mid-1984, and by the end of 1986, that deficit—U.S. assets abroad less foreign assets in the United States—stood at a negative $200 billion. An economist at Merrill Lynch noted, "If the securities buying from abroad were to dry up, we would be in a pickle."[4]

Other voices add to the chorus. The *New York Times* ran a headline on April 5, 1987: "In Global Financial Circles, Everyone Is Growing Frantic."[5] The article describes the world economy in terms of a "three ring circus." The rings are the precipitous fall of the dollar, the foreign debt crisis (Brazil had just suspended payment on $68 billion in debt), and the United States–Japan trade war. The *Times* attributes the U.S. economic problems to three linked phenomena: inadequate national savings, insufficient investment in productive capacity, and the resultant growing dependence on foreign capital. The latter point goes beyond natural feelings of patriotism; it could have severe economic impact on the United States and the global economy. With the dollar falling, the flow of foreign capital could be stemmed, driving up interest rates in the United States, fueling inflation, recession, and worse. Some think this process has begun. The market "meltdown" of October 19, 1987, was blamed in part on Treasury Secretary Baker's expressed unwillingness to support the dollar.[6]

What is at the heart of these problems or, perhaps more important, behind the sense of unease that these problems highlight? Opinions differ, of course. O'Toole reports on a survey of U.S. managers and scholars—their assessment of the root causes of U.S. economic difficulties since the oil crisis.[7] One view looks beyond economics and business practices to the larger cultural shifts in our society. This camp points us toward a potpourri of cultural changes: growing affluence, rising expectations, the influence of TV, the effects of the Vietnam War, the women's movement. All these changes have created new cultural values, and people have become more concerned with the quality of life than with economic efficiency. We have shifted more from production to consumption; we tend more toward immediate personal gratification than toward the long-term sacrifices required for sustained economic growth. The U.S. educational system is faulted; our educators are considered responsible for an overall decline in discipline—a psychology of entitlement, zero risk, narcissism. We shall return to these cultural factors in the next section.

Clearly, we are undergoing a change whose roots are profound and complex. Let us turn to the future—the new economic world that these forces are likely to engender. Cetron's 1985 work, *The Future of American Business*, provides some clues. He repeats some of the themes we have already covered. The outlook is not encouraging for U.S. "smokestack" (i.e., heavy) industries; but even our new manufacturing industries—electronics and biotechnology—face stiff challenges from abroad.[8] The bright spot in the U.S. economy—the services sector—is not without its downside as well. The jobs in this sector tend to be low-paid—considerably lower than a unionized factory job. And the factory jobs are vanishing: In the 1950s and 1960s, one-third of U.S. jobs were in manufacturing. That figure is 24 percent today, and Cetron projects it to be 8 percent in the year 2000.[9]

The increasing importance of service industries and service jobs is, of course, the essence of the postindustrial society—the concept first popularized by Daniel Bell. We are already a postindustrial society under the narrow definition: More than half of the U.S. GNP and half of the U.S. jobs are in the service sector. In fact, we have been in this mode since at least 1970—some say as early as 1940.[10] Bell sees postindustrialization as a natural step from industrialization itself. Once a nation has gained the material benefits of industrialization, economic forces lead it inexorably along the trajectory toward a service economy. Higher productivity in manufacturing leads to fewer jobs, but as incomes rise, there is a greater demand for education, health services, recreation, and so forth, so jobs are created in those sectors.[11]

Today, 60 percent of the U.S. GNP is in services and 70 percent of nonfarm workers are in service industries. In the past ten years, the United States created 18 million jobs in services and only 2.5 million in manufacturing.[12] In the third world, services are also growing faster than other sectors; service jobs there absorb most of the new entrants into the labor force, mainly in wholesale, retail, and government. (Recall that government is classified as a "service industry," and government everywhere grows apace.) This picture of the third world is arresting. Bell and the other "postindustrialists" have tended to idealize this new economy; we catch the vision of a clean, orderly environment, a highly paid and highly educated work force, "knowledge workers" and technocrats serving one another. Gunnar Myrdal showed us the reality of third-world "postindustrialism" in his analysis of India, an exceptionally poor country with more than half its workers in service trades.[13] As Myrdal showed, they were in services because there were few manufacturing jobs, and the alternative was to starve in the countryside. These were not knowledge workers; rather, they were peddlers and shoeshine men—an army of underemployed scratching for a living.

Pre-, post-, present-industrialization—call it what you will—Myrdal demonstrated that it is difficult to sustain an economy based on everyone taking in one another's laundry. But the projections for the U.S. economy are a continuation of the services trend, with a manufacturing sector composed of new industries—especially electronics and biotechnology.

The new economy means new jobs but also new types of work—a great deal of service work, as we have seen, and most of that low paid, but also a great deal of engineering and software development, a great demand for technical knowledge of all types. These new industries and service establishments are a radical change from the past—the old factory environment with its rigid demands for discipline and drill. It seems inevitable that these new circumstances will affect the workers' attitudes toward work as well as the businessman's concept of his operations, his paradigm, and his metaphors. This is a point to which we shall return.

Let us look now at another scholar, Herman Kahn, who devoted his working life to projections of the future. In 1974, Kahn focused his attention on the prospective U.S. economy in the year 2000. He foresaw substantial economic growth and a very high level of personal income but an economy quite different from that of 1974 or, indeed, 1989. Recall that economists differentiate economic sectors as primary (agriculture and mining), secondary (manufacturing), and tertiary (services). Most of the talk of postindustrialism has been about the tertiary sector—services to the other two sectors, such as insurance, transportation, and professional services. Kahn predicted that by 2000, most economic activity will be in a *quaternary* sector—largely personal services, such as entertainment, travel, and other aids to self-actualization.[14]

To sum up: We are in a period of distinct uncertainty and uneasiness vis-à-vis the U.S. economy and our industrial society. America has become dependent on foreign capital and trade—not necessarily a bad thing in itself, but deeply disturbing to a society and an economy that has prized independence. The U.S. economy is in transition: heavy industry generally dwindling, new industries growing rapidly but threatened from abroad, and more and more economic activity shifting toward services—traditional "tertiary" services, but "quaternary" services as well. There are many reasons for these changes, and we have seen a number of thinkers searching for their sources. There is a substantial body of opinion that attributes the new directions to changes in culture. Let us turn to that subject.

Cultural Trends

We live in an age when change is on everyone's lips; there is an obsession with change in society at large, as well as in business— new values, new mores. We are reluctant today to accept the words of the Preacher, "There is no new thing under the sun,"[15] or those of Marcus Aurelius, "He who has seen the present day has seen all—for all things are of one kind and of one form."[16] Rather, we see new things and new forms all around us.

The coupling of economic and social change is a very close one, so close that the cause-and-effect relationship is difficult to discern. There is the Marxist view that cultural change stems from economic conditions, a view defended by Mark Harris in his book *America Now*. Harris cites the familiar litany of problems: the American worker losing pride in his work, a new culture of permissiveness and libertarianism. But Harris finds the cause in our economic organization. Very simply, people no longer earn their living as they did in the past, and anthropological studies show that when people change their way of making a living, there are always unintended consequences in a broad range of customs and institutions.[17]

Harris has a simple point. America has changed in its values and work ethics because America has become "bureaucratized" and "oligopolized"; work has become more oriented to people processing and information processing, less oriented to the production of goods—the postindustrial society again. Harris thinks that bureaucratic work, a product of our new economic organization, has produced attitudes and alienation that throw people into the arms of permissiveness and hedonism. Cause and effect are clearly postulated here by Harris.[18]

Herman Kahn sees the same phenomenon—what he calls an increasingly "sensate" culture, a culture to which he applies a long string of adjectives: "empirical, this-worldly, secular, humanistic, pragmatic, utilitarian, epicurean, hedonistic." The culture is also characterized by the decline, even the extinction, of sacred and religious authority. But Kahn sees this culture as but one part of a "multi-fold" trend—a complex of changes that he makes no attempt to sort into cause and effect. The other critical components of this trend are familiar to us: accumulation of technical knowledge, worldwide industrialization and urbanization, increased leisure and affluence, growth of the quaternary sector, the increasing tempo of change.[19]

If there is any driver among there factors, any cause for all those effects, Kahn would probably choose a key Western trait: rationality. Much of what we see today and will see tomorrow can be attributed to man's manipulative rationality, applying logic and science to the full scope of human activities—cultural, political, social, and economic. This has literally transformed the world; the process did not begin yesterday, but its effects are accumulating. Kahn cites man's rationality applied to man himself—man in his social role. William Barrett has expressed his concern for this trend:

> For a long time the labor of a good part of our culture has been reductive; the effort to undermine in one way or another the spiritual status of the human person.[20]

But this can be viewed in another light; we need not see all darkness in man's attempt to understand his nature and remake his society and culture. We have learned from Vico that man makes history and society—that he has that power, even that imperative. Daniel Bell dwells on the positive aspect of this, citing the Meiji Restoration and the industrialization of Japan as but one example of a deliberate—and positive—intervention in a society's direction.[21]

Mentalities have changed, and values have also clearly changed. Kahn has specified a set of "societal levers"—the means that the society has to effect social control. He finds that all these levers are having less and less effect as time goes on, and he forecasts that their power will continue to decline. Each of us can judge how effective these levers are today and how effective they were in the past. Kahn's levers are:[22]

- Religion, tradition, authority
- The stress of the physical environment
- The need to earn a living
- The defense of the frontiers, economy, and political institutions
- The martial virtues
- The manly emphasis (team sports, heroic types)
- The Puritan ethic
- Loyalty
- Repression of instincts
- Taboos, rituals, myths, and customs

Kahn has tried to crystallize the erosion of these levers—the change in mentality—in a parable about a job-hunter. Our applicant in 1930 would have asked only about salary and chances for advancement. His grandson (Kahn wrote in 1974) would ask: "What are the fringe benefits? What is your product? What kind of an organization are you? What kind of people do you produce? How are decisions made? Will I enjoy it here? Will I mature? Will I exercise most of my skills?"[23] These are not bad questions. Evidently, Kahn is not entirely unhappy to see the societal levers lose some of their potency.

But what of the old values—the values that got us this far? It is popular to look back today and condemn those who built this industrial society. We have seen their metaphors and their purposes, but what were their basic values? We have one answer from a study of business leaders in the period 1945–55.[24] The leaders of that day held to the following:

- Individualism, moral responsibility and freedom

- Materialism

- Action based on realism

- The goal of progress

- Optimism

- Competitiveness

- Democracy, equal opportunity

- Service and social responsibility

Not a bad list. But if they were sincere, either these ideas changed dramatically or the public perception of them changed. Daniel Yankelovich surveyed Americans throughout the period 1969–75 and found that over 90 percent of young people thought that business was overly concerned with profits and unconcerned with its public responsibility. And one-third of the business executives agreed. By 1976, the Harris poll showed that only 21 percent of the American people had confidence in corporate leadership.[25]

Somehow a disconnect occurred between corporate values, respectable as they were, and public values—the expectations of people about business. Cavanagh has sought the nature of this disconnect in his book *American Business Values in Transition*.[26] First, he thinks that the world has finally caught up with Adam Smith's invisible hand: An acquisitive materialism has been encouraged by a system that provides a rationalization for selfishness.

Second, people have begun to sense the lack of purpose or, perhaps, the inappropriate purpose of business. The values of the business leaders—individualism, freedom, progress—are admirable, but to what purpose will that freedom be applied, and what is the goal of progress?

Cavanagh projects a set of new values, both for society and for business:

- The central role of the person

- Participation in decision making

- The corporation as a servant of society

- Harmony with the environment

And he cites concepts that will occupy us later: new measurements of business success and the necessity for a new legitimacy. This is a set of values that would probably satisfy Kahn's 1974 job-hunter—a corporate credo that would appeal to a person seeking more than a salary and a chance for advancement.

A change has taken place; perhaps there *is* some new thing under the sun. The values of the larger society have changed; Kahn's societal levers are weakening; individual needs are supplanting society's—and business's—needs. These value changes have placed new demands on the business enterprise. The demands come from outside, of course—from the consumers and the citizens, all of whom bring powerful pressure on the corporation. But they come from inside the business as well. Business leaders are not janissaries—cultureless people raised from childhood to serve the organization. The leaders breathe in the same culture as their fellow citizens, attend the same schools, read the same books, see the same news. As the culture changes, the new business leaders grow up with it like everyone else, and their actions in the future must reflect the basic ideas that they have imbibed from earliest childhood. Let us turn to these ideas.

Trends in Thought

As we have seen throughout this work, there have been changes in the views that business leaders have of their organizations and changes in the metaphors they apply. In the period since 1975, there have been radical shifts in metaphor usage: War has become a much more common image than in the earlier periods, and the once popular society metaphor (Peters and Waterman to the contrary) has become a great deal less popular. In a very similar manner, the purposes for business have undergone a sea change; in our own time, none of the paradigms of business can hold a majority: wealth, 29 percent; production, 41 percent; institution, 29 percent. In all other historical periods, one of the paradigms was always a clear favorite. It would appear that the ferment in society, the economic as well as the cultural uncertainties, have had their impact on business thought. It is tempting to speculate that we are in a period of paradigm transition, that as we grapple with new economic orders and new values, the purpose of business is also undergoing a major transition.

The nature of this transition, and what might emerge as a new business paradigm, is not at all clear at this time but will almost certainly be rooted in the economic and cultural changes that we see around us. We are nearing the completion of the twentieth century—the *fin de siècle*. It could be useful to reflect on the last turn of the century, the era that popularized the term *fin de siècle* itself.

The beginning of the twentieth century was also a period of great intellectual and cultural change. Most of what we now call "modern"—modern philosophy, music, art, architecture, and so on—began in this era; it is a paradox that "modernism" refers to movements that are now nearly a century old. By a quirk of history, many of the makers of the modern world lived in turn-of-the-century Vienna; the Viennese giants of modernism include Schoenberg in music, Freud in psychology, Wittgenstein in philosophy, Wagner in architecture, and Klimt in painting. These men and their successors throughout the world transformed culture and thought; none of the higher arts and sciences would ever be the same after the breakthroughs of the turn of the century. Nowadays, we see human behavior through the prism of Freud's work; we are accustomed to architecture that is functional; we view paintings as objects rather than representations. The world is a different place since the experience of modernism. But how has modernism affected the thinking of business leaders? Hardly at all, it would first appear. If there has been any impact at all, it would be a better understanding of human motivation through the discoveries of psychology. But the other changes in modern thought had left business virtually untouched until very recently.

Business thinking has been largely fixed in the mode of scientific materialism, a way of thinking that runs back to Descartes in the seventeenth century. Scientific materialism is probably still the dominant mentality in the West, especially among business people. It is the belief that the ultimate facts of nature are bits of matter in space and that all the phenomena of our experience can be explained by the movement and configuration of this matter.[27] A bit more intellectual baggage has been added since then: Social Darwinism and positivism, neither of which are incompatible with scientific materialism.

But there have been profound changes in thought since Descartes, Darwin, and Comte. One rather corrosive stream of thought in philosophy is the logical positivism movement, an offshoot of Wittgenstein's early work but a movement that he renounced and condemned. The philosophy is rooted in language, a compelling concern for Wittgenstein throughout his life. Within language, which is to say within the limits of man's thought, there are really only two types of statements. The first type is statements about the world, statements that can be verified by logic or experiment. The other type is all the others—statements on metaphysics, ethics, aesthetics, values. To the logical positivist, these latter statements are—literally—nonsense; they are unverifiable. Wittgenstein's heirs forgot his key qualification: These are the statements that are really the only important ones—provable or not. But it is very likely that logical positivism has taken its toll on modern consciousness as an intellectually respectable means to relegate values and religion to nonissues. The "societal levers" of Kahn may well be losing their effect under the onslaught of this type of thinking. And perhaps some in business have lost the vision of a transcendent purpose because of the influence of this doctrine.

Wittgenstein's work helped found another twentieth-century movement: structuralism. His insight that human beings are prisoners of language suggested the existence of some other prisons, or structures, in the world—structures that determine man's being and his reality. The anthropologist Lévi-Strauss found a rigorous pattern in a host of primitive customs and rituals and attributed them to a fundamental structure in the human mind that was manifested in these practices. Chomsky followed up on Wittgenstein's language insight and claimed to have found a deep structure underlying the forms of sentences—some kind of built-in human capacity to understand basic grammatical principles: Structuralism is

> a hidden harmony of things, generating language, patterns of culture, ideologies and institutions. . . . The structures which determine language and culture are determinants of individuals.[28]

This is a rather dark picture—nothing less than man's behavior and culture determined by his biological makeup, his genes. We could stress this determinism and unfreedom, or we could stress another aspect of structuralism—its insight into the ultimate reality of existence. For what structuralism is saying is that the view of knowledge as a reflection within someone of the "real" contents of the environment is incorrect; scientific materialism, the presumed faith of the average businessman, is plainly misguided. Rather than mirroring some external "reality," our minds, through their structure—the wiring of our brains, if you will—actively participate in creating a reality.[29]

Structuralism and logical positivism show a family resemblance and a distinct dissimilarity to scientific materialism. The new thought is radically relativistic, denying both ultimate values and ultimately knowable "reality." Such are some of the currents of modern thought that are starting to touch business thinking. We shall return to these matters.

Failures of the Paradigms

I have sketched out just a few strands of modern thought to demonstrate modernism's radical departure from the past, its new ways of looking at the world. And let us recall that that is what a paradigm is really all about—a way of looking at the world, a way of making sense of experience. The notions about business that I have called paradigms are in this sense derivative; they are derived from the actors' most profound assumptions about the nature and structure of reality. Should those assumptions shift radically, we would expect a corresponding shift in the attitudes toward business. As I have tried to show, there have been radical changes in philosophy, thinking that proposes a new view of reality. In the main, these ideas are relativistic; they unmoor man from an ultimate ground for reality. These new ideas are slowly making their way into popular consciousness, and we could expect that the ideas will affect business thought.

We may already be experiencing this impact. If I was able to demonstrate anything in our long march through the business paradigms, I hope that I showed that none of them is very satisfactory, that all create a certain uneasiness in our minds. None has a firm hold on a majority of business people; there is little consensus anymore on the fundamental purpose of business. In one way, this can be read as a critique of industrialization and capitalism—not a Marxist critique, but a humanistic one. As we have seen, one of the fundamental concerns is the moral basis of capitalism, not its efficacy. Michael Novack takes the high road in his defense of capitalism:

> The inherent nature of capitalism as a system is not the well-being of the individual. It is the well-being of the entire human race.[30]

This is, of course, a restatement of Adam Smith's thought. To Smith, capitalism's purpose was—literally—the wealth of nations; individual wealth and individual greed were necessary by-products, but the system was for the betterment of mankind. It is precisely on this ground that Karl Polanyi mounted his attack on the market system of capitalism: Has it been for man's benefit or will it lead to his destruction? Polanyi is another of the *fin de siècle* Viennese, actually Wittgenstein's close contemporary, born in 1886. I have already touched on Polanyi's critique of capitalism (he calls it the market system), but I want to cover his ideas a little further, since they can help illuminate the failures of the current paradigms. Polanyi's fundamental quarrel with capitalism stems from the inner logic and dynamic of the system itself. Capitalism is based on the notion, as we have seen, that labor, land, and capital are commodities—objects produced for sale. They must be considered as such for the market system to work, since a market, by its nature, consists of buyers and sellers of objects produced for sale. But these "commodities"—especially labor and land—are the very substance of society itself, so the society becomes subordinated to the market system.[31] Polanyi strikes at the heart of the basic assumption: "None of them is produced for sale. The commodity description of labor, land and money is entirely fictitious."[32]

The argument really comes down to the primacy of society over economics. In Polanyi's view, capitalism has reversed this primacy; the economic order has absorbed all of society. And it has not always been so. Polanyi tries to show that our market system is a historical anomaly. In all times and places, man organized himself into societies, and the prime function of those societies was to serve the needs of its members. One aspect of every society is, of course, the economic one—the need to make a living—but this had always been subordinated to society, made an element of life that was to serve man's needs.[33]

For Polanyi, this child of society swallowed its father; capitalism, in order to function as a market system, incorporated society—man and nature—into itself. Polanyi stresses the distinctiveness of our market system, finding it historically unprecedented and potentially destructive in the extreme. His is definitely a fear of the apocalypse; in fact, Polanyi on the market system reminds us of the apocalyptic prophet Daniel:

> The fourth beast shall be the fourth kingdom upon earth, which shall be diverse from all kingdoms and shall devour the whole earth, and shall tread it down, and break it in pieces.[34]

Polanyi's critique can be applied especially to the paradigm of wealth. As we saw, that paradigm fails us in its ultimate nihilism, the essential futility of piling up those treasures upon earth, carrying those ingots to the grave. Polanyi does not find this flaw in Adam Smith; rather:

> Wealth was to him merely an aspect of the life of the country, to
> the purpose of which it remained subordinate. . . . There is no
> intimation in his work that the economic interests of the capital-
> ists laid down the law to society.[35]

But of course, later capitalists did in fact put their own wealth
above the needs of society—they did justify themselves by Smith's
invisible hand. And in doing so, they coarsened society and debased
civilization's values; as Engels said, they created the notion that
men and things had value only if they could be used to make money.

Polanyi was a radical thinker; his critique of capitalism is fundamental: He believed that Western civilization simply chose the
wrong path when industrialization came and that Western man
created a monster that would consume him—a "fourth beast" and
a "fourth kingdom" that would devour the whole earth. But much
more moderate voices have also condemned the paradigm of wealth,
not least a staunch defender of capitalism, Peter Drucker. Writing
in 1974, Drucker took dead aim at the very exemplar of the paradigm of wealth, Alfred Sloan:

> General Motors has stayed with Sloan's legacy. And in Sloan's
> terms, i.e., in terms of sales and profits, it has succeeded admi-
> rably. . . . But, it has also failed abysmally—in terms of public
> reputation, of public esteem, of acceptance by the public.[36]

The paradigm of wealth has spun out its usefulness. Perhaps
the final word on the paradigm—its effects on society and the
individual—was written 2,500 years ago in the *Bhagavad Gita*:
"Anger and lust is their refuge; and they strive by unjust means to
amass wealth for their own cravings."[37]

Let us turn now to the paradigm of production—the bright
promise of an endless stream of necessary goods, so vitally important to mankind struggling with scarcity—Ford's new Messiah. The
paradigm seems to have lost its way; the inner logic of its development has now left us with a surfeit of questionable consumer
goods and the threat of irreparable environmental damage. The
environmental threat was foreseen by Polanyi; it was the logical
result of the commodization of land—that is, nature. If nature is
an object produced for sale, it will certainly be sold, exploited, used

for any purpose that will maximize its profit potential. Polanyi wrote:

> What we call land is an element of nature inextricably interwoven with man's institutions. To isolate it and form a market out of it was perhaps the weirdest of all the undertakings of our ancestors.[38]

But let us not forget that production of necessities is still a critical issue for humanity and that capitalism—the market system—has given man the means to satisfy material needs. Having those means presents us with an imperative, a moral imperative. As Novack said: "Today, famines are no longer God's responsibility, but man's."[39] We cannot turn our backs on industrial civilization; we cannot even be indifferent to it. It is now our duty to use the enormous productive capacity of that system to produce the goods that men need. But Galbraith's critique is sound; clearly, the notion of production for production's sake, producing goods regardless of their merit, is senseless. And if in the process we destroy our habitat, it is worse than senseless—it is criminal.

Now let us see what has happened to the paradigm of the institution. I believe that the failure of this paradigm has become apparent as well. The stakeholder view of the firm, once a very promising concomitant of the institutional view, has become bankrupt: institutional managers now seek autonomy from their stakeholders, rather than power sharing or interest balancing. Agency costs have become a serious issue with the institutional paradigm, as managers and employees use the institution for their own purposes. The Grand Inquisitor, not the vicar, is the image we find in present-day institutional leadership. This poses a threat not just to the owners of these institutions but to the society at large. Managers have control of enormous economic and productive power and are becoming less and less answerable to society for their use of that power. This is a serious disconnect. Polanyi's insight on this subject is true: The economic element of society exists for society's purposes, not the other way around.

The *New York Times* reported on the attitudes of some American CEOs—attitudes that can only be categorized as the perversion of the institutional ideal. Under the threat of foreign competition and corporate raiders, many CEOs are "adopting a new credo that puts corporate survival above all else." The *Times* stated:

> The new order eschews loyalty to workers, products, corporate structure, businesses, factories, communities, even the nation. With survival at stake, only market leadership, strong profits and a high stock price can be allowed to matter.[40]

This is a truly astonishing departure from the institutional ideals: little thought given to building or preserving the business, no sense of a responsibility to create jobs or help communities. The "stakeholders" arc definitely gone. Even the institution that Reg Jones served has undergone this profound change. Jones's hand-picked successor, John F. Welch, Jr., has been called "Neutron Jack" at GE. In five years, he closed scores of plants and idled tens of thousands of workers; like the impact of the neutron bomb, the buildings remain, but the people are gone. Welch has jettisoned more than 150 GE businesses and has reduced employment by more than 25 percent. This has been called "a searing change for a company whose loyalty to employees and communities had seemed an inviolate part of its culture."[41]

But Welch is not alone in his views or in his actions. In fact, we may now be starting to see, from relatively young business leaders like Welch, the impact of modern thought—especially the extreme relativity of that thought, the lack of an ultimate grounding.

The shape of things to come may be discernible in a recent article by McDonald in the *Harvard Business Review*.[42] McDonald first paints a familiar picture for us, reminding us of almost everyone's commonsense idea of a business: plants—fixed, of course, in a community—with long-term employees and long-term ties to the community; similarly enduring relationships with suppliers, banks, and other institutions. At one time—and McDonald says it has passed—markets were the opposite of those fixed institutional components: Markets were elastic, transient, something the business dealt with and solicited, but certainly not a *part* of the business. Now, it is precisely the reverse. The managers see their market as the fixed compass point, the true essence of the business—the thing that is fixed and tangible. Employees, plants, and institutional relationships—these are now fluid, disposable things; market share is now a corporate asset, as a factory once was.

This trend will probably accelerate; already there is a growth business in independent corporate services. Large companies will increasingly "farm out" costly staff functions—such as personnel, legal, and real estate—to independent contractors.[43] And what is left? In the blind urge to survive—the impulse to capture a market, to sell something—we have the spectacle of wholesale divestiture of nearly everything we once thought of as a business: plants, people, staff. It is almost like the infamous remark of the U.S. officer in Vietnam: "It was necessary to destroy the village in order to save it."

Legitimacy

This discussion of the paradigms and their failures really centers on the problem of legitimacy—the problem that Gilder addressed with the wealth paradigm, Galbraith exposed with the production paradigm, and North tried to solve with the institution paradigm. Simply put: How does a business justify its economic power, its actions toward society? There is a basic argument, rooted in the wealth paradigm, that, after all, business is private property; and the institution of private property is a well-established and fundamental right in a free society. But private property is not an absolute right. We do not need Karl Polanyi to tell us that business must be subordinated to society for the latter's self-defense; every business operates under a charter from the state. The right of private property is formally subjugated to society's interests by our very legal system. So business does require more of a justification than the exercise of private rights.

This question of legitimacy is becoming more important. In the early part of the Reagan era, public criticism of business was muted; government became a staunch ally. But times are changing; one straw in the wind is a headline: "On the Brink of an Anti-Business Era."[44] The article points out that businessmen have failed to realize how fragile the public's confidence is, how fundamentally suspicious people are. Without the spur of adverse public opinion or government opposition, businesses have become more ready to shift production abroad, abandoning communities and workers. But public confidence in business ebbs and flows. We have been in a period of either indifference or support for business; that can and will change, because the question of legitimacy has yet to be answered satisfactorily.

Given that a corporation is chartered by society, its legitimacy clearly must flow from society's agreement to an acceptable purpose for the business. We have spent some time elaborating on some fundamental purposes, and we have found them all wanting. Wealth as a purpose was acceptable only so long as people believed in the "invisible hand," so long as people believed that private greed served public purpose. I am not convinced that this is a sustainable belief today, certainly not in the sense that the sole purpose of a business is to make money.

The institutional purpose for business—a purpose that can be and has been reduced to mere survival—cannot gain widespread acceptance in society. By its nature, the purposes served are only those of the institutional members; society, if it is served at all, is served indirectly through Ackoff's new "invisible hand"—the spur on the managers to perform so that the institution can survive.

Production in one sense comes as close as possible to a purpose that society can find acceptable. Daniel Bell expressed that thought:

> The justification of the corporation is no longer . . . in the natural right of private property, but in its role as an institution for producing more and more goods.[45]

But as we have seen, this production can become uncontrolled. Neither the nature of the goods produced nor the extent of environmental damage is logically of any concern to the corporation whose justification is production alone. In and of itself, the paradigm of production is not a sound basis for legitimacy.

The problem of legitimacy is not a new one; it seems always to have been an issue for capitalism—the issue of finding a theoretical and moral ground for the undertaking. At the root of the problem is the fact that capitalism has never had an adequate ideology; it is fundamentally a pragmatic system; it just *works*—pretty well most of the time.

Paul Samuelson called capitalism "an effective but unloveable system with no mystique to protect it."[46] And Joseph Schumpeter has pointed out that the more successful capitalism has been, the more it is criticized—the more our material needs are satisfied, the less we think we need industrialization and the more we become critical of capitalism's ambivalent nature. Capitalism was conceived for only one purpose: economic growth.[47] But in achieving that, it transformed society—in Polanyi's view, it *became* society—and when that occurred, the ideology, or lack of one, became of central importance.

Adolph Berle, writing in 1932, framed the issue of legitimacy for us, if he did not solve the problem:

> Whenever there is a question of power, there is a question of legitimacy. . . . These institutions of tremendous power have the slenderest claim to legitimacy, which also means finding a field of responsibility and a field of accountability.[48]

Responsibility and accountability—these fit well the new values that we covered earlier; the corporation as a servant of society; the concern for the individual as well as society; harmony with the environment. But how can this all be achieved? Is there a purpose for business that can provide true legitimacy—a purpose that is practical and sustainable? Or will the problem of legitimacy continue to beset us in the future? We will speculate on these questions in the final chapter.

Summary

- There is a general uneasiness about the U.S. economy: a volatile stock market, increased dependence on foreign economies and financial markets, a *fin de siècle* air of uncertainty, a fear of the apocalypse.

- It is difficult to account for the U.S. malaise; some find the cause in new societal values that favor quality of life over economic efficiency.

- The United States is a postindustrial society; 70 percent of nonfarm workers are in service industries. This type of work is radically different from the manufacturing environment that sustained the old values.

- A "sensate culture" has been created—empirical, this-worldly, hedonistic, utilitarian. Herman Kahn's societal levers—religion, authority, the Puritan ethic—are losing their effect.

- New values for business have emerged, at least among the working populace: the central role of the person; participation; the corporation as society's servant; the need for environmental protection.

- Trends in modern thought are beginning to be felt in business. Business people had largely been fixed in a seventeenth-century mentality of scientific materialism, with a nineteenth-century admixture of Social Darwinism and positivism. The radically relativistic philosophies of the twentieth century, which deny any ultimate grounding, are beginning to influence business thinking.

- The "old" paradigms are failing; none holds a majority position among contemporary business leaders.

- The wealth paradigm has been exposed as essentially nihilistic—the futile piling up of treasures on earth; the creation of a "fourth beast," which could consume society, as Polanyi foresaw. The paradigm's metaphors suggest dangerous leader roles—the gambler and the "bad" shepherd. "Anger and lust is their refuge; and they strive by unjust means to amass wealth."

- The production paradigm has failed as well in its fall into the output of useless goods and its harm to the environment. Galbraith's critique is telling. The paradigm's leader roles—the captain of a *voyage sans but*, the omniscient creator/designer—have proved pernicious.

- The institutional paradigm has foundered on the issue of agency costs. The Grand Inquisitor, not the vicar, has emerged as the preferred leader role. To keep independence, institutional leaders are eschewing loyalty to workers, products, and communities; only market leadership, profits, and high stock prices matter anymore.

- With the failure of the paradigm, legitimacy has become the central issue. The corporation's right to control vast assets has been called into question.

- Adolph Berle has framed the legitimacy question for us: Legitimacy stems from responsibility and accountability.

Now let us turn to the future—a future conditioned by the economic, cultural, and philosophical trends; a future in the wake of the paradigms' shipwrecks; a future that must deal with the problem of legitimacy. In the next chapter, we will explore some new paradigms and their new metaphors and see whether these hold any promise or whether the issue of legitimacy will continue to elude us.

15
Voyaging, Voyaging, Voyaging

But O the ship, the immortal ship!
O ship aboard the ship!
Ship of the body, ship of the soul,
voyaging, voyaging, voyaging!

—Walt Whitman[1]

Things Fall Apart

In this last chapter, I will speculate on new paradigms and new metaphors. Of course, predictions are always hazardous; more often than not, we fail to see the great changes when we are in the midst of them. I am reminded of Otto Wagner's diary entry on the day that the Archduke Franz Ferdinand was assassinated. Now, the great modernist Wagner and the conservative archduke did not see eye-to-eye on an architectural aesthetic. So when Franz Ferdinand was shot at Sarajevo—the proximate cause of a war that utterly transformed European history, culture, and society—Wagner thought that he saw the historical impact:

> I consider that the death of the Crown Prince has removed the greatest single obstacle to the practice and further development of modern architecture in Austria.[2]

Perhaps I am being as myopic. Nonetheless, I am hazarding the opinion that we are in the midst of a transition in business thought—

a transition toward a new paradigm and new metaphors. We have largely left the old patterns behind us: Sloan's idea of wealth and his favorite metaphor, the organism; Ford's and Taylor's paradigm of production and Taylor's key metaphor, the machine; Reg Jones's institutional paradigm and the metaphor of society. We are in a time that Yeats characterized as "things fall apart, the center cannot hold."[3] The currents in economics, culture, and thought have swept us from our old moorings in the paradigms of business. We are adrift, but we must still seek legitimacy for business. Is there a purpose that can provide true legitimacy, a paradigm that is sustainable and practical? Peter Drucker has proposed one such. We shall examine it but, I regret to say, find it impractical; then we shall explore another new paradigm, which seems to move more with the tides of history than Drucker's but will leave us no closer to a basis for business legitimacy.

Drucker's Paradigm: The Eclectic

Drucker attempted an answer to the legitimacy question in the last chapter of his book *Management*.[4] As we shall see, he has in fact attempted a grand synthesis of our paradigms—wealth, production, and institution. Drucker begins with the basic task of management: to make the organization perform—perform for the economy, the society, the community, and the individual. He strongly emphasizes managing the business for the purpose for which it was designed—in his view, economic performance. This is "job one"; it must be done or nothing else can follow. Drucker would probably say that Alfred Sloan also saw this as "job one" but failed to see anything further.

According to Drucker, economic performance must be achieved first:

> The manager who believes that social consciousness is a substitute for managing his business so that it produces the results for the sake of which it exists, is either a fool or a knave.

But economic performance is necessary, not sufficient. The manager has additional tasks: to make work productive and the worker "achieving." And further, the manager must provide for the quality of life for the society and the individual. To achieve these things, Drucker also sees the need for legitimacy; the community must accept the power of managers in order to accomplish these goals. Legitimacy must stem from a principle of morality. The old basis for justification—Smith's invisible hand—was, in Drucker's view, never accepted by society: "Profit maximization and profit motive are not only anti-social. They are immoral."

Drucker's formula is one that we have already touched on: Corporations must convert public needs into business terms—that is, profitable opportunities. But in his mind, even that is not sufficient. The foundation—the moral principle—must be "to make human strength productive." To accomplish this, Drucker argues for the autonomy of management, a feature of the institutional paradigm. His argument is pragmatic. Experience has shown that "totalitarian" approaches, even under the most benevolent governments, do not work. Freely competitive, autonomous business managers simply do a better job of managing an economy than centralized institutions do. The need for business autonomy is purely practical: It is a better means to serve society's purposes. Let me quote Drucker's peroration:

> What is needed . . . is management performance. This first requires performance as a technocrat. It requires performance that makes the manager's organization capable of supplying to society and the economy the contribution for the sake of which it exists, such as economic goods and services and the capital fund for tomorrow. . . . It also requires . . . performance in making work productive and the worker achieving and performance with respect to the quality of life. . . . If he is to remain—as he should— the manager of an autonomous institution, he must accept that he is a public man. He must accept the moral responsibility of making individual strengths productive and achieving.

Let us see what he has done. He has actually synthesized our three paradigms of business: The business must produce wealth, for it has an obligation to fund the capital stock needed for future growth; the business must produce necessary goods and services— society demands that; and the business must be managed as an autonomous institution that will endure—that is how the job can be done most effectively. And in doing these things, attention is also given to the human needs of the institution members—their need for a moral purpose and for work that is meaningful, "achieving." A neat compound of the paradigms we have reviewed—an eclectic paradigm.

If this is a new paradigm, we should expect that it would engender new metaphors. I have not heard Drucker propose one, nor have I seen any metaphor applied that could fit the eclectic. If I could speculate on one that could be used, it would be "cathedral building." The cathedral builders of the late Middle Ages built for the future; few of them saw the completed work or expected to. They worked on an edifice that had great value to society—nothing less than the house of God. And the work was "achieving," in Drucker's word: The effort called forth the best that people were capable of, both in art and in engineering. In fact, the stained glass work of these anonymous people has never been equaled; and many of the cathedrals—Chartres is the best example—stand undamaged after 800 years.

Cathedral building is an excellent metaphor for business and inspires an excellent role for the leader. The problem, though, is that no one uses this metaphor—I think, at bottom, because no one really sees a practical way to operate a business as Drucker proposes in his paradigm. Today's metaphors are voyage, war, and organism—feebly matched to cathedrals or to the eclectic. But before we reject this paradigm out of hand, let us look at it from the standpoint of legitimacy, from Adolph Berle's criteria of responsibility and accountability.

In Drucker's eclectic paradigm, responsibility is at the very heart of the business. The manager's essential responsibility is to mankind; his job is to make human strength productive. But he must also build for the future by adding to the capital stock, and he must produce things of value to society. These are certainly responsible activities and surely meet Berle's criterion: Management has found a field of responsibility. If it were possible to do business this way, the eclectic paradigm would provide all the right goals— the best features of the old paradigms: a field for human aspirations, an increase in the capital stock, and the goods and services mankind needs.

Berle's other criterion, accountability, is not so easily fulfilled by the eclectic view. Drucker insists on autonomy, and for very good reasons—it cannot work otherwise. His point is very valid; our experience clearly shows the value of decentralized economic management. But we are back to an old dilemma. If it is agreed that society must exercise some degree of control over economic institutions, how can that be achieved? Drucker is silent on this point but implies that the control will come from within the managers themselves—a sort of societal superego will steer the managers toward right action. He is relying on the good faith and goodwill of a new generation of managers who recognize their responsibility under the eclectic paradigm and are accountable to society only insofar as they accept the paradigm and its goals of service to society and the individual. I'm almost afraid to say it, but we have another "invisible hand" here—in this case, not the greed of the capitalist but quite the reverse, the moral sense of the manager. We are relying on these cathedral builders to build true cathedrals, not to build private palaces or make off with the money and materials. (I guess it has to be said that the old cathedral builders *did* build them.)

I have implied throughout this discussion that I don't believe that Drucker's scheme will work. It sounds right and probably is right in the best of worlds; the difficulty is in seeing how it could be realized today or in the foreseeable future. The cultural, philosophical, and economic trends seem to be carrying us away from any hope of realizing Drucker's noble purpose—for it *is* noble; I have no quarrel with that.

First, let us look at the impact of economics on Drucker's model. Black Monday—October 19, 1987—wiped out *$1 trillion* in corporate valuation.[5] What does that mean to the leaders of these companies? Well, by chance, the editor of *Industry Week* had a breakfast meeting scheduled for the next day with twenty CEOs. They were not panicked or desperate; rather, they were angry and frustrated. Their excellent performance of the past several years— performance in terms of wise investment and solid operations— was not rewarded by the stock market. *Au contraire.* All expressed a feeling of vulnerability toward the financial sector.[6] And this is a general feeling among company leaders. The capital markets are no longer seen as business partners, as the providers of necessary funding; they are seen as "the other"—a capricious and merciless master, not a part of their community. After Black Monday, the CEOs said that the crash was Wall Street's problem, not corporate America's. Typically, when J.W. Marriott was asked by a shareholder, "What's wrong with Marriott?" he replied, "Nothing. What's wrong with Wall Street?"[7]

The financial markets have become exceptionally volatile. The weekend I write—January 10, 1988—follows a 140-point drop in the Dow. The explanation this time was that *good* news (a drop in the unemployment rate) was at fault; the investors feared a return of inflation. Good news or bad news, share prices are fluctuating at unprecedented rates. And the corporate manager—the leader whom Drucker urges to perform—feels betrayed. Management performance (in earnings, revenue growth, production goals, whatever) is no longer enough, and management performance is at the very core of Drucker's paradigm. How can we ask leaders to base their objective solely on business performance when they are so vulnerable to arbitrary stock market prices?

The cultural trends I sketched in chapter 14 also speak against the eclectic. Drucker seeks leaders who can deal with the enormous power he grants them—remember, he posits almost total autonomy. The control mechanism in his scheme—the method that society must use to govern business—is no more than the goodwill and just instincts of corporate managers. Now, these leaders are not janissaries; they are products of the same culture as all of us. And that culture is becoming "sensate," in Herman Kahn's term— more hedonistic, more selfish, more individually oriented. Kahn's societal levers—tradition, religion, the pull of authority—are loosening as the sensate culture comes to the fore. Where, then, does Drucker expect to find the people who will operate corporate America in the highly responsible, self-sacrificing way that he prescribes? I would argue that we are producing people of quite a different stripe. How atypical is Ivan Boesky, recently sentenced to three years in prison and fined $100 million for illegal trading? In 1985, Boesky spoke to a group of business students—precisely the types that Drucker hopes will rule responsibly. Boesky's message: "I think greed is healthy. You can be greedy and still feel good about yourself."[8]

In the same manner, trends in thought pull us away from the eclectic. We saw earlier that business people were mainly fixed in the seventeenth-century mentality of scientific materialism—a method of thinking that posits a fixed and knowable reality. Drucker's magnum opus, *Management,* is a handbook infused with that philosophy. It is all rational and predictable, an image of an orderly world filled with rational people. Pfeffer has shown us that this rational model is seldom right; ambiguity and, consequently, politics in business are much closer to the truth. Today's philosophies of radical relativism—the denial of any ultimate grounding—are in Pfeffer's mode; and sadly, I believe that Pfeffer is right.

I wish Drucker were right. His is a world I want for my work life, and those of my children and grandchildren. Cathedral building is one of the noblest expressions of the human spirit, and we should cherish the builders' ideals as well as their products. But the cathedral builders are dead—gone many ages ago—gone with feudalism, divine right, scholasticism, and the other cultural features of that day. We live in a world that is simply not congenial to Drucker's model for business.

The Shape-Changers

I want to propose that a new paradigm is emerging. It is not the noble purpose that Drucker sought—far to the contrary; it is more a figure like a "rough beast . . . slouch[ing] toward Bethlehem to be born."[9] We saw something of this paradigm in chapter 14—the degeneration of the institutional ideal. These are the new leaders who "eschew loyalty to workers, products, corporate structure, business, factories, communities." To survive, "only market leadership, strong profits and a high stock price can be allowed to matter."[10]

These are the same people McDonald wrote about in the *Harvard Business Review*[11]—leaders who have reversed the old logic of business. In the past, a business was people, factories, and a network of relationships with banks, customers, suppliers. The firms's markets were an abstraction—fluid, ephemeral things, logically not a part of the business. But now, markets largely *are* the business, the entire focus of the business, the "real" assets of the company. The old assets—workers, plants, relationships—are now viewed almost as liabilities, certainly as transient and disposable things. The managers that the *New York Times* and McDonald describe stand ready to effect any transformation of the corporation to assure its continuance. The only purpose is the indefinite duration of some abstraction, some ethereal "corporate entity."

We might liken these new leaders to the "shape-changers" of Norse mythology—men capable of free transformation of their forms to suit their purpose. A shape-changer could become a bear for combat, a bird for flight, anything to ensure his survival. Our modern-day shape-changers want the same magic power; they want to jettison their plants, people, communities, nations—anything—if it aids their survival. The watchword is extreme flexibility. Only markets are fixed; markets are the new lodestone.

I proposed a medieval analogy to match Drucker's paradigm, and another image from that era will perhaps fit the style of business I have been describing: the medieval fair. The "business" people of that day made no goods, employed no people, and had no fixed base—they merely bought and sold. The only truly fixed economic units were the great market fairs across Europe—from Stourbridge in England to Novgorod in Russia. The most famous and popular fairs were the Champagne region's six-week affairs, which moved about the province with the change of the seasons. The earliest originated in Troyes in the fifth century, and that fair continued for nearly a thousand years, every September and November. In time, other Champagne towns added their own fairs: Lagny in January, Bar-sur-Aube during Lent, Provins in May and September.[12]

These fairs and their counterparts across Europe—Lyon, Ypres, Douai, Bruges, Leipzig, Lübeck, Geneva—were the fixed economic units, literally the "markets." Business in those days was a matter of buying and selling at these markets and had little to do with fixed sites for manufacturing, large numbers of employees, or even governmental regulation, since trade was international. Business had achieved complete flexibility. Only the markets mattered. *Plus ça change, plus c'est la meme chose.*

But we are still concerned with the problem of legitimacy—Adolph Berle's field for responsibility and accountability. How do the shape-changers and their "fairs" rate against Berle's criteria? Not well. The field of responsibility that these managers assume has now become extremely limited—limited to the continuance of the firm, regardless of how many of the component parts must be left behind. Responsibility to communities, even to the nation, has largely been eschewed. The imperative is merely to continue; the strategy is to dominate certain markets. I choose the word *dominate*, rather than *serve*, deliberately. The strategy nowadays is to find markets that can be dominated in the sense of achieving a large market share. "Serving" markets is becoming a passé concept. Responsibility? No.

On the score of accountability, the shape-changers score equally badly. The trend, as we saw, is in just the other direction. Every effort is bent to reduce or eliminate accountability to anyone: privatization to keep the public out of the business or high stock prices so that the "owners" will leave them alone; fewer workers, so fewer obligations to them; plants in countries whose governments are more compliant. Accountability? Never.

The shape-changer paradigm thus seems to come no nearer legitimacy than the past paradigms; in fact, the trend is all in the opposite direction—more of an escape from responsibility and accountability toward society. How did we arrive at this pass?

First, let us return to the economic conditions that face our new leaders. October 19, 1987, only highlighted a trend that has been accelerating for some time. The power of Wall Street over business leaders has grown enormously, and the volatility of the markets has accentuated that power. In large part, I believe, Wall Street—driven by its own logic and dynamic—has actually *produced* the shape-changers. Many in the financial sector firmly adhere to the wealth paradigm in its extreme form; their goal has become "money and more money," no less than Andrew Carnegie's. In the pursuit of this paradigm, corporations—those marvelous combinations of people, technology, and real assets—have been reduced to commodities. I use the word *commodities* in its literal sense: goods that have no intrinsic value but whose value is set by the market—that is, whatever anyone will pay for them. The idea that a business has intrinsic worth—as an engine of progress, an immortal institution, or even a money machine—has been totally lost on Wall Street.

We saw this conflict between the financial sector and corporate America when the Allen Group's Walter Kissinger decried the "financial wizards" and "arbitrageurs who may be in the stock for a few hours" and have "the same moral claim and rights as an investor who has dedicated his whole life to the building of a company."[13]Kissinger is an institutional man; his metaphor is a human being with transcendent purposes. His conflict with Wall Street is profound—a true Kuhnian *dialogue des sourdes*. His suggestion that the arbitrageurs have a moral claim is, in their world-view, literally nonsense. Allen Group's stock—but, more important, Allen Group itself—is to them a commodity. Who has a "moral claim" on a commodity? Who has any claim at all on a shipment of wheat or a barrel of oil, except the one who can meet the asking price? Why does Kissinger have any more right to the company than a speculator with ready cash? You can see the *dialogue*—an impossible conversation between those who see the company as a commodity and Kissinger, who sees it as a member of his family.

The commoditization of the corporation has put enormous pressure on business managers. The only sensible goal for a public company has become high stock prices. If prices lag the market, the end is in sight: takeover, acquisition, death to the human organism or immortal institution. This is a real fear; the rate of acquisitions, mainly unfriendly, has accelerated. In 1976, businesses worth $590 million changed hands: in 1986, that number was $1.7 trillion.[14] This fear, this preoccupation with financial matters, can only be injurious. Consider the time that CEOs must spend on just this one issue. *Business Month* surveyed the leaders of their "best-managed" businesses after Black Monday. All reported an absorption in stock buy-back plans, relooks at capital budgets—in short, their financial position.[15] Who was attending to the product strategies, the market signals, the customers? Or consider a famous case, the Texaco/Pennzoil dispute—a case that highlights old Henry Ford's concern about a view of business that he thought had passed but has reappeared today:

The most surprising feature of business as it was conducted then was the large attention to finance and the small attention to service. That seemed to be reversing the natural process."[16]

A look at the Texaco/Pennzoil case shows that Ford's point is still with us. Pennzoil and Texaco both attempted to acquire Getty Oil; Pennzoil argued that Texaco's actions illegally quashed their deal, sued, and won a judgment of $10.53 billion. All of this goes back to 1985. Note the date. The parties finally settled for $3 billion in late 1987.[17] Can you imagine the time and attention the CEOs spent on this transaction over that period? Could they think of anything else? Where in the prosaic operations of their businesses—exploration, production, distribution—could they see earnings of the magnitude of $10 billion, or even $3 billion? Were the interests of Texaco and Pennzoil—as economic units producing goods—well served by all this? Ford was right; they have "reversed the natural process."

The shape-changers are a product of Wall Street and both are products of the sensate culture, the striving for individual gain alone, the acceptance—indeed, the embrace—of Ivan Boesky's dictum: "You can be greedy and still feel good about yourself." And the shape-changers are also products of the corrosive effects of modern thought. Their attitude—extreme relativism—bears a family resemblance to logical positivism, which postpones, or rather shunts aside, any questions of transcendent purpose. The approach is purely pragmatic: Let us solve the problems we have before us today, not be concerned with issues—values, duties, service—that may, as logical positivism teaches, not be realities at all, but merely words. These are not the people that Drucker needs for his paradigm, but I'm afraid they are what we have.

Metaphors

I have suggested the metaphor of the market fair—an idea that fits the shape-changers' exclusive focus on markets and their disdain for the responsibility and accountability of "ordinary" business.

Now, the stock metaphors of the day are journey (50 percent of the actors use it), organism (50 percent), and war (38 percent). These all suit the Norsemen and, I believe, spring from the new paradigm. Recall that the shape-changers were raiders—warriors who sailed on voyages of plunder. They were seafaring men; they had "shipped aboard the immortal ship," in Whitman's phrase.[18] And like our new business leaders, their goal was survival, regardless of the transformation required. The ship—and the voyage—were immortal; the human being would survive, and war was his means.

Today's metaphors are best expressed as verb forms, as we saw in Harold Geneen's apt metaphorical choice—cooking on a wood stove. Even the title of his autobiography is appropriate—not *Management* (Drucker's choice) or *Manager*, but rather the verb, *Managing*. We can look back to Pepper and his set of "root metaphors" in Western thought.[19] One of this limited set Pepper called "contextualism"—descriptions of processes. The principal categories of these metaphors are novelty and change—quite congenial to today's ferment in business. So, more properly, today's metaphors should be *voyaging, warring,* and *surviving*.

Let me suggest an image that perhaps will capture the new paradigm for us. Imagine our new business leader, our warring shape-changer, in his ultimate metamorphosis—shed of his responsibilities for plants in demanding communities, his recalcitrant labor force, his regulation-minded government, his troublesome shareholders—off on the journey to the new market fair, to the new Novgorod and Bar-sur-Aube. Voyaging, voyaging, voyaging—shipped aboard the immortal ship.

And we who must live in this new world? We must find the means to control this shape-changer—to tame this bear, ground this bird. We must find a way to reorient business from the market fair, from *le voyage sans but*, and get it back to its proper role—assuring a better life for everyone, spiritually and materially.

We need a new paradigm, and we need new metaphors for business—enough of massacres, ships of fools, and children's games. We need new "invisible powers" to set our leaders in a better direction. We need a modern version of "cathedral building," or Carse's infinite game, to inspire people to the challenging, rewarding, and socially responsible calling that business should be.

Notes

Chapter 1: Introduction

1. Stromberg (1986), p. 317.

Chapter 2: The Web of Language

1. Kenny (1984), p. 42, quoting Wittgenstein.
2. Weick (1979), p. 5.
3. Ibid., p. 3.
4. Kuhn (1962), p. 111.
5. Pepper (1948), p. 91.
6. Weick (1979), p. 42.
7. Rosenberg and Birdzell (1986), p. 127.
8. Wedgwood (1965), p. 46.
9. Sanford (1984).
10. Geneen (1984), pp. 29–30.
11. Weick (1979), p. 51.
12. Davis (1986).
13. Stromberg (1986), p. 262.
14. Steiner (1978), p. 127.
15. Sacks (1978), p. 82.
16. Burton (1976), p. 115.
17. Wedgwood (1965), p. 128.
18. Burton (1976), p. 31.
19. Ibid., p. 115.
20. Ibid., p. 194.
21. Wedgwood (1965), p. 81.
22. Ibid., p. 81.
23. Burton (1976), p. 11.
24. Ibid., p. 11.

25. Engels (1958), p. 311.
26. Merrill (1960), p. 21.
27. Engels (1958), p. 312.
28. Merrill (1960), p. 40.
29. Ibid., p. 45.
30. Ibid., p. 51.
31. O'Toole, et al. (1973), p. 186.
32. Merrill (1960), p. 67.
33. Ibid., p. 92.
34. Ibid., p. 110.
35. Augustine (1950), p. 693.
36. Merrill (1960), p. 85.
37. Ibid., p. 201.
38. Kotter (1985), p. 5.
39. Ackoff (1981), pp. 27–28.

Chapter 3: The Bearer of Truth

1. Connell (1973), p. 156. Reprinted by permission.
2. Campbell (1977), p. 188.
3. Sacks (1978), p. 49.
4. Ibid., p. 10.
5. Lakoff and Johnson (1980), p. 5.
6. Sacks (1978), p. 31.
7. Pepper (1948), p. 91.
8. Lakoff and Johnson (1980), p. 3.
9. James (1956), p. 119.
10. Lakoff and Johnson (1980), p. 115.
11. Ibid., p. 8.
12. Ibid., p. 25.
13. Ibid., p. 31.
14. Ibid., p. 33.
15. Ibid., p. 10.
16. Cowley (1985), p. 34. Copyright © 1962 by Malcolm Cowley. All rights reserved. Reprinted by permission of Viking Penguin, Inc.
17. Lakoff and Johnson (1980), p. 96.

Chapter 4: The Journey

1. Homer (1946), p. 26
2. Roppen and Sommer (1964), p. 108.

3. Ibid., p. 17.
4. Ibid., p. 173.
5. Baudelaire (1975).
6. Yeats (1983), p. 193. Reprinted with permission of Macmillan Publishing Company. Copyright 1928 by Macmillan Publishing Company, renewed 1956 by Georgie Yeats.
7. Ibid., p. 248. Reprinted with permission of Macmillan Publishing Company. Copyright 1933 by Macmillan Publishing Company, renewed 1961 by Bertha Georgie Yeats.
8. Ford (1923), p. 43.
9. Sloan (1965), p. 437.
10. Douglas (1954), p. 146.
11. Merrill (1960), p. 297.
12. Chester (1936–37).
13. Nichol (1940–41).
14. Levinson and Rosenthal (1984), p. 69.
15. Ibid., p. 167.
16. Iacocca (1986), p. 94.
17. Ibid., p. 196.
18. Ibid., p. 121.
19. Burke (1984).
20. Roppen and Sommer (1964), p. ii.
21. Guicciardini (1965), p. 82.
22. Nordhoff and Hall (1946).
23. DeVoto (1953).

Chapter 5: The Game

1. Winkler (1931), p. 95.
2. Ibid., p. 17.
3. Ibid., p. 3.
4. Ibid., p. 58.
5. Ibid., p. 95.
6. Ibid., p. 124.
7. Klein (1986), p. 67.
8. Ibid., p. 128.
9. Ibid., p. 129.
10. Ibid., p. 179.
11. Merrill (1960), p. 111.
12. Ibid., p. 29.
13. Petre (1986).
14. Levinson and Rosenthal (1984), p. 69.
15. Ibid., p. 110.

16. Ibid., p. 100.
17. Ibid., p. 201.
18. Burke (1984).
19. Iacocca (1986), p. 59.
20. Ibid., p. 100.
21. Ibid., p. 161.
22. Ibid., p. 166.
23. Ibid., p. 166.
24. Ibid., p. 188.
25. Ibid., p. 195.
26. Ibid., p. 331.
27. Levin and Ingrassia (1986).
28. Iacocca (1986), p. 60.
29. Geneen (1984), p. 99.
30. Donaldson and Lorsch (1983), p. 25.
31. Hamilton (1973), p. 22.
32. Carse (1986), p. 3.
33. Ibid., p. 21.
34. Ibid., p. 20.
35. Ibid., p. 9.
36. Ibid., pp. 17–18.
37. Ibid., p. 19.
38. Ibid., p. 12.
39. Hesse (1969).

Chapter 6: War

1. Kahn (1974), p. 67.
 2. Oxford Dictionary of Quotations (1955), p. 248.
 3. Barzun (1981), p. 92.
 4. Ibid., p. 93.
 5. Byron (1954), p. 25.
 6. Barzun (1981), p. 93.
 7. Nietzche (1966), p. 47.
 8. Wedgwood (1965), p. 126.
 9. Klein (1986), p. 67.
10. Ibid., p. 81.
11. Ibid., p. 109.
12. Ibid., p. 123.
13. Ibid., p. 113.
14. Ibid., p. 109.
15. Donaldson and Lorsch (1983), p. 22.
16. Clifford and Cavanagh (1985), p. 35.

17. Prokesch (1986). Copyright © 1986 by The New York Times Company. Reprinted by permission.
18. *Wall Street Journal,* June 11, 1986.
19. Iacocca (1986), p. 55.
20. Ibid., p. 242.
21. Fisher (1988).
22. Reis and Trout (1986).
23. Ashley (1962), pp. 231.
24. Hale (1969), p. 127–28.
25. Vaughan (1978), p. 95.
26. Shakespeare, *Julius Caesar,* Act III, Scene i, p. 61.
27. Oxford Dictionary of Quotations (1979), p. 323.
28. Ford (1923), p. 43.
29. Merrill (1960), p. 174.
30. Weick (1979), p. 50.
31. Oxford Dictionary of Quotations (1979), p. 251
32. *The Bible,* Psalms 68:30.

Chapter 7: The Machine

1. Merrill (1960), p. 337.
2. Burton (1976), p. 31.
3. Merrill (1960), p. 23.
4. Ibid., p. 254.
5. Cook (1984).
6. Stromberg (1986), p. 26.
7. Ibid., p. 106.
8. Golding (1985), p. 97.
9. Ibid., p. 26.
10. Pepper (1948), p. 242.
11. Ford (1923), p. 92.
12. Ibid., p. 80.
13. Stromberg (1986), p. 211.
14. Carse (1986), p. 122.
15. Pfeffer (1981), p. 8.
16. Peters and Waterman (1984), p. 29.
17. Morgan (1986), p. 13.
18. Merrill (1960), p. 45.
19. Guicciardini (1965), p. 139.
20. Morgan (1986), p. 34.
21. Ibid., p. 34.
22. Peters and Waterman (1984), p. 44.
23. Kahn (1974), p. 45.

24. Ford (1923), p. 264.

Chapter 8: The Organism

1. Wilson (1984), p. 1.
2. Morgan (1986), p. 39.
3. Pepper (1948), p. 120.
4. *The Bible, Genesis*, 1:28.
5. Bourke (1974), p. 164.
6. Merrill (1960), p. 92.
7. Ibid., p. 174.
8. Ibid., p. 221.
9. Ibid., p. 232.
10. Sloan (1965), p. xxi.
11. Robertson (1946–47).
12. Geneen (1984), p. ix.
13. Levinson and Rosenthal (1984), p. 69.
14. Ibid., p. 204.
15. Anderson (1984).
16. Iacocca (1986), pp. xvii, 180, 196.
17. Stromberg (1986), pp. 35–36.
18. Ibid., p. 17.
19. Ibid., p. 78.
20. Aiken (1956), p. 162.
21. Yeats (1983), p. 207. Reprinted with permission of Macmillan Publishing Company. Copyright 1928 by Macmillan Publishing Company, renewed 1956 by Georgie Yeats.
22. Winkler (1931), p. 16.
23. Merrill (1960), p. 396.
24. Thomas (1981), pp. 295–96.
25. Peters and Waterman (1984), pp. 13–15.
26. O'Toole (1986), p. 18.
27. Porter (1980).
28. Carse (1986), p. 129.
29. Morgan (1986), p. 72.
30. Peters and Waterman (1984), p. 114.
31. Morgan (1986), p. 74.
32. *Wall Street Journal*, December 15, 1986, pp. 25–26.
33. Gould (1986).
34. Drucker (1974), pp. 572ff.
35. Morgan (1986), p. 76.
36. Peters and Waterman (1984), p. 96.

37. Kissinger (1986). Copyright © 1986 by The New York Times Company. Reprinted by permission.

Chapter 9: The Society

1. Stromberg (1986), p. 142.
2. Aristotle (1962), p. 56.
3. Leroi-Gourhan (1982), p. 75.
4. Berlin (1976), p. 80.
5. Morgan (1986), p. 112.
6. Selznick (1957), p. 91ff.
7. Stromberg (1986), p. 174.
8. Merrill (1960), p. 158.
9. Ibid., p. 217,
10. Sward (1948), pp. 58–59.
11. Douglas (1954), p. 149.
12. Petersen (1955–56).
13. Levinson and Rosenthal (1984), p. 20.
14. Ibid., p. 54.
15. Ibid., p. 69.
16. Ibid., p. 74.
17. Ibid., p. 105.
18. Ibid., p. 122.
19. Harnischfeger (1984).
20. Iacocca (1986), p. 103.
21. Ibid., p. 161.
22. Ibid., p. 161.
23. Donaldson and Lorsch (1983), p. 29.
24. Clifford and Cavanagh (1985), p. 132.
25. Ibid., p. 13.
26. Peters and Waterman (1984), pp. 14–15.
27. Berlin (1969), p. 162.
28. O'Toole (1986), p. 15.
29. Ibid., p. 49.
30. Becker (1975), p. 4.
31. Bettelheim (1977), p. 3.
32. Stromberg (1986), p. 106.
33. Montague (1984), p. 18. © Wake Forest University Press, Winston-Salem, N.C., 1984.
34. Peters and Waterman (1984), p. 75.
35. O'Toole (1986), p. 61.
36. Carse (1986), p. 40.
37. Frost et al. (1985), pp. 60–61.

38. Merrill (1960), p. 74.
39. Frost et al. (1985), pp. 62–64.
40. Selznick (1957), p. 55.
41. Langer (1942), p. 160.
42. Carse (1986), p. 41.
43. Weber (1958), p. 26.
44. Peters and Waterman (1984), p. 60.
45. Ibid., p. 75.
46. Becker (1973), p. 3.
47. Connell (1962), p. 3. Reprinted by permission.
48. Langer (1942), p. 93.
49. Ibid., p. 153.
50. Bettelheim (1977), p. 26.
51. Selznick (1957), p. 151.
52. Carse (1986), p. 6.
53. Rimbaud (1973), p. 54.
54. Pfeffer (1981), p. 1.
55. Ibid., p. 7.
56. Ibid., p. 8.
57. Ibid., p. 32.
58. Ibid., p. 184, quoting Pondry.
59. Ibid.
60. Morgan (1986), p. 144.
61. Selznick (1957), p. 40.
62. Marcus Aurelius (1945), p. 20.
63. Leroi-Gourhan (1982), p. 32.
64. Campbell (1972), p. 100.
65. Ibid., pp. 256–57.
66. Clifford and Cavanagh (1985), p. 95.
67. Prokesch (1986). Copyright © 1986 by The New York Times Company. Reprinted by permission.
68. Levinson and Rosenthal (1984), p. 118.
69. Peters and Waterman (1984), p. 74.
70. Selznick (1957), p. 151.
71. Peters and Waterman (1984), p. 29, quoting Athos.
72. Ibid., p. 104, quoting Peltigan.
73. Pfeffer (1981), p. 184.
74. Petersen (1955–56).
75. Douglas (1954), p. 155.
76. Ibid., pp. 127–28, quoting Sloan.
77. Sloan (1965), p. 191.
78. Iacocca (1986), p. 103.
79. O'Toole (1986), p. 42.
80. Ackoff (1981), p. 31.

81. Webber (1986a).
82. Webber (1986b).
83. Klein (1986), p. 329.
84. Ortega y Gasset (1961), p. 149.
85. Gilder (1981), p. 36.
86. Ibid., p. 23.
87. Ibid., p. 93.
88. Weber (1958), p. 54.
89. Petre (1986).
90. Connell (1962), p. 8. Reprinted by permission.
91. O'Toole (1986), p. 61.
92. Langer (1942), p. 165, quoting Durkheim.
93. Morgan (1986), pp. 134–35.
94. Ibid.
95. Pfeffer (1981), p. 341.
96. DeMott (1986).
97. Ford (1923), p. 92.
98. Ibid, p. 263.
99. Ibid., p. 112.
100. Stromberg (1986), p. 216, quoting Lenin.
101. Sward (1948), p. 110.
102. Kahn (1974), p. 81.
103. *Wall Street Journal* December 15, 1986, pp. 25–26.
104. Langer (1942), pp. 48–49.
105. O'Toole (1986), p. 275.
106. Ibid., p. 289.
107. Morgan (1986), pp. 134–35.
108. Peters and Waterman (1984), p. 77.
109. Langer (1942), pp. 175–76.

Chapter 10: Purposes and Paradigms

1. Langer (1942), p. 9.
2. Ackoff (1981), pp. 27–28.
3. Asprey (1986), pp. 577–78.
4. Pepper (1948), p. 1.
5. Stromberg (1986), p. 25.
6. Kuhn (1962), p. 139.
7. Ibid., p. 17.
8. Ibid., p. 36.
9. Carse (1986), p. 102, quoting Heisenberg.
10. Kuhn (1962), p. 59.
11. Ibid., p. 4.

12. Ibid., p. 85.
13. Ibid., p. 94.
14. Ibid., p. 48.
15. Ibid., p. 78.
16. Ibid., p. 103.
17. Ibid., p. 184.
18. Iacocca (1986), p. 8.

Chapter 11: The New Messiah

1. Galbraith (1958), p. 101.
2. Merrill (1960), p. 271.
3. O'Toole (1986), p. 8.
4. Heilbroner (1966), p. 40.
5. Ibid., pp. 107–9.
6. Ibid., p. 119.
7. Ibid., p. 198.
8. Ibid., p. 204.
9. Ibid., p. 203.
10. Ibid., pp. 228–39.
11. Galbraith (1958), pp. 102–3.
12. Gilder (1981), p. 31.
13. Wedgwood (1965), p. 81.
14. Burton (1976), p. 86.
15. Ibid., p. 115.
16. Merrill (1960), p. 158.
17. Ibid., p. 92.
18. Ford (1923), p. 12.
19. Ibid., p. 2.
20. Ibid., p. 37.
21. O'Toole (1986), p. 147, quoting Draper-Dayton.
22. Douglas (1954), p. 172.
23. Azzato (1984).
24. Prokesch (1986).
25. O'Toole (1986), p. 233, quoting Hanson.
26. Monosson (1987).
27. Sward (1948), pp. 104–5.
28. Ford (1923), p. 7.
29. Sward (1948), p. 62.
30. Ibid., p. 22.
31. Ibid., p. 4.
32. Ibid., p. 23.
33. Ibid., p. 20.

34. Ibid., p. 23
35. Ibid., p. 24.
36. Ibid., p. 42.
37. Ibid., p. 77.
38. Ibid., p. 197.
39. Ibid., p. 195.
40. Ibid., p. 1.
41. Ford (1923), p. 159.
42. Sward (1948), p. 76.
43. Ibid., p. 43.
44. Ibid., p. 35.
45. Ibid., p. 39.
46. Ford (1923), p. 103.
47. Ibid., p. 77.
48. Ibid., p. 80.
49. Sward (1948), p. 10.
50. Ibid., pp. 51–56.
51. Douglas (1954), p. 139.
52. Langer (1942), p. 4.
53. Ford (1923), p. 71.
54. Sward (1948), p. 41.
55. Ibid., p. 47.
56. Ibid., p. 175.
57. Ibid., p. 305.
58. Ibid., p. 76.
59. Ibid., p. 198.
60. Ibid., p. 196.
61. Ibid., p. 198.
62. Ibid., pp. 194–95.
63. Ibid., p. 199.
64. Iacocca (1986), p. 47.
65. Ibid., p. 66.
66. Prokesch (1986).
67. Ford (1923), p. 37.
68. Ibid., p. 41.
69. Ibid., p. 20.
70. Ibid., p. 162.
71. Ibid., p. 176.
72. O'Toole (1986), p. 145.
73. Chester (1936–37).
74. Azzato (1984).
75. Stone (1984).
76. Robertson (1946–47).
77. Sanford (1984).

78. Merrill (1960), p. 54.
79. Ibid., p. 92.
80. Ibid.
81. Ibid., p. 111.
82. O'Toole (1986), p. 233.
83. Galbraith (1958), p. 109.
84. Ibid., p. 114.
85. Ibid., p. 124.
86. Ibid.
87. *New York Times*, February 15, 1987.
88. Byron (1954), p. 98.

Chapter 12: Treasures upon Earth

 1. *The Bible*, Matthew 6:19,21.
 2. Sloan (1965), p. 49.
 3. Heilbroner (1966), pp. 11ff.
 4. Rice (1970), p. 54, quoting Thomas Aquinas.
 5. Weber (1958), p. 43.
 6. Ibid., p. 51.
 7. Heilbroner (1966), p. 98.
 8. Smith (1970), p. 44.
 9. Ibid., p. 43.
10. Heilbroner (1966), pp. 228–37.
11. O'Toole (1986), p. 144.
12. Gilder (1981), p. 23.
13. Ibid., p. 36.
14. Wedgwood (1965), p. 46.
15. Burton (1976), p. 11.
16. Merrill (1960), p. 21.
17. Winkler (1931), p. 58.
18. Merrill (1960), p. 52.
19. Nichol (1940–41).
20. Geneen (1984), p. ix.
21. Ibid.
22. Ibid., p. 34.
23. Iacocca (1986), p. 9.
24. Ibid., p. 42.
25. Ibid., p. 48.
26. Ferris (1987).
27. O'Toole (1986), p. 145.
28. *Wall Street Journal*, March 5, 1987.
29. Douglas (1954), pp. 129–45.

30. Ibid., p. 154.
31. Sloan (1965), p. 283.
32. Douglas (1954), p. 177.
33. Ibid., p. 168.
34. Sloan (1965), p. 64.
35. Ibid., p. xxiii.
36. Ibid., p. 4.
37. Aacker (1984), p. 8.
38. Sloan (1965), p. 59.
39. Iacocca (1986), p. 69.
40. Ibid., p. 150.
41. Sloan (1965), p. xxi.
42. Sward (1948), p. 195.
43. Sloan (1965), p. 163.
44. Winkler (1931), p. 58.
45. Ibid., p. 93.
46. Klein (1986), p. 128.
47. Geneen (1984), p. ix.
48. Iacocca (1986), p. xvii.
49. Ibid., p. 152.
50. Ibid., p. 180.
51. Ibid., p. 196.
52. Ibid., p. 222.
53. Ibid., p. 55.
54. Wedgwood (1965), p. 46.
55. Anderson (1984).
56. Sloan (1965), p. xix.
57. Ibid., p. xxi.
58. Ibid.
59. O'Toole (1986), p. 143.
60. Kahn (1974), p. 173.
61. Arnoff and Ward (1984), p. 133, quoting Smith.
62. Weber (1958), p. 17.
63. Arnoff and Ward (1984), p. 11.
64. Ibid.
65. *The Bible*, Matthew 19:24.
66. Ibid., 19:21.
67. Shakespeare, *Measure for Measure*, Act III, Scene i, p. 47.
68. Engels (1958), pp. 311–12.
69. Weber (1958), p. 52.
70. Polanyi (1944), p. 73.
71. Ibid.
72. Kahn (1974), p. 66.

Chapter 13: Stonecutters Fighting Time

1. Jeffers (1963), p. 3 Copyright 1924. Renewed 1952 by Robinson Jeffers. Reprinted from *Selected Poetry of Robinson Jeffers*. By permission of Random House, Inc.
2. Levinson and Rosenthal (1984), p. 91.
3. Marcuse (1969), p. 205.
4. Selznick (1957), p. 55.
5. Becker (1975), p. 3.
6. Montague (1984), p. 18.© Wake Forest University Press, Winston-Salem, N.C., 1984.
7. Becker (1973), p. 26.
8. Pascal (1976), p. 110.
9. Shelley (1956), p. 107.
10. Carse (1986), p. 26.
11. Ibid., p. 32.
12. Clifford and Cavanaugh (1985), p. 13.
13. Ibid., p. 232.
14. Donaldson and Lorsch (1983), p. 28.
15. Ibid., p. 31.
16. Levinson and Rosenthal (1984), p. 49.
17. Ibid.
18. Ibid., p. 131.
19. Ibid., p. 133.
20. Ibid., p. 172.
21. O'Toole (1986), p. 50.
22. Kissinger (1986). Copyright © 1986 by The New York Times Company. Reprinted by permission.
23. Levinson and Rosenthal (1984), p. 18.
24. Ibid., p. 13.
25. Ibid., p. 20.
26. Ibid., p. 53.
27. Ibid., p. 49.
28. Selznick (1957), pp. 62–63.
29. Levinson and Rosenthal (1984), p. 24.
30. Ibid., pp. 18–19.
31. Ibid., p. 17.
32. Ibid., p. 54.
33. Ibid., p. 69.
34. Ibid., p. 150.
35. Ibid., p. 162.
36. Ibid., p. 167.
37. Ibid., p. 100.
38. Ibid., p. 131.

39. Ibid., p. 122.
40. Petersen (1955–56).
41. Levinson and Rosenthal (1984), p. 21.
42. Ibid., p. 25.
43. North (1981), pp. 201–2.
44. Arnoff and Ward (1984), pp. 54–57.
45. Pfeffer (1981), p. 32.
46. Drucker (1988).
47. Ackoff (1986).
48. Dostoyevsky (1980), pp. 227–244.
49. *The Bible*, John 8:32.
50. Connell (1962), p. 15. Reprinted by permission.
51. Anders (1986), p. 6.

Chapter 14: Fin de Siecle

1. Berman (1982), p. 3.
2. Barrett (1987), p. xiv.
3. Ortega y Gasset (1968), p. 136.
4. Malabre (1986).
5. Silk (1987).
6. Nathans (1987), p. 79.
7. O'Toole (1986), pp. 166ff.
8. Cetron (1985), p. xi.
9. Ibid., pp. xii–xiv.
10. Ibid., p. 137.
11. Arnoff and Ward (1984), p. 18.
12. Cetron (1985), p. 137.
13. Myrdal (1968), pp. 467–71.
14. Kahn (1974), p. 141.
15. *The Bible*, Ecclesiastes 1:9.
16. Marcus Aurelius (1945), p. 63.
17. Harris (1981), pp. 8–11.
18. Ibid., pp. 166ff.
19. Kahn (1974), pp. 107–10.
20. Barrett (1987), p. 157.
21. Arnoff and Ward (1984), p. 151.
22. Kahn (1974), p. 130.
23. Ibid., p. 149.
24. Cavanaugh (1976), pp. 57–59.
25. Ibid., pp. 136–37.
26. Ibid., p. 25.
27. Barrett (1987), p. 7.

28. Stromberg (1986), pp. 295–96.
29. Gardner (1981), p. 255.
30. Arnoff and Ward (1984), p. 11.
31. Sievers (1949), p. 19.
32. Polanyi (1944), p. 72.
33. Sievers (1949), p. 40.
34. *The Bible*, Daniel 7:23.
35. Polanyi (1944), p. 111.
36. Drucker (1974), pp. 809ff.
37. *Bhagavad Gita*, ch. XVI, verses 11–12.
38. Polanyi (1944), p. 178.
39. Arnoff and Ward (1984), p. 17.
40. Prokesch (1987). Copyright © 1987 by The New York Times Company. Reprinted by permission.
41. Potts and Behr (1987), pp.1–2.
42. McDonald (1986).
43. Cetron (1985), p. xx.
44. Reich (1987).
45. Cavanaugh (1976), p. 172, quoting Daniel Bell.
46. Ibid., p. 56, quoting Paul Samuelson.
47. Ibid., p. 55, quoting Joseph Schumpeter.
48. Ibid., p. 25, quoting Adolph Berle.

Chapter 15: Voyaging, Voyaging, Voyaging

1. Whitman (1950), p. 392.
2. *Vienna 1900* (1986), p. 39.
3. Yeats (1983), p. 187. Reprinted with permission of Macmillan Publishing Company. Copyright 1924 by Macmillan Publishing Company, renewed 1952 by Bertha Georgie Yeats.
4. Drucker (1974), pp. 807–11.
5. Nathans (1987).
6. Pascarella (1987).
7. Nathans (1987).
8. Prokesch (December 13, 1987).
9. Yeats (1983), p. 187.
10. Prokesch (January 25, 1987).
11. McDonald (1986).
12. Durant (1950), p. 615.
13. Kissinger (1986). Copyright © 1986 by The New York Times Company. Reprinted by permission.
14. Prokesch (December 13, 1987).
15. Nathans (1987).

16. Ford (1923), p. 12.
17. Salpukas (1987).
18. Whitman (1950), p. 392.
19. Pepper (1948), pp. 232–33.

Bibliography

Acker, D. *Strategic Market Management*. John Wiley and Sons, New York, 1984.

Ackerman, P. "Our Common Stake." *Vital Speeches*, 24: 762, 1957–58.

Ackoff, R.L. *Creating the Corporate Future*. Wiley, New York, 1981.

———. "Profit as a Means." *New York Times*, August 31, 1986, p. 2F.

Aiken, H.D. *The Age of Ideology*. Mentor Books, New York, 1956.

Anders, G.O. "Perot's Departure From GM Dismays Big Holders as Firm's Shares Tumble," *Wall Street Journal*, December 2, 1986, p. 6.

Anderson, R. "Through Turbulent Times." Pub. No. 1223, Newcomen Society of the U.S., New York, 1984.

Aristotle. *The Politics*, I ii (Trans. T.A. Sinclair). Penguin Books, New York, 1962.

Arnoff, C., and Ward, J. (Eds.). *The Future of Private Enterprise*. Georgia State University, Atlanta, 1984.

Ashley, M. *The Greatness of Oliver Cromwell*. Collier Books, New York, 1962.

Asprey, R.B. *Frederick the Great*. Ticknor and Fields, New York, 1986.

Augustine. *The City of God* (Trans. M. Dods). Modern Library, New York, 1950.

Azzato, L.E., "Foster Wheeler Corporation." Pub. No. 1232, Newcomen Society of the U.S., New York, 1984.

Barrett, W. *Death of the Soul*. Anchor Press, Garden City, N.Y., 1987.

Barzun, J. *Darwin, Marx, Wagner: Critique of a Heritage*. University of Chicago Press, Chicago, 1981.

Baudelaire, C. *Selected Poems*. Penguin Books, Harmondsworth, England, 1975, p. 206.

Becker, E. *The Denial of Death*. Free Press, New York, 1973.

———. *Escape from Evil*. Free Press, New York, 1975.

Berlin, I. *Four Essays on Liberty*. Oxford University Press, London, 1969.

———. *Vico and Herder.* Vintage Books, New York, 1976.

Berman, M. *All That Is Solid Melts into Air.* Simon and Schuster, New York, 1982.

Bettelheim, B. *The Uses of Enchantment.* Vintage Books, New York, 1977.

Bhagavad Gita, The (Trans. J. Mascaro). Penguin Books, Middlesex, England, 1962.

Bible, The, Authorized (King James) Version.

Bonoma, T.V. "Marketing Subversives." *Harvard Business Review,* 64(6), November-December 1986.

Bourke, V. (Ed.). *The Essential Augustine.* Hackett, Indianapolis, 1974.

Burke, W.W. "Conversation with H. K. Sperlich." *Organizational Dynamics,* Spring 1984, pp. 23–36.

Burton, A. *Josiah Wedgwood: A Biography.* Andre Deutsch, London, 1976.

Byron, G.N.G., Lord. *Poems.* Penguin Books, Harmondsworth, England, 1954.

Cameron, W.J. "Shovel Leaners." *Vital Speeches,* 5:384, 1938–39.

Campbell, J. *The Hero with a Thousand Faces.* Bollingen Series, Princeton University Press, Princeton, N.J., 1972.

———. *The Masks of God: Creative Mythology.* Penguin Books, New York, 1977.

Carse, J.P. *Finite and Infinite Games.* Free Press, New York, 1986.

Cavanaugh, G.F. *American Business Values in Transition.* Prentice-Hall, Englewood Cliffs, N.J., 1976.

Cetron, M. *The Future of American Business.* McGraw-Hill, New York, 1985.

Chester, C.M. "The Great Highway." *Vital Speeches,* 3: 57, 1936–37.

Clifford, D.K., and Cavanagh, R.E. *The Winning Performance.* Bantam Books, New York, 1985.

Connell, E. *Notes from a Bottle Found on the Beach at Carmel.* North Point Press, San Francisco, 1962.

———. *Points for a Compass Rose.* North Point Press, San Francisco, 1973.

Cook, W.S. "Union Pacific Railroad.", Pub. No. 1228, Newcomen Society of the U.S., October 18, 1984.

Cowley, M. *Blue Juniata.* Penguin Books, New York, 1985.

Davis, W. "Interfacing with Biz Speak." *New York Times,* June 8, 1986, p. 86.

DeMott, B. "Threats and Wimpers", *New York Times Book Review,* October 26, 1986. p. 1.

DeVoto, B. (Ed.). *The Journals of Lewis and Clark.* Houghton Mifflin, Boston, 1953.

Donaldson, G., and Lorsch, J.E. *Decision Making at the Top*. Basic Books, New York, 1983.

Dostoyevsky, F. *The Brothers Karamazov* (Trans. C. Garnett). NAL Penguin, New York, 1980.

Douglas, P. *Six Upon the World*. Little, Brown, Boston, 1954.

Drucker, P. *Management: Tasks, Responsibilities, Practices*. Harper and Row, New York, 1974.

————"Leadership: More Doing Than Dash." *Wall Street Journal*, January 6, 1988, p. 15.

duPont, H.B. "That No Man Shall be Poor." *Vital Speeches*, 12: 587, 1946–47.

Durant, W. *The Age of Faith*. Simon and Schuster, New York, 1950.

Engels, F. *The Condition of the Working Class in England* (Trans. and ed. W.O. Henderson and W.H. Chalomer). Macmillan, New York, 1958 (originally published 1845).

Ferguson, J.L. "General Foods Corporation." Pub. No. 1232, Newcomen Society of the U.S., New York, 1985.

Ferris R.J. Fellow Address at Cornell University, *Executive Speaker*, 8(1), January 1987, p. 3.

Fisher, L., "Oracle Hurtles Past Rivals' Teams," *San Jose Mercury News*, March 21, 1988, p. 3C.

Ford, H. *My Life and Works*. Doubleday, Page, New York, 1923.

Ford, H., II. "The Challenge of Human Engineering." *Vital Speeches*, 12:271, 1946–47.

Frisbee, D.C. "The PacifiCorp Story." Pub. No. 1232, Newcomen Society of the U.S., New York, 1984.

Frost, Moore, Louis, Lundbers, and Martin (Eds.). *Organizational Culture*. Sage, Beverly Hills, Calif., 1985.

Galbraith, J.K. *The Affluent Society*. New American Library, New York, 1958.

Gardner, H. *The Quest for Mind*. University of Chicago Press, Chicago, 1981.

Geneen, H. (with Moscow, A.). *Managing*. Doubleday, Garden City, N.Y., 1984.

Gilder, G. *Wealth and Poverty*. Bantam Books, Toronto, 1981.

Golding, J. *Boccioni: Unique Forms of Continuity in Space*. Tate Gallery, London, 1985.

Gould, S.J. "Of Kiwi Eggs and the Liberty Bell." *Natural History*, 95(11), November 1986.

Guicciardini, F. *Maxims and Reflections (Ricordi)* (Trans. M. Domandi). University of Pennsylvania Press, Philadelphia, 1965.

Hale, W. *The World of Rodin*. Time-Life Books, Alexandria, Va., 1969.

Hamilton, E. *The Greek Way.* Avon Books, New York, 1973.

Harnischfeger, H. "Harnischfeger Corporation." Pub. No. 1234, New-comen Society of the U.S., New York, 1984.

Harris, M. *America Now.* Simon and Schuster, New York, 1981.

Heilbroner, R.L. *The Worldly Philosophers.* Simon and Schuster, New York, 1966.

Hesse, H. *Magister Ludi.* Bantam Books, New York, 1969.

Homer. *The Odyssey* (Trans. E.V. Rieu). Penguin Books, Middlesex, England, 1946.

Iacocca, L. *Iacocca.* Bantam Books, New York, 1986.

James, W. *The Will to Believe.* Dover, New York, 1956.

Jeffers, R. *Selected Poems.* Penguin Books, New York, 1963.

Kahn, C.H. (Ed.). *The Art and Thought of Heraclitus.* Cambridge University Press, Cambridge, 1979.

Kahn, H. (Ed.). *The Future of the Corporation.* Mason and Lapscomb, New York, 1974.

Kenny, A. *The Legacy of Wittgenstein.* Basil Blackwell, Oxford, 1984.

Kissinger, W. "The Word for Take-Overs: Pernicious," *New York Times,* December 5, 1986, p. 15.

Klein, M. *The Life and Legend of Jay Gould.* Johns Hopkins University Press, Baltimore, 1986.

Kotter, J.P. *Power and Influence.* Free Press, New York, 1985.

Kuhn, T.S. *The Structure of Scientific Revolutions.* University of Chicago Press, Chicago, 1962.

Lakoff, G., and Johnson, M. *Metaphors We Live By.* University of Chicago Press, Chicago, 1980.

Langer, S.K. *Philosophy in a New Key.* Harvard University Press, Cambridge, Mass., 1942.

Leroi-Gourhan, P. *The Dawn of European Art.* Cambridge University Press, Cambridge, 1982.

Levin, D.P., and Ingrassia, P. "Now on the Inside, Ross Perot Tells GM and its Rivals How they Must Change," *Wall Street Journal,* November 8, 1986, p. 7.

Levinson, H., and Rosenthal, S. *CEO: Corporate Leadership in Action.* Basic Books, New York, 1984.

Malabre, A.L. "Dependent Nation: U.S. Economy Grows Even More Vulnerable to Foreign Influences." *Wall Street Journal,* October 27, 1986, p. 1.

Marcus Aurelius. *Meditations.* Walter J. Black, Roslyn, N.Y., 1945.

Marcuse, H. *One-Dimensional Man.* Beacon Press, Boston, 1969.

McDonald, A.L. "Of Floating Factories and Mating Dinosaurs." *Harvard Business Review,* 64(6), November-December 1986.

Merrill, H.F. *Classics in Management.* AMA, New York, 1960.

Monosson, A. *Monosson on DEC.* Monosson, Boston, Mass., March, 1987.

Montague, J. *The Dead Kingdom.* Wake Forest University Press, Winston-Salem, N.C., 1984.

Morgan, G. *Images of Organization.* Sage, Beverly Hills, Calif. 1986.

Myrdal, G. *Asian Drama* (Vol. I). Pantheon, New York, 1968.

Nathans, L. "Bleak Monday's Ripples Begin to Show Up," *Business Month,* Dec. 1987, 1.

Nichol, F.W. "Advice to Young Men Entering Business." *Vital Speeches,* 7: 668, 1940–41.

Nietzsche, F. *Thus Spoke Zarathustra* (Trans. W. Kaufmann). Viking Press, New York, 1966.

Nordhoff, C., and Hall, J. *Men Against the Sea.* Pocket Books, New York, 1946.

North, D.C. *Structure and Change in Economic History.* Norton, New York, 1981.

Ortega y Gasset, J. *Meditations on Quixote.* Norton, New York, 1961.

———. *The Dehumanization of Art and Other Essays.* Princeton University Press, Princeton, N.J., 1968.

O'Toole, J. *Vanguard Management: Redesigning the Corporate Future.* Doubleday, Garden City, N.Y., 1986.

O'Toole, J., et al. *Work in America: Report of the Special Task Force to the Secretary of HEW.* MIT Press, Cambridge, Mass., 1973.

Pascal, B. *Pensées.* Garnier-Flammarion, Paris, 1976.

Pascarella, P. Editorial. *Industry Week,* December 14, 1987, p. 7.

Pepper, S.C. *World Hypotheses.* University of California Press, Berkeley, 1948.

Peters, T., and Waterman, R. *In Search of Excellence.* Warner Books, New York, 1984.

Petersen, T.S. "Philosophy of American Management." *Vital Speeches.* 22:141, 1955–56.

Petre, P. "America's Most Successful Entrepreneurs." *Fortune,* October 27, 1986.

Pfeffer, J. *Power in Organizations.* Pitman, Boston, 1981.

Polanyi, K. *The Great Transformation.* Farras and Rinehart, New York, 1944.

Porter, M. *Competitive Strategy.* Free Press, New York, 1980.

Potts, M., and Behr, P. *The Leading Edge.* McGraw-Hill, New York, 1987.

Prokesch, S. "Can Don Burr Go Back to the Future?" *New York Times,* July 6, 1986, p. 21.

————. "Remaking the American CEO." *New York Times,* January 25, 1987, Section 3, p. 1.

————. "Stunning Blow to the Age of Improvidence," *New York Times,* December 13, 1987, p. 1.

Reich, R.B. "On the Brink of an Anti-Business Era." *New York Times,* April 12, 1987, p. F3.

Reis, A., and Trout, J. *Marketing Warfare.* McGraw-Hill, New York, 1986.

Rice, E.F., Jr. *The Foundations of Early Modern Europe: 1460–1559.* Norton, New York, 1970.

Rimbaud, A. *Une Saison en Enfer.* Oxford University Press, Oxford, 1973.

Robertson, A.W. "Modern Business Giants." *Vital Speeches.* 12:184, 1946–47.

Roppen, G., and Sommer, R. *Strangers and Pilgrims: An Essay on the Metaphor of the Journey.* Humanities Press, New York, 1964.

Rosenberg, N., and Birdzell, L.E. *How the West Grew Rich.* Basic Books, New York, 1986.

Sacks, S. (Ed.). *On Metaphor.* University of Chicago Press, Chicago, 1978.

Salpukas, A. "Icahn Role in Texaco-Pennzoil Deal," *New York Times,* December 20, 1987, p. 18.

Sanford, F.P., Jr. "Torchmark Corporation." Pub. No. 1226, Newcomen Society of the U.S., New York, 1984.

Selznick, P. *Leadership in Administration.* Row, Peterson, Evanston, Ill., 1957.

Shakespeare, W. *Julius Caesar.* Yale University Press, New Haven, Conn., 1954.

————. *Measure for Measure.* Yale University Press, New Haven, Conn., 1954.

Shelley, P. *Poems.* Penguin Books, Harmondsworth, England, 1956.

Sievers, A.M. *Has Market Capitalism Collapsed?* Columbia University Press, New York, 1949.

Silk, L. "In Global Financial Circles, Everyone Is Growing Frantic." *New York Times,* April 5, 1987.

Sloan, A.P., Jr. *My Years with General Motors.* (Ed. J. McDonald). McFadden Books, New York, 1965.

Smith, A. *The Wealth of Nations.* Penguin Books, New York, 1970.

Steiner, G. *Martin Heidegger.* Penguin Books, New York, 1978.

Stone, E.E., III. "Stone Manufacturing Company." Pub. No. 1222, Newcomen Society of the U.S., New York, 1984.

Stromberg, R.S. *European Intellectual History Since 1789.* Prentice-Hall, Englewood Cliffs, N.J., 1986.

Sward, K. *The Legend of Henry Ford.* Rinehart, Toronto, 1948.

Thomas, D.M. *The White Hotel.* Pocket Books, New York, 1981.

Vaughan, W. *Romantic Art.* Oxford University Press, New York, 1978.

Vienna 1900. Exhibition Catalog, Museum of Modern Art, New York, 1986.

Webber, A.W. "Helmut Schmidt: The Statesman as CEO." *Harvard Business Review,* 64(4), p. 71, July-August 1986a.

———. "James Callaghan: The Statesman as CEO." *Harvard Business Review,* 64(6), November-December 1986b.

Weber, M. *The Protestant Ethic and the Spirit of Capitalism* (Trans. T. Parsons). Scribner, New York, 1958.

Wedgwood, J. *Selected Letters* (Ed. A. Fine and G. Savage). Cory, Adams and MacKay, London, 1965.

Weick, K.E. *The Social Psychology of Organization,* Addison Wesley, Reading, Mass., 1979.

Whitman, W. "Aboard at a Ship's Helm." In *Oxford Book of American Verse* (Ed. F.O. Mattieson). University Press, New York, 1950.

Wilson, E.O. *Biophilia.* Harvard University Press, Cambridge, Mass., 1984.

Winkler, J.K. *Incredible Carnegie.* Vanguard Press, New York, 1931.

Wittgenstein, L. *The Blue Book.* Harper and Row, New York, 1965.

Yeats, W.B. *The Poems of W.B. Yeats.* (Ed. R.J. Finneran). Macmillan, New York, 1983.

Zenger, J.H. *Leadership: Management's Better Half.* Zenger-Miller, Los Angeles, 1985.

Index

Ackoff, R., 19–20, 170, 258, 282
Agency costs, 83, 259, 262, 279
Anderson, R., 93, 230
Animism, 92
Anthropomorphism, 92, 100
Aristotle, 117, 118, 129, 141, 257
Augustine of Hippo, St., 93, 241
Azzato, L., 189, 203

Babbage, C., 16
Barrett, W., 263, 269
Barzun, J., 63
Baudelaire, C., 36
Becker, E., 128, 130, 135–136, 241–242, 243
Bell, D., 266, 267, 270, 282
Berle, A., 283, 285, 290, 291, 295
Berlin, I., 127, 144
Berman, M., 263
Bettelheim, B., 128, 137
Bhagavad Gita, 278
Blake, W., 97
Bligh, W., 39, 56
Boccioni, U., 79
Boesky, I., 234, 292, 297
Burke, E., 97, 118, 161
Burr, D.; and war, 66; and society, 146–147; and production, 189, 201
Byron, G., 35–36, 64, 210

Callagahan, J., 151
Campbell, J., 23, 146
Carnegie, A., 45, 62, 98, 219, 221,
229, 255, 295; and game, 47; and wealth, 221, 229
Cathedral builders, 290, 291, 293, 299
Carse, J., 50–52, 53–54, 60–62, 80, 106, 131, 138, 244, 247, 253
Cavanagh, G., 271–272; and Clifford, D., 66, 71, 126, 245
Cetron, M., 266
Chomsky, N., 275
Chester, C., 38, 203
Clausewitz, Karl von, 67, 68
Coleridge, S., 35, 97
Comte, A., 78, 274
Connell, E., 23, 136, 153–154, 260
Cook, W., 77
Cowley, M., 27
Crane, S., 64
Cromwell, O., 70
Crouch, G., 66
Culture, 130–134

Daimler, G., 191
Darwin, C., 63, 98, 274
Davis, W., 12.
DeMott, B., 158–159
Descartes, R., 96, 274
Domestication, 92, 93, 99, 113
Donaldson, G., and Lorsch, J., 126, 245
Dostoyevsky, F., 259
Draper-Dayton, G., 189
Durkheim, E., 154
Drucker, P., 124, 236, 257, 278, 288–293, 298

Duryea, C., 191, 192

Eclectic paradigm, 288–293
Einstein, A., 175, 191, 192
Ellison, L., 67
Engels, F., 15, 185, 216, 278
Entailment; definition of, 27
Erasmus of Rotterdam, 260, 261
Experience curve, 195

Fayol, H.; and organism, 94; and society, 122
Ferris, R., 221–222
Finite games, 50–51, 62
Fitzgerald, F. S., 222
Fisk, J., 66
Follett, M., 18, 77
Ford, H., 1, 17, 19, 88, 159, 173, 188–189, 194–197, 203, 220, 222, 223, 224, 225, 226, 227, 228, 240, 247, 248, 255, 296–297; and distribution, 199–200; exemplar of production, 190–193; and journey, 37; and machine, 80; and organism, 112; and people, 198–199; and production, 189, 278; and puzzles of production, 194–197; and society, 123, 159
Ford, H., II, 125, 200
Francis of Assisi, St., 93, 233, 234
Franklin, B., 235
Frederick the Great, 170
Freud, S., 87, 101, 130, 273
Frick, H., 43, 185
Friedman, M., 217, 222
Futurism, 78–79

Galileo, G., 76
Game metaphor; business usage, 48–50; and entailments, 52–55; and Greeks, 50; historical usage, 171; and institution, 252–253; leader roles, 58–60; and production, 203, 204, 205; strengths, 56–57; weaknesses, 57–58; and wealth, 229–230
Galbraith, J. K., 183, 186, 207–209, 217, 279, 281

Gantt, H., 18; and production, 188; and society, 122
Geneen, H., 11, 152, 298; and game, 49; and organism, 95; and wealth, 221, 225, 229–230
Géricault, T., 39, 64, 97
Gibbon, E., 1
Gilder, G., 152–153, 186, 218, 232, 281
Gilbreth, F., 18; and machine, 77; and production, 183, 204
Goethe, J., 93
Gould, J., 58, 151, 185, 219, 220, 255; and game, 46; and war, 65; and wealth, 219, 229
Gould, S. J., 109–110, 115
Goya, F., 71
Grand Inquistor, 259–260, 285
Guicciardini, F., 39, 53, 84

Hamilton, E., 50
Hanley, J., 38, 246, 252, 255
Hanson, R., 189, 207
Harnischfeger, H., 125
Harris, M., 268–269
Hegel, G., 97
Heidegger, M., 13, 264
Heisenberg, W., 173
Heraclitus, 63, 88, 161
Hesse, H., 58
Hobbes, T., 63, 74, 117
Homer, 35

Iacocca, L., 1, 152, 200–201, 227; and game, 48–49, 53; and journey, 38; and organism, 96; and society, 125–126, 150, 156; and war, 67; and wealth, 178, 221, 227, 229–230
Infinite games, 51–52, 62, 160–161, 244, 253
Institutional paradigm; and business proponents, 245–247; degeneration, 257–258, 279–281, 282; and Jones, 19, 247–251; leader roles, 255–256; metaphors, 251–253; origins, 241–244; puzzles, 249–251; strengths, 254, 256; weaknesses, 257–260

James, W., 9, 24

Jeffers, R., 239, 243, 244

Jones, R., 19, 261, 280; and institution, 247–251, 252, 288; and society, 124

Journey metaphor; business usage, 37–38; entailments, 38–40; historical usage, 168–169; impulse toward order, 35; and institution, 251–253; leader roles, 41–42, 210; and production, 203, 204–205; and shape-changers, 298; strengths and weaknesses, 40–42; *voyage sans but,* 36, 169, 253, 257, 298

Kahn, H., 267–268, 269–270, 272, 292

Kant, I., 172

Keynes, J. M., 185–187, 208

Kierkegaard, S., 242, 255

Kissinger, W., 113, 247, 296

Kroc, R., 112

Kuhn, T., 1, 2, 3, 27, 171–177, 201, 207, 213, 226, 249, 296

Lakoff, G., and Johnson, M., 24, 25–28.

Langer, S., 133, 136–137, 167

Laplace, P., 78, 81, 96

Lavosier, A., 175

Legitimacy of Business, 281–283, 285, 288, 295

Lenin, N., 159

Levi-Strauss, C., 275

Lewis, M., and Clark, W., 40

Locke, J., 1, 168

Logical Positivism, 274, 275, 297

Lombardi, V., 49

Luther, M., 153, 260

Macaulay, T., 72

McDonald, A., 280–281

McHenry, J., 66

Machine metaphor; business usage, 75; entailments, 79–82; historical usage, 169; impact, 82–84; leader roles, 87–88; and production,

205–206; strengths, 84; weaknesses, 84–85, and wealth, 220

MacGregor, I.; and game, 48, 53; and institution, 246, 252; and society, 125, 147

McNamara, R., 200–201

Mailer, N., 65

Marcus Aurelius, 145, 268

Marcuse, H., 240

Marinetti, M., 78

Marriott, J., 112, 292

Marshall, G., 73

Marx, K., 117, 214, 268

Mason, G., 254

Matthew, St., 213, 233

Maya, 243–244

Mayo, F., 87, 174

MBO, 83, 85

Mergers and acquisitions, 2–3, 139–140

Metaphor; business use, 28–33; definition, 24; entailments, 27; historical usage, 29–32, 168–171; limiting experience, 26; misapplication, 26; ontological, 25–26; and poetry, 23; its power, 12, 23; psychology of, 23–24; and understanding, 9–10

Metcalfe, H., 16, 83

Mill, J. S., 184–185, 208

Moltke, H., Graf von, 64

Montague, J., 129, 156, 242, 256, 264

Montesquieu, C., 121

Morgan, G., 89, 119

MRP, 83

Myrdal, G., 267

Newton, I., 77, 173, 175, 191, 192

Nietzsche, F., 64

Nichol, F. W., 36, 220, 221

North, D., 254, 281

Novack, M., 232–233, 276, 279

Olsen, K., 153; and game, 47–48; and organism, 112; and production, 189–190, 204

Operations Research, 83–84

Organism metaphor: business usage,

93–96; definition, 91; entailments, 91, 98–102; historical usage, 169–170; leader roles, 110–112, 229–230; and production, 204, 206; strengths, 106–107; weaknesses, 107–110; and wealth, 229–231
Ortega y Gasset, J., 152, 264
Orwell, G., 12, 82
O'Toole, J., 128, 130, 231, 265
Ouchi, W., 120
Owen, R., 15–16, 77, 219

Paradigm, 2, 172–176; and business purpose, 176; and metaphor, 2,3, 176
Pascal, B., 242–243, 255, 264
Patton, G., 73
Pepper, S., 24, 79, 92, 298
Perot, R., 47, 149, 170, 260–261
Peters, T., and Waterman, R., 81, 87, 102–104, 111, 115, 126–127, 130, 135, 137, 147, 157, 158, 161, 171, 177, 273
Petersen, T., 124, 252
Pfeffer, J., 141–143, 148, 156, 257, 293
Poincaré, H., 192
Poincaré, R., 192
Polanyi, K., 235, 276–278, 281
Politics, 141–143, 253, 257, 293
Porter, M., 104–106, 226, 227
Positivism, 78
Production paradigm; business proponents, 186–190; degeneration, 278–279, 282; economic basis, 184–186; and Ford, 190–201; leader roles, 210; metaphors, 203–206; puzzles, 193–197; strengths, 207; weaknesses, 207–209
Process metaphors, 33
Profit motive, 214
Purposes of business; historical trends, 181; link to metaphor, 181–182

Quinn, J. B., 147

Rank, O., 153
Remarque, E. M., 65

Rimbaud, A., 140
Robb, R., 73, 94
Robertson, A., 95, 203–204
Roderick, D., 202, 222
Rodin, A., 70–71
Romanticism, 35, 37, 96–97
Rousseau, J. J., 97, 117, 127

Saint, 152–153
Samuelson, P., 283
Sanford, F., 11, 204
Schumpeter, J., 245, 283
Scientific Management; and Babbage, 16; and game, 54; and machine, 80; and Metcalfe, 16; and society, 156; and Taylor, 16–17; and Towne, 16; and wealth, 220
Schmidt, H., 151
Selznick, P., 119, 137–138, 143, 147, 240
Shakespeare, W., 71, 233–234
Shaman, 145–149, 257–258, 262
Shape-changer paradigm, 293–297
Sheldon, O., 38
Shelley, P., 243
Sik, O., 231
Sloan, A., 1, 13, 19, 152, 220, 240, 247, 248, 278; and Ford, 197, 223, 224, 225; and journey, 37; and organism, 94, 288; and production, 189, and society, 121, 124, 149; and wealth, 222–229, 288
Smith, A., 153, 182, 184, 208, 215, 216, 217, 218, 232, 235, 277–278, 289
Smircich, L., 131, 132–134
Snider, B., 146
Society metaphor; business usage, 122–128; and culture, 130–134; entailments, 128–145; historical usage, 171; and institution, 251, 252, 253; leader roles, 145–154; and meaning, 128–130; modern, 121; strengths, 154–157; traditional, 120–121; weaknesses, 157–162
Social Darwinism, 63–64, 98, 100, 145, 233, 274

Spencer, H., 98
Sperlich, H., 38, 48
Stakeholder theory, 124, 150–151, 249
Statesman, 149, 152, 256
Stone, E., 203
Strategy, 104–106; Sloan's, 226–229
Structuralism, 274–275
System metaphors, 33

Taylor, F., 16–18, 87, 93, 107, 177, 188, 189, 194; and game, 47; and machine, 77, 81, 288; and production, 186, 220, 288; and society, 133–134, 139

Thomas à Kempis, 93
Thomas Aquinas, St., 214
Thomas, D. M., 101
Tolstoy, L., 64
Towne, H., 16, 220

Veblen, T., 185, 234
Vico, G., 118, 119, 160
Vonnegut, K., 10
Voyage sans but, le, 36, 169, 253, 257, 298

War metaphor; business usage, 65–
67; entailments, 67–72; historical usage, 170–171; leader roles, 72–73; and shape changers, 298; strengths, 67–69; weaknesses, 71–72
Watson, T., 48, 85, 112
Wagner, O., 273, 287
Wealth paradigm; business proponents, 219–222; definition, 213; degeneration, 277, 278, 282; economic basis, 214–218; leader roles, 237; metaphors of, 229–231; and Sloan, 19, 222–229; strengths, 231–232; weaknesses, 232–236
Weber, M., 80, 85, 107, 134, 153, 215, 232, 235
Wedgwood, J., 11, 15, 65, 190; and machine, 77; and production, 186–187; and wealth, 219, 230
Weick, K., 73–74
Welch, J., 280
Whitman, W., 287, 298
Wittgenstein, L., 9, 13, 274, 276
Wriston, W., 255; and institution, 239, 252; and journey, 38; and game, 48; and organism, 95; and society, 124–125, 145

Yankelovich, D., 271
Yeats, W. B., 35, 36–37, 98, 288

About the Author

John Clancy is an information systems industry executive who spent twenty-five years with a major corporation in R&D, sales, marketing, and general management, including the presidency of a $200 million division. He is currently president and CEO of a Silicon Valley start-up software company.

Mr. Clancy frequently speaks at computer industry conferences in the United States and abroad. He holds bachelor and master's degrees in engineering, an MBA, and a master of liberal arts.